SmartStorming®

The Game-Changing Process for Generating
Bigger, Better Ideas

By

Mitchell Rigie and Keith Harmeyer

First published by Dog Ear Publishing
4010 W. 86th Street, Suite H
Indianapolis, IN 46268
www.dogearpublishing.net

ISBN: 978-1-4575-1662-7

This book is printed on acid-free paper.

Printed in the United States of America

SS.8.6.2013.V38

To Elizabeth, Amanda, and Max...
my greatest source of love, inspiration, and joy.

—Mitchell

To Vivian, Jacqueline, and Doedy...
my three beautiful Muses.

—Keith

CONTENTS

This Book and How to Use It   vii

Introduction
Chapter 1: Innovation: The New Darwinism   3
Chapter 2: Brainstorming and Why We Love to Hate It   11
Chapter 3: SmartStorming—The 21st-Century Evolution of Brainstorming   17

Part One: SmartStorming Fundamentals
Chapter 4: SmartStorming Principles and Best Practices   25

Part Two: The Six-Step SmartStorming Process
Chapter 5: Step 1—Creating Your Blueprint for Success   47
Chapter 6: Step 2—Aligning Your Group for Collaboration   57
Chapter 7: Step 3—Creating a Springboard for the Imagination   67
Chapter 8: Step 4—Generating Ideas! Unleashing Your Group's Creative Genius   79
Chapter 9: Step 5—Harvesting Your Group's Most Innovative Ideas   97
Chapter 10: Step 6—Transforming Ideas into New Realities   115

Part Three: SmartStorming Leadership Skills
Chapter 11: Inspiring and Guiding Your Group to Greatness   125
Chapter 12: Managing Divergent and Convergent Thinking   133
Chapter 13: The Art of Asking Powerful Questions   139
Chapter 14: Escaping the Box—The Power of Challenging Assumptions   151
Chapter 15: Maximizing Your Group's Productivity   157
Chapter 16: Getting Your Group Off to a Fast Start   161
Chapter 17: Engaging the "Silent Thinkers"   165
Chapter 18: Managing Groups of Different Sizes   169
Chapter 19: SmartStorming Leadership—Frequently Asked Questions   175

Part Four: SmartStorming Pilot's Toolkit

Chapter 20: Idea-Generation Techniques and Tools 181

  1-4-All 185

  Bad2Good 187

  Brainwriting 190

  Channeling Genius 192

  Escaping the Box 196

  Frankensteining 200

  Group Graffiti 203

  Idea Mashup 205

  Idea Speed Dating 207

  Idea Sprinting 209

  In Their Shoes 212

  Mind Mapping 215

  Pre-Storming 219

  Pump Up the Value 221

  Reimagine It! 224

  SCAMPER 228

  SmartSWOT 234

  Think Much, Much Bigger 241

  Vision Boards 244

  What If...? 246

  SmartStorming Value Compass 249

  SmartStorming Idea Selection Diagnostic Matrix 250

Chapter 21: Guides, Planners, and Worksheets 251

  Rules of the Game 253

  Rules for Selecting Ideas 254

  25 Great Icebreaker Activities 255

  25 Piloting Questions for Any Challenge 259

  SmartStorming Pre-Session Planner 260

  Solo SmartStorming Pre-Session Planner 261

  Determining Your Challenge, Goals, and Objectives Worksheet 262

  SmartStorming Participant Selection Planner 263

Idea Selection Criteria Worksheet   264

SmartStorming Next Steps: 5-As Action Planner   266

SmartStorming Six-Step Session Flowchart   267

Piloting Your First Session Checklist   268

Part Five: Solo SmartStorming

Chapter 22: Solo SmartStorming—Liberating Your Own Creative Genius   271

Part Six: Open Innovation and Virtual SmartStorming

Chapter 23: Open Innovation and Virtual SmartStorming   285

Part Seven: A Bird's-Eye View

Chapter 24: SmartStorming: Putting It All Together   299

Chapter 25: Welcome to a New Paradigm in Idea Generation   315

Notes   318

References   319

About the Authors   320

Index   321

THIS BOOK AND HOW TO USE IT

"Innovation distinguishes between a leader and a follower."
—Steve Jobs

Thinking up ideas now and then is not all that difficult for most people.

Generating lots of ideas—bold, new, innovative ideas, on a consistent basis—is a different story. It takes a measure of vision, knowledge, skill, and experience.

Unfortunately, most of us have had little to no education about how to think differently, solve challenges creatively, or think outside the box. And in today's chaotic, innovation-driven world, that missing expertise can put individuals, groups, and entire organizations at a distinct disadvantage.

In our training and consulting practice, we've had the honor of working with many of the most innovative companies in fields such as advertising and media, information and technology, sporting goods and apparel, pharmaceuticals, health care and medical devices, publishing, and education. We have trained an international audience of thousands of corporate professionals, as well as graduate students at the MIT Sloan School of Management. And now we are pleased to offer our highly effective process, tools, and techniques to you.

This book was written to help fill the void and empower you, the reader, with everything you will need to become a leader in the innovation economy.

During the nearly twenty-five years we each spent in the highly creative, innovation-driven fields of advertising and marketing communications, we saw firsthand the frustration many people face when called upon to generate ideas on a consistent basis. This was especially true when working in groups, where the challenges that arise from interpersonal dynamics compounded the problem. It was clear that something was missing: a simple, reliable, systematic process for generating innovative, game-changing ideas whenever needed.

The information contained in this book is designed to help make the idea-generation process easier, even foolproof. The SmartStorming® process and all of its supporting tools and materials have been carefully designed to systematically guide you in planning and leading your most successful brainstorms ever.

How you use this book depends on who you are and what you are looking to achieve. Some of you may be brainstorming novices, looking for a fundamental understanding of all that's involved in the process. Some may have a bit more experience under your belts. Perhaps you've attended or led a number of brainstorming sessions and might have learned an idea-generation technique or two. Still others will be highly experienced brainstorm facilitators, seeking to expand your knowledge and skill sets.

Our goal in writing this book was to make it a valuable resource for each of you and to fulfill all of those needs. The book has been designed to serve as an instructional guide to the SmartStorming methodology; a resource with a wealth of tips, tools, and techniques for those seeking to strengthen their expertise; and a ready-to-use reference you can come back to, time and again, whenever you need a refresher or need to find just the right tool or technique for the task at hand.

The book is divided into seven main sections, each building sequentially upon the last:

Introduction—Here we explain the importance and value of brainstorming skills in today's often chaotic, innovation-driven world.

Part One: SmartStorming Fundamentals—Here you will learn some of the fundamental SmartStorming principles and concepts that underlie the process, all of which are vital for success.

Part Two: The Six-Step SmartStorming Process—Focusing on the first of the "three pillars of brainstorming success," this is the core instructional section of the book, which guides you through each of the six steps in the SmartStorming process.

Part Three: SmartStorming Leadership Skills—The second pillar of success, addressed here, focuses on the specific, real-world leadership skills necessary for masterfully inspiring and guiding a group through the SmartStorming process.

Part Four: SmartStorming Pilot's Toolkit—The third and final pillar of success provides a valuable collection of proven tools and techniques for more effectively generating ideas, as well as planning and leading sessions. These are included here, in your Pilot's Toolkit.

Part Five: Solo SmartStorming—In this fifth section, we provide the structure and tools for unlocking more of your creative problem-solving genius so you can generate more fresh, innovative ideas on your own.

Part Six: Open Innovation and Virtual SmartStorming—Here you will learn how to apply the power, principles, and tools of SmartStorming to open innovation and virtual online platforms.

Part Seven: A Bird's-Eye View—In this final section, we provide an overview of the SmartStorming process in its entirety.

If you are seeking a complete education in effective brainstorming, we encourage you to read this book cover to cover. (If you do, you will be better equipped to plan and lead highly effective brainstorming sessions than over 90 percent of those doing so now, in any industry!) Afterward, place this book prominently on your bookshelf as a reference guide, ready whenever you need it.

If you are interested in selectively identifying those elements that are of greatest use for your specific needs, we suggest starting with Part Seven: A Bird's-Eye View. Then, based on a top-line understanding of the SmartStorming methodology, you can turn to the table of contents to find those topics you're more interested in.

And if you are simply hoping to add some new skills and techniques to your current brainstorming abilities, go right to the table of contents and search for the sections and topics you can make best use of.

Above all, we hope you will make regular use of this book. There is a wealth of information here, something to help every individual, group, and organization become more effective at innovative thinking, creative problem solving, and idea generation.

Happy SmartStorming!

The dramatic challenges facing our world
will not be solved through traditional linear thinking.
They will be solved through bold leaps
of insight and imagination.

For more information about the SmartStorming® process and tools that appear in this book, or to learn how you can bring SmartStorming Brainstorm Leadership Training to your organization, please visit our website at http://www.SmartStorming.com, or contact us via email at Partners@SmartStorming.com.

Introduction

CHAPTER 1

Innovation: The New Darwinism

*"It is not the strongest of the species that survives,
nor the most intelligent that survives.
It is the one that is the most adaptable to change."*

—Charles Darwin

In case you haven't noticed, chaos and disruptive change are the new business-as-usual.

The upheaval over the past several years in business, the economy, politics, technology, education, and society in general are not anomalies. They are the new world order (or lack thereof). The speed at which things change is faster than ever, and accelerating every day.

If you get the sense that no one knows what is going to happen next, like it or not, that is probably the case. Decades-old, global organizations, once viewed as invincible, tumble overnight. Yesterday's disruptive technology leaders suddenly become irrelevant. And highly skilled business professionals, once coveted by their loyal employers, are out of work with little notice and with few viable prospects—except to reinvent themselves.

Reinvention has become the new, critical skill set—for corporations, start-ups, governments, educational institutions, workgroups, and individuals.

Of course, none of this should come as a surprise. We have actually been hearing about this evolutionary shift for years on television news, in magazines, in newsletters, and in countless blogs. Scores of books have addressed it and Harvard Business School professors have lectured on it. The topic: Innovation.

Of course, "innovation" doesn't sound quite so intimidating as "continuous reinvention" or worse, "chaos." But in today's world, they are all one and the same.

While it might seem counterintuitive, choosing to ignore this state of continuous change actually means assuming even greater risk than embracing it. Whatever the economy may be doing, however unstable the markets may be, change will rage on. Spending time, energy, and resources desperately searching for some long-term stability will be fruitless, because while you are striving to maintain the status quo, the wave of change will be passing you by. The only real choice facing us today is to innovate or slip into irrelevance.

Innovation, or the ability to not only handle but also embrace continuous change, is the new Darwinism in business. Where not long ago, "survival of the fittest," at least in business terms, was all about operational efficiency—faster plus cheaper equaled better— today the big dogs at the top of the corporate food chain are those who are willing to continuously reinvent themselves, proactively reevaluate their product or service offerings, and redirect their efforts. Today's market leaders are the companies that introduce us to the new, new thing, the bleeding-edge technology, the better mousetrap, the reinvented wheel, even before we know we want it. This new paradigm of chaos is just as challenging for them; the only difference is, they dive right in—and use it to their advantage. Risky? To be sure. But not nearly as risky as standing still.

Who are they, these more evolved corporate organisms that seem to have adapted so masterfully to the chaotic, 21st-century economic environment? We hesitate to even name them, for fear that, by the time you read this, they will be yesterday's news. But for the moment, they are companies we all know and revere—Apple, Facebook, Google, Amazon, Starbucks, Nike. And there are hundreds and even thousands more you've never heard of, visionary companies that are taking risks, breaking the rules, establishing new standards, delivering incredible value, delighting their customers, and then starting the process all over again and again and again. These companies come in all shapes and sizes, and exist in every industry—technology, biotech, pharmaceuticals, automotive, consumer packaged goods, even your favorite local or online retailer. You name it, they're out there out-thinking and outdoing everyone else in their field. But they all have one thing in common: *They passionately pursue innovation.*

In this new innovation frontier, everything is possible. Old, limiting assumptions are no longer perceived as boundaries, but rather as new points of departure for discovery, and the unknown is transformed from a treacherous place of risk into a playground of new possibilities. The battle cry for this brave new world is *"Create Forward!"*

The intersection of the consumer and technology

If you're wondering what brought about this cataclysmic shift in the modern business environment, this absolute, unequivocal requirement for innovation, just take a look in a mirror. It's you. And me. All of us. Armed with today's all-empowering technology that provides not only knowledge but also control over virtually every commercial and personal interaction, consumers are the driving force behind the relentless demand for innovation. By consumer, we mean anyone who makes a decision to purchase or otherwise acquire something from someone else. The woman shopping for the best, most comfortable, performance-enhancing running shoe available today. The young urbanite researching the lightest, most durable bicycle for city riding. The guy deciding which toothpaste to buy, the one that whitens teeth, reduces tartar, promises fewer cavities, or all of the above. A purchasing manager choosing a new materials supplier. The head of corporate marketing searching for a new ad agency and then demanding only the best, freshest, most unexpected thinking from them once they're engaged. They are all consumers; they are all in the market for something from someone. And they hold all the cards.

As it ends up, knowledge really is power, and consumers have knowledge like they've never had it before—knowledge that ultimately gives them virtually limitless choices for anything they want or need. In the not-so-distant past, it was a different story. Consumers had relatively limited access to information when they were in the market for a product or service—a company's reputation (gleaned through referrals or word of mouth); advertising, public relations, and editorial press coverage (in print publications, TV, radio, outdoor ads, or direct mail); and/or facts gained through the direct selling efforts of the company being considered. Yesterday's consumers did the best they could, but in fact, it was always pretty much a seller's market. "I have what you need, Mr. and Ms. Consumer. Come and get it—on my terms—or do without." This was the unspoken message delivered by most businesses in the past.

What ultimately turned the tables were computers, and specifically, the Internet, with its virtually unlimited access to information and ultimately vast, powerful social networks. Today, in a nanosecond, with just a few small movements of the fingers, anyone, anywhere can discover everything there is to know about anything, right now, this second, 24/7/365. They can compare and contrast, find reviews, prices, special promotions and discounts, specifications, and detailed accounts of others' experiences. And then they can share all of this information and personal perspective with hundreds, thousands, even millions of others with whom they are directly or tangentially connected.

What, at this precise moment in time, is the best, most innovative offering out there? Which companies compete in this space? Which have the best reputations? Which offer the best prices? Which provide the best customer service? Which are financially secure? In short, who and what can provide exactly what I need—with absolutely no compromise whatsoever—right now? If you aren't at the top of the list of responses to that question, you are out of the game.

Technology and connectivity have made competition fiercer than ever before. The other guys are always right there, lurking in the shadows, waiting to step in and steal your customer at the first opportunity. And consumers aren't just shopping in their own neighborhoods. This instantaneous accessibility of information and options is global. Depending on your need and circumstances, your number one choice might be in any state or country, on any continent, in any time zone. They are all just a click, an email, a text message, a phone call, and an overnight shipment away.

All this power makes consumers remarkably fickle. Customer loyalty? Don't count on it. What consumers love today, they will lose interest in tomorrow and disdain next week. Consider the PalmPilot, the BlackBerry, and the iPhone. Are you Mac or PC? Starbucks or Dunkin' Donuts? Whatever happened to Krispy Kreme and Kodak? Remember when AOL ruled the online world? (No, really, it did.)

Today's consumers are constantly moving targets. Their tastes, interests, and demands evolve, not every day, but every moment. If companies are to survive and thrive, they must make every effort to stay ahead of those consumers—zigging, zagging, ebbing, flowing, and doing whatever it takes to keep up the pace and sustain the evolutionary momentum. It's exhausting and it's exhilarating. But make no mistake, it's non-negotiable.

Chaos or opportunity? For those willing to do the dance, it is both.

Today's consumers are more knowledgeable, more sophisticated, more discriminating, more demanding, less forgiving, less devoted, and less willing to compromise than ever before. They understand that they call the shots and expect total compliance from the companies they give their business to. They are king of the jungle, and they know it.

But the smartest business leaders know it, too. In survey after survey, corporate executives rank creativity and innovation as among the most critical elements of contemporary business success. Yet in one study, only one in eight CEOs surveyed said their companies were innovating very well.[1] And it's no wonder. This shift in power from company to consumer, from provider to acquirer, has happened rather suddenly. Many companies have been caught with their corporate pants down, and they aren't really sure how to pull them back up.

Many companies, especially larger, more established ones, have deeply entrenched cultures and massive operational infrastructures that make it difficult to be nimble. Plans need to be formulated, systems need to be redesigned, roles and responsibilities need to be reconsidered, processes need to be adapted. It takes time. It costs money. It needs to be studied, evaluated, tested, and fine-tuned. Such companies try to slow down change because change takes time. And meanwhile, the consumer forgets they exist.

Today, companies face an important choice:

1. Embrace change, innovate continuously, and stay ahead of their competition, doing whatever it takes to meet constantly evolving consumer demand;

2. Wait for others to break new ground and then play catch-up, forever scrambling to match the latest development introduced by the market leaders; or

3. Do nothing. Stay right where they are and quickly slip into irrelevance and, finally, extinction.

By the way, this requirement for innovation doesn't only apply to global market leaders. It is a challenge facing all businesses, from Wall Street to Main Street, as well as schools, governments, entrepreneurs, sole proprietors, and even individuals, who must also continually reinvent themselves, upgrading the value they deliver to their employers or customers. It is often noted that the top careers a decade from now don't even exist today. How does one prepare for such a future? *Not by learning how to perform a specific job function, but by learning how to think more creatively and reinvent oneself every day.*

What is innovation, and how do we do it?

All this talk about innovation and the fact that it's an absolute imperative for success! So just what is innovation, anyway? We have already introduced the notion that innovation involves reinvention. To go a bit further, innovation can be defined as *the introduction of something new or different that provides greater value or benefit.* In fact, there are many different ways to drive innovation; three of the most common approaches are:

1. Do or create something new that has never been done before.

2. Do or create something that has been done before, but do it better.

3. Take two or more different things and combine them in a way that has never been done before.

So for example, when the Internet was first made available to the public, it was a true innovation in the sense that it offered something that had never been offered before. When eBay first launched its website, it was innovative in that it provided something that had been around for a long time, public auctions, but in a better, more accessible way, in an easy-to-use online venue. And the iPhone took a number of things that had been available to consumers—a mobile phone, contact database, online calendar, wireless Internet access, digital music and photography, and other capabilities—and combined them all in a single, revolutionary device that was unquestionably innovative. In each case, something new was introduced, and it provided greater value or benefit.

As for how the magic of innovation actually takes place, well, it's not exactly magic. Innovation is the end product of an idea. Without an initial idea, there can be no "doing something that hasn't been done before," "doing something better," or "combining things in a way that has never been done before."

Innovation always starts with a great idea.

But to be an innovation leader in today's world requires more than a great idea. To stay ahead of the pack, you must have lots of great ideas. Where once a company could thrive for decades with just one breakthrough concept for a successful product or service, today they must have a great idea every year, every quarter, in some cases, every month. Because if they don't, someone else surely will.

In short, it takes a continuous stream of fresh, new thinking to power the engines of innovation.

Which leads us to brainstorming

When it comes to innovation, it generally takes more than a single person or one way of thinking about things to turn a good, creative idea into a new reality. Even legendary innovators like Thomas Edison, Henry Ford, and Steve Jobs collaborated with other colleagues to bring their ideas to life.

It seems that while some people are really good at coming up with that original creative thought, others are great at figuring out all the details about just how that idea might actually work. Some people are excellent at planning how to implement the idea, others at how to make it happen efficiently and affordably, and still others at how to make the idea aesthetically pleasing or how to market it effectively. The point is that different people have different creative-thinking strengths. Put them all together, and the whole becomes greater than the sum of its parts. It seems two (or even more) heads really are better than one.

All of those people working together to produce or develop an idea? Sounds a lot like a brainstorm. It is hard to imagine any group of individuals trying to solve a problem or capitalize on an opportunity that doesn't rely heavily on some form of group idea-generation process to conceive, develop, and refine new ideas. In fact, brainstorming is the number one methodology used by groups to innovate. Every day, in offices, conference rooms, classrooms, living rooms, and garages across the globe, tens of thousands of brainstorming sessions are held. For our purposes, we define brainstorming as two or more people getting together to generate and/or develop new ideas. You do it. I do it. We all do it.

The goal of this book is to help you rethink forever the way you approach creative problem solving and, specifically, group brainstorming, by learning, understanding, and applying a methodology we call SmartStorming. Once you learn how to SmartStorm, you will never brainstorm the same way again. SmartStorming is an innovative, step-by-step process for producing fresh, new, creative ideas. It is comprehensive, easy to understand and apply, and has been proven effective.

How does SmartStorming fit into our world of chaotic change? Ironically, in order to successfully navigate in this unpredictable new environment, you must have somewhat predictable structures, tools, and methodologies you can depend on. Of course, in such a world, truly useful processes must be not only dependable but also practical and flexible. And so, while SmartStorming does provide a proven, consistent process, its various planning methods, tools, and techniques are timeless and infinitely customizable for any situation, problem, or opportunity. In a way, it adapts to any challenge.

SmartStorming is an evolutionary advance in the area of creative problem solving and idea generation, and it is going to revolutionize the way you work. It is more efficient, more effective, and more enjoyable. It is that better mousetrap.

Before we get into SmartStorming specifics, however, we need to take a look at the current state of things: traditional, old-school brainstorming—what it is, what's good about it, what's not so good, and why.

Hopefully, this will be the last time you ever look at brainstorming in quite the same way.

What to remember

- Today, chaos and disruptive change are the new business-as-usual.

- Business success is based on your ability to innovate. *You must innovate or slip into irrelevance.*

- Innovation can be defined as *the introduction of something new or different that provides greater value or benefit.*

- There are many different ways to drive innovation; three of the most common are:

    1. Do or create something new that has never been done before.

    2. Do or create something that has been done before, but do it better.

    3. Take two or more different things and combine them in a way that has never been done before.

- Innovation is fueled by new ideas—lots and lots of ideas. No ideas, no innovation.

- Brainstorming is the most widely used method for generating new ideas.

- SmartStorming provides a better way to brainstorm in our world of continuous reinvention…an evolutionary advance in the area of creative problem solving and idea generation.

CHAPTER 2

Brainstorming and Why We Love to Hate It

"It is easier to tone down a wild idea than to think up a new one."

—Alex Osborn

The father of brainstorming

Alex Osborn, to whom the above quote is attributed, was one of the founders of the legendary advertising agency BBDO.

In 1939, a team led by Mr. Osborn coined the term "brainstorm." The word, as they conceived it, literally means using one's brain to "storm" a creative problem, to attack it in "commando fashion." The objective of brainstorming was to take the ideation process outside the realm of the solitary thinker and into a group environment, where ideas might be more rapidly and efficiently generated and developed.

Osborn originally identified four essential criteria for successful brainstorming.

1. **Defer judgment.** In order for people to feel free to express ideas, there must be no criticism during the brainstorming session.

2. **Wild ideas are encouraged.** While outlandish concepts might not be ultimately usable, they often lead to other innovative ideas.

3. **Quantity over quality.** Groups should strive to generate as many concepts as possible, the idea being that this increases the odds that high-quality, usable ideas will be in the mix.

4. **Ideas should be improved and combined.** Participants are encouraged to suggest ways to make an idea better and to suggest combining two or more ideas.

He also outlined a creative problem-solving process in terms of a series of procedures that included:

Fact-Finding—accurate "Problem-definition" and "Preparation" (the gathering and analyzing of relevant data).

Idea-Finding—a two-step process that included "Idea-production" (generating ideas as possible leads) and "Idea-development" (selecting promising ideas, adding new ones, and reprocessing/modifying ideas).

Solution-Finding—consisting of the processes of "Evaluation" (verifying possible solutions via testing) and "Adaption" (implementing the final solution).[2]

Clearly Alex Osborn was onto something. Over the past seventy-plus years, his brainstorming process has become the most widely utilized methodology for generating ideas within workgroups. Anytime two or more people get together to throw some ideas around, they're participating in some type of brainstorm. They may or may not adhere to each of Osborn's four criteria or procedures, but the net result is much the same: A group of individuals share, enhance, extrapolate, extend, twist, bend, combine, and otherwise develop a series of ideas with the objective of generating as long a list of good concepts as they can.

Alex Osborn was one clever guy. The concept of brainstorming was nothing short of brilliant. It is based on a simple and well-accepted principle: Two (or more) heads are better than one. It is one thing to sit alone in a room and think up a bunch of neat ideas. It is another one altogether to generate ideas collaboratively. The very act of having a group work together, bringing a diverse range of perspectives to the table, leads to more fully developed thinking.

By nature, each individual sees things differently. Each sees facets of meaning and potential that others may miss. One might recognize the shortcomings in an idea that another participant is blind to, because of either personal attachment to the idea or a lack of knowledge and background. By combining diverse backgrounds, experiences, and talents, the group capitalizes on their combined strengths and minimizes individual weaknesses. And by doing so, they become capable of exploring a wider range of perspectives, making more connections and generating more new ideas than would be possible by any one of them working individually.

So if brainstorming is such a valuable creative problem-solving tool, then what's this book all about? Where's the problem? Why aren't we all absolutely thrilled with the prospect of another brainstorming session tomorrow at nine o'clock sharp? Well, like so many other great ideas before and after it, the breakdown of brainstorming takes place in its execution. In concept, it's pure genius. In practice, however, somewhat less so.

The fact is, traditional brainstorming as actually practiced today is often a loosely structured and improvised affair. Many people, in an effort to avoid restricting creativity, purposely impose little or no structure on a brainstorming session, generally with disappointing results. Many people don't enjoy brainstorms. And the final product is often as unsatisfying as the process itself. Strong language, to be sure, and perhaps not entirely fair; certainly some good thinking comes out of brainstorming sessions and may even be carried through to final execution. But as a whole, you will be hard-pressed to find many individuals who believe brainstorming is an efficient, effective, and enjoyable way to help an organization drive its innovation initiative.

Why does brainstorming so often fall short? The problem is that the very thing that makes brainstorming such a dynamic concept—the power of group dynamics—is the same one that can bring about its unraveling. Groups are made up of individuals with egos (both overinflated and fragile); diverse, sometimes conflicting opinions and perspectives; and personal agendas that are often out of sync with those of others. The people who make up groups, and particularly groups in the workplace, can often be territorial, political, or insecure; have established alliances or competitive relationships with others; and are often subject to a preexisting pecking order in terms of their respective roles. Any one of these aspects of the group dynamic can be detrimental to a brainstorming session. Throw several of these issues into the room, and it becomes very difficult to achieve any level of success, even a modest one.

Multigenerational workgroups, increasingly common in today's business world, only make the problem worse. Often three different generations are represented: Baby Boomers, Gen X, and Gen Y or Millennials. Boomers and their younger, free-thinking counterparts express ideas very differently. Gen-Xers have very specific views regarding work style and collaboration that are different from both groups. All have disparate ideas about just what personal contribution means and what acknowledgment of authority looks like. A group ideation methodology as casual and unstructured as traditional brainstorming simply does not provide the necessary tools for navigating such diverse perspectives, attitudes, and communication styles, and rarely, if ever, leads to a dynamic exchange of information and ideas.

No one at the helm

The Achilles' heel of brainstorming as a dependable innovation and ideation process can be attributed to one predominant shortcoming: lack of formal training for group facilitators. In our experience, fewer than 10 percent of those surveyed have ever had any formal training of any kind in creative problem solving or brainstorming[3]—those who have typically learned only one or two ideation techniques to use during sessions. But this in no way addresses the remaining elements identified by Alex Osborn as necessary for successful groups—that facilitators need strong questioning skills, that leaders should thoroughly plan sessions in advance, that rules for session participation need to be developed and established with participants, that group warm-up activities should be utilized, and that specific attention needs to be given to the process for following through on the ideas generated.

And more recent research seems to support many of these points. A study published in 1996 revealed that when group facilitators receive formal training, their groups produce a greater number of concepts.[4] A separate study, also published in 1996, went further, and looked at the level of training a facilitator receives. The conclusion: Groups with highly trained facilitators perform better than groups whose facilitators have had less training.[5] And a more recent study, conducted at North Carolina State University in 2010, found that "the benefits of high quality brainstorming" kicked in only when a number of best practices were incorporated.[6]

Success doesn't just happen

Successful group ideation sessions do not happen by accident; they are designed, planned, and executed—by group leaders who know what they're doing from start to finish. It's not enough to have good intentions or a strong sense of optimism, a belief in the power of camaraderie, or even abundant talent and creativity. You must have all of that, and more. Thorough, big-picture planning, advance preparation, a sound process, and strong, active leadership throughout the process are essential.

Specific failings of typical brainstorms

In our work we have identified the following eight most common failings of typical brainstorming sessions:

1. **Little to no planning**—Most brainstorms take place with only a vague idea of what will actually happen during the session.

2. **No structure/process**—Some believe, erroneously, that since brainstorming is a "creative" process, it should remain free and unstructured. The result can be an unproductive session that meanders off purpose.

3. **Lack of skilled leadership**—This is really the underlying source of most brainstorming issues. A trained facilitator will generally have the expertise and experience to correct any challenge that arises.

4. **Poorly defined goals and objectives**—Leaders and groups rarely, if ever, take the time to fully understand and clarify the challenge at hand, running the very real risk that they are working to solve the wrong problem. They are also rarely clear about specifically what they plan to produce in a session, in terms of number and types of ideas.

5. **Lack of stimuli**—No fresh input of inspiration (information, facts/data, images, experiences, etc.) to help stimulate new creative problem-solving connections.

6. **Lack of rules**—To believe that a group of individuals can work together, in concert, toward a common goal with no agreed-upon guidelines for participation is naïve. Think *Robert's Rules of Order*.

7. **Few ideation techniques**—Different challenges require different problem-solving approaches. Being familiar with a range of proven, effective ideation techniques enables a facilitator to guide a group's thinking in new and different ways.

8. **Poor follow-through**—One of the most common complaints voiced about brainstorm sessions is that once participants leave the room, they never hear about their great ideas again.

So the question we need to ask is, if traditional group brainstorming, as typically practiced, is as flawed and ineffective a process as it appears to be, why on earth do we keep using it?

Around the world, businesses invest thousands, hundreds of thousands, in some cases even millions of dollars in this inefficient practice every year. Highly paid professionals sit through countless hours of brainstorming sessions, often delivering questionable value to those who pay them. The quantity and quality of ideas generated are often disappointing, and on those occasions when good ideas are produced, only a small fraction of them are ever acted upon.

The reason we keep doing it, over and over again, is simple. It's the best we've got. Those innovation-focused organizations we referred to earlier realize that in order to innovate, they need a continuous supply of fresh, new ideas. And brainstorming is the best tool available for the job.

But very little attention has been given to the total group ideation process, from start to finish. Most of the best work in this area has focused on how to generate more ideas, ways of viewing issues from different perspectives, and methods for freeing the mind and fostering greater creativity. All crucially important; but what about the critical preplanning process, those things that must take place before the session ever begins? What about specific skills to help someone masterfully guide a session through its various peaks and valleys? What about an overall approach to idea generation that allows more effective use of different creative ideation techniques? What about specific, detailed processes for idea selection and effective follow-through?

SmartStorming was developed to help answer all of these questions. In the upcoming chapters, you will be introduced to this innovative, truly comprehensive, step-by-step creative problem-solving process for planning and leading highly effective group ideation sessions. And it will transform forever the way you think about and approach brainstorming.

What to remember

- Brainstorming, as typically practiced, is a flawed and incomplete process.

- Effective brainstorming requires a number of critical elements for guaranteed success, such as preplanning the session, clarifying the goals and objectives, following a structured process, new stimuli for the imagination, a variety of idea-generation techniques, etc.

- More than 90 percent of those individuals leading brainstorms, in any industry, have had little to no training in how to do so effectively.

- SmartStorming provides a foolproof, step-by-step process, designed to solve the most common failings of traditional brainstorming.

CHAPTER 3

SmartStorming—The 21st-Century Evolution of Brainstorming

"The way to get good ideas is to get lots of ideas, and throw the bad ones away."
—Dr. Linus Pauling

SmartStorming is not just a better way to brainstorm; it is an evolution in group ideation methodology. It is something you've never experienced before, and when learned and practiced, it eradicates all of the fundamental weaknesses of traditional brainstorming.

After working nearly twenty-five years each in the fields of advertising and strategic marketing communications—industries that demand fresh, innovative ideas on a daily basis—we have sat through more than our share of disappointing, ineffective, unproductive (and yes, even dysfunctional) brainstorms. We have witnessed rudderless facilitation and ego-driven, territorial battles. We have seen younger, less experienced group members shut down when their idea was ridiculed by the boss. We have looked on as groups meandered off topic and got lost in diversions. We have marveled at how few truly original ideas were generated after an hour, two hours, two days of brainstorming, and wondered, weeks after a session, whatever happened to the big breakthrough concept that was offered up.

It became all too clear to us that something was badly broken. And we weren't the only ones who felt this way. Over the years, the hundreds of professionals we've spoken to about this topic have pretty much universally shared the same experiences, opinions, and frustrations.

In an effort to create a better way to brainstorm, we asked these people what they felt was missing in the brainstorming process. We analyzed all of the best practices in innovation, creative problem solving, and group ideation. We researched the topic, all the way back to Alex Osborn's own commentary from the 1930s. We uncovered a lot of great thinking. In fact, as we mentioned earlier, Osborn did develop his own highly respected Creative Problem Solving process for brainstorming along the way.

But still, we found that a number of practical, real-world principles, steps, tools, and techniques were missing; specifically, there was little written about pre-session planning (blueprinting a great session), creating group alignment, or the specific types of leadership skills required to inspire and manage groups productively in today's fast-paced, time-crunched, innovation-driven world.

This book was written to help fill the void. It is not just an instructional guide to the SmartStorming process, but a valuable reference tool for anyone who leads, or hopes to lead, successful group idea-generation sessions. In this book you will find everything you need to plan and lead highly effective SmartStorming sessions, time after time.

Group genius

As creative professionals ourselves, we realized that any effective group-ideation technology must focus on three critical elements: creative problem-solving productivity, positive group dynamics, and effective interpersonal communication.

Obviously productivity is at the core of any ideation process; if a system is to be viewed as successful, it must result in an abundance of new, innovative ideas. Since we are talking about working in groups, the system must also provide for a positive group dynamic; people have to work together in an efficient, productive, and pleasant manner if the group is going to succeed. And finally, without the ability to easily, clearly, and confidently communicate among group members, nothing will ever get achieved; effective interpersonal communication is critical to the success of any group enterprise.

With these three elements at its core, SmartStorming allows groups to function much in the way highly creative individuals do. Creativity is an elusive process for many. How does someone make new connections and think of something that's never been imagined before? But this is precisely what creative types do every day. And SmartStorming allows groups to do the same, collectively and cooperatively. The process facilitates the generation, development, and clear expression of innovative ideas—with the added power of group thinking (the "two heads are better than one" advantage we wrote about earlier). The result is a powerful force often referred to as *group genius,* and SmartStorming is uniquely capable of helping to maximize it in any group.

When groups have been trained in the SmartStorming system, they are delighted at how much more productive they are, how much more efficient their use of time is, how much more enjoyable their sessions are, and how much more often they develop winning ideas that move their businesses forward and give them a competitive edge in the marketplace. Traditional brainstorming as widely practiced today tends to be a relatively passive approach: *Let's get together and hope something happens.* SmartStorming is a dynamic and proactive process: *Let's work systematically to ensure we achieve or surpass our goal.* It is the power of group genius unleashed, whenever and wherever you need it.

The three pillars for success

The SmartStorming system is built on three pillars necessary for effective group ideation:

Structure—Unlike traditional brainstorming, which by its nature is often loosely structured, SmartStorming utilizes a proven, repeatable, six-step process designed to optimize the flow of ideas and energy and to ensure consistent results. Like the carefully sequenced acts in a tightly choreographed play, each SmartStorming step builds momentum on the one before, helping to maximize a group's creative performance and productivity. Groups stay on schedule and make the best possible use of time.

Leadership Skills—The vast majority of individuals leading brainstorms have had little to no formal training whatsoever in how to do it. SmartStorming provides the principles and specific skills a session leader needs to help inspire and guide a group more productively and with less effort from start to finish.

Idea-Generation Techniques—SmartStorming includes a library of proven effective idea-generation techniques that can be used by any group for any creative, strategic, tactical, or planning challenge.

How SmartStorming is different

In the previous chapter we listed the eight most common failings of traditional brainstorming sessions. SmartStorming was specifically designed to address and eliminate each of these weaknesses.

Traditional brainstorming	vs.	SmartStorming
Little to no planning	>	Comprehensive session blueprint
No structure/process	>	Proven structure/process
Lack of skilled leadership	>	Skillful leadership
Poorly defined goals	>	Clearly defined goals
Lack of stimuli	>	Stimuli for making new creative connections
Lack of rules	>	Defined rules/guidelines
Few ideation techniques	>	Collection of proven ideation techniques
Poor follow-through	>	Step-by-step follow-through and action steps

The result is a repeatable system that ensures increased efficiency (through a proven structure and facilitation skills), greater productivity (thanks to proven ideation techniques and tools), and vastly improved group participation, contribution, and morale.

Why SmartStorming works

While many brainstorming sessions can lapse into haphazard, hit or miss affairs, SmartStorming sessions are consistently effective and highly productive. Our clients who have implemented the SmartStorming methodology throughout their organizations consistently report immediate, dramatic improvement in the areas of innovation and employee morale.

There are a number of key factors contributing to SmartStorming's effectiveness: a clear statement of session goals and objectives; a structural blueprint designed to build success; agreed-upon rules and guidelines for group behavior and participation; alignment of group energy and focus; massive idea generation; unambiguous idea selection criteria based on defined objectives; and a thorough, systematic process for follow-through, to ensure great ideas actually get implemented.

The fun factor

But there is another reason SmartStorming works so well. People like it.

When a group finds a collaborative process pleasurable, when it makes them feel good about the job they're doing and the contribution they're making, and when it helps them work more effectively and productively, both individually and with their colleagues, they embrace it. Only ideas that are embraced and utilized can be successful. SmartStorming is just such an idea. In every sense, it is evolutionary and transformational. And as you will see in the coming chapters, the real beauty of it is that it is incredibly easy to learn and apply.

What to remember

- Effective brainstorms must succeed in three areas: Creative problem-solving productivity, positive group dynamics, and effective interpersonal communication.

- SmartStorming is built on the three pillars necessary for brainstorming success: Structure, Leadership Skills, and Idea-Generation Techniques.

- SmartStorming directly addresses each of the eight most common weaknesses of traditional brainstorming.

- One of the key reasons SmartStorming is so effective is that it makes brainstorming a more enjoyable and productive process for everyone involved.

Part One
SmartStorming
Fundamentals

CHAPTER 4

SmartStorming Principles and Best Practices

"I have an existential map. It has 'You are here' written all over it."

—Steven Wright, comedian

You are here…at the start of your SmartStorming journey. In order to get from where you are now to where you want to go—being able to plan and lead dynamic, highly productive group ideation sessions, time after time—you will be following a carefully designed course, a clear, well-traveled path to success. Stay on that path, don't wander off, perform the tasks required, enforce a few rules, and listen to some advice from those who have traveled before you, and you will absolutely reach your desired destination. Before we actually begin the journey, however, there are a few things you will need to know.

First, every successful journey requires a map, and SmartStorming is no exception. You will need to familiarize yourself with that map, the Six-Step SmartStorming Process. Thoroughly understanding this structure, and the meaning and value of each step, is important for success.

Second, by definition, you will not be taking this journey alone. Group idea generation involves, well, a group. In order for your endeavor to be successful, there are certain roles that must be defined. And so, before you depart, you will need to understand what you and those traveling with you will be doing.

Finally, there are those rules we mentioned—not many, but they are extremely important. In order to stay on the path, and in order for everyone in your group to do what is required of them, rules must be established and adhered to. In this chapter, you will receive your Rules of the Game.

So let's get started. You have some very interesting ground to cover.

The SmartStorming process

SmartStorming is built on a proven six-step structure that optimizes the flow of ideas and energy and delivers consistent results.

Like the carefully sequenced acts in a tightly choreographed play, each Smart-Storming step builds momentum on the one before, helping to maximize a group's creative performance and productivity. Groups stay on schedule and make the best possible use of time. SmartStorming leaves nothing to chance. Each step of the process is clearly defined, with specific action items provided. The steps are sequential and flow naturally from one to the next.

By having a clearly defined process to follow, the group leader is free to focus attention on the group dynamics, allowing him or her to more effectively inspire and guide the group's exploration.

The six SmartStorming steps

Here is a brief explanation of the six SmartStorming steps, each of which will be covered in great detail later.

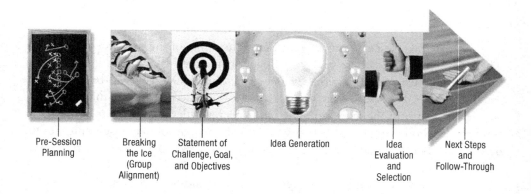

| Pre-Session Planning | Breaking the Ice (Group Alignment) | Statement of Challenge, Goal, and Objectives | Idea Generation | Idea Evaluation and Selection | Next Steps and Follow-Through |

1. Pre-Session Planning

The majority of traditional brainstorms begin with little or no detailed thought beforehand about what will actually take place in the session. Pre-planning a SmartStorming session has a number of valuable benefits: Session leaders have a blueprint indicating exactly how to most effectively conduct the brainstorm; groups stay focused and on track, and the likelihood of wandering off course or lethargy is minimized; and most important, the ultimate creative yield of the group (the breadth, depth, and number of new ideas the group generates) is maximized. Issues to be addressed by the leader prior to the start of a session include: clarifying goals and objectives; identifying the best participants to invite; determining what background information, stimuli, and resources may help participants generate ideas; choosing the best icebreaker and ideation techniques for the task at hand (more on these later); developing a list of criteria for evaluating and selecting the best ideas; and planning the next steps and follow-through tasks that will take place once the session is complete. In Chapter 5, we have included a comprehensive checklist you can use to ensure you address each of these topics.

2. Breaking the Ice (Creating group alignment)

At the start of a typical brainstorm, a group's attention is often scattered. Participants may be in the room physically, but their minds tend to be elsewhere, thinking about outside concerns, totally unrelated to the brainstorming session about to take place. This is especially true if participants are juggling multiple projects or work in a busy, fast-paced business or in an organization that is lean on staff. The key to a successful SmartStorming session is to first transform a room full of individuals into a collaborative team, aligned toward a common goal, and to do so as quickly as possible, to make the most of your allotted time. The fastest, most effective way to do this is to engage the group in an enjoyable activity that releases attention from outside distractions, breaks down interpersonal boundaries, and gets the creative juices flowing. This is often referred to as "breaking the ice." In this book, you will discover a number of engaging ice-breaking activities.

3. Statement of Challenge, Goal, and Objectives

How often have you participated in a brainstorm, only to see it quickly derailed by off-topic conversation, failure to meet expectations in terms of the quality and quantity of ideas generated, and disruptive behavior? In order to avoid these types of problems, the leader needs to set the stage by clearly and provocatively summarizing the brainstorm challenge, clearly defining the goals and objectives of the session, establishing the rules by which the session will be conducted, and posting them all prominently in the room. This step is critically important in order for the group to be fully aligned toward a common goal and focused, and to remain on track.

4. Idea Generation

Of course, idea generation is the heart of any brainstorm, and the SmartStorming system is no exception. This is when participants are doing what they came to do—generate fresh, new ideas! The difference is that in a SmartStorm, they will generate more, better, executable ideas than ever before—first, because the other steps in the SmartStorming process help to ensure the ultimate effectiveness of your group's idea generation, and second, because you, the leader, will be armed with a portfolio of proven ideation techniques designed to inspire new and different ways of thinking about any challenge.

5. Idea Evaluation and Selection

In a typical brainstorm, idea selection is a largely subjective process; the ideas selected are the ones liked most by those in charge, or by group preferences. SmartStorming provides a more effective approach. A SmartStorming session can easily generate hundreds of ideas, only a few of which might successfully address the challenge. So how does one efficiently and accurately separate the wheat from the chaff, and ensure that the best ideas are harvested and carried forward? This step incorporates a systematic process for evaluating ideas against a predetermined set of objective selection criteria. It not only simplifies and speeds up the process, it makes it far more balanced and productive.

6. Next Steps and Follow-Through

Most brainstorms end when a range of promising ideas are generated. But even the best ideas are worthless if they aren't carried forward and brought to life. The final step in the SmartStorming process takes a systematic approach to recognizing the contribution of the group and establishing timelines, action steps, roles, and responsibilities to ensure accountability and compliance in taking the final step: implementing the idea.

As you can see, the Six-Step SmartStorming Process offers a comprehensive and systematic approach to brainstorming. It is built on the principle that a successful brainstorm involves much more than just idea generation; it is a process that should be planned, actively and expertly led, and carried through to completion. You will be learning more about each of the steps in subsequent chapters. But first, there are some additional fundamentals to cover.

The three SmartStorming roles

Individuals participating in SmartStorming sessions play one of three roles: Pilot (session leader), Reporter (scribe/idea catcher), and SmartStormer (idea generator). Each plays a different, critical part in the process; each is equally important.

The Pilot

In SmartStorming, the session leader is referred to as the Pilot. Why a pilot? Because his or her role is to confidently and skillfully navigate the group through the SmartStorming process as smoothly and efficiently as possible. The Pilot determines the point of departure (creative challenge), plots the course (designs the session for maximum group productivity), and makes sure the endeavor reaches the desired destination (the achievement of the goals/objectives). The Pilot navigates the group through the inevitable ups and downs, twists and turns, and any turbulence encountered during the ideation process. If the energy level of the group drops too low, the Pilot helps elevate it. If the discussions veer off the subject, the Pilot quickly guides them back on course. A good Pilot makes the SmartStorming journey a smooth, pleasurable, and productive experience.

It is recommended that the Pilot *not* contribute his or her own ideas during the session, however tempting it might be to do so. Why? Because it's extremely difficult to have one's attention fully focused (outwardly) on inspiring and guiding a group's efforts while simultaneously fishing around for ideas in the inner recesses of one's own head. A multitasking Pilot runs the risk of becoming so absorbed in the content of the session that he or she can lose effectiveness in managing the process itself. So while the Pilot may be intimately involved with the challenge at hand, he or she will actually reduce the productivity of the session if preoccupied with thinking up and contributing ideas.

Don't worry, though—as Pilot, you will be able to guide your group's exploration of ideas in any direction you find interesting or fruitful, and even suggest certain specifics to inspire new thinking.

In Part Three of this book, SmartStorming Leadership Skills, you will learn a set of valuable principles and skills that will help you confidently inspire and guide groups to higher levels of productivity.

The Reporter

The Reporter is a volunteer team member selected to write down the ideas generated by the group, thereby freeing up the Pilot to focus exclusively on leading the group in achieving its goals. The Reporter's role is essential for running an effective SmartStorming session, as he or she helps to bring order, structure, and clarity to the process. The Reporter's duties include writing down all ideas quickly, accurately, and legibly for the entire group to see and reference later. He or she should also number each idea to provide continuity and spatial memory, as well as make note of any ideas worth coming back to for further discussion. It is the Pilot's job to ask for a volunteer to serve as the Reporter. If someone is a particularly good Reporter, that person can serve throughout the SmartStorming session; or a number of different group members can volunteer and take turns if that is a better solution for your group.

A word of advice: At times, it may seem tempting to simply have the Pilot also serve as Reporter. This can be even more disruptive to a Pilot's effectiveness than actively contributing ideas, and virtually ensures a less productive session. It is more difficult for a Pilot to effectively monitor, inspire, and lead a group while simultaneously listening and writing down ideas flying by at a fast and furious pace.

We will discuss different methods you can use to capture your group's ideas later in this chapter.

The SmartStormers

The role of the SmartStormers is to understand the goals, objectives, and rules of the session; enthusiastically contribute insights and ideas; and participate in selecting the most promising ideas (if appropriate). The more diversity there is among the participants, in terms of personality type, age, gender, culture, personal/professional background, job function, etc., the wider the range of insights and innovative ideas the group will generate.

Selecting your SmartStormers

The quality and creative yield of ideas in any SmartStorming session will only be as good as the people who make up the group—the SmartStormers. SmartStorming at its best is a group activity. Even the revered innovator Thomas Edison, who was awarded over a thousand patents in his day, had a small army of assistants and fellow inventors collaborating with him on his numerous projects. Success in today's highly competitive, innovation-driven marketplace is fueled by collaboration and connection.

In his book *Group Genius: The Creative Power of Collaboration,* author Keith Sawyer explains, "...the lone genius is a myth; instead, it's group genius that generates breakthrough innovation. When we collaborate, creativity unfolds across people; the sparks fly faster, and the whole is greater than the sum of its parts. Collaboration drives creativity because innovation always emerges from a series of sparks—never a single flash of insight."[7]

This is the essence of group creativity. And it is precisely what we want to tap into with SmartStorming.

Group creativity and flow

The most productive SmartStorming sessions occur when the group becomes so absorbed in their activity that they slip into a state of *flow*. Flow is that peak performance state athletes refer to as "The Zone." The term "flow" was coined by Mihaly Csikszentmihalyi, one of the world's leading researchers on positive psychology and states of optimal experience. When a group becomes single-mindedly focused in its creative problem-solving activity, all sense of time, place, and self-consciousness (ego) disappears. Everyone feels highly alert and on top of their game. It is under these conditions that a unified sense of effortless collaboration emerges; the group begins to function as a single, collective mind that intuitively knows the best ways to build upon, amplify, or refine one another's ideas.

For group flow to take place, there needs to be a balance between the difficulty of the challenge and the group's (both individual and collective) ability to overcome that challenge. If the challenge is greater in scope than the knowledge, skills, or expertise of the group, the result will be stress and anxiety—that uncomfortable feeling that the group is not up to the task. Conversely, if the challenge is perceived as too easy, the group will quickly become bored and lose interest. In short, the group must be sufficiently challenged, but not to a degree that is beyond their abilities.

Selecting the most appropriate and effective group of SmartStormers for your specific challenge is the key to an enjoyable, super-productive idea-generation session.

Creating a dream team vs. inviting the usual suspects

If you were a basketball coach striving to win a championship, you would go to great lengths to assemble an all-star, powerhouse team of accomplished players. You wouldn't settle for a mixed bag of amateurs who just happened to be nearby and easy to recruit. To assemble this dream team, you would comprehensively scout for the most talented athletes who possess the specific skills, talent, and experience your team needs to win. Likewise, when faced with a tough business or situational challenge, shouldn't you carefully evaluate who in your organization or network possesses the best knowledge, skills, and experience to successfully tackle the challenge? Shouldn't your goal be to assemble the smartest, most capable, most creative problem-solving all-stars you can find?

But surprisingly, few brainstorm leaders invest adequate time or effort in this important step. They forego the due diligence of a scouting effort and more often than not extend invitations to the usual suspects. The term "usual suspects" here refers to those individuals who work in the same department or division, or work on the same product, service, or client account. It's all too easy to ask yourself why you should invite outsiders when you already know and feel comfortable with the usual suspects. After all, they understand your product, service, goods, or process and they understand the underlying issues, situation, and challenges right? Aren't these people the best qualified to help you develop innovative solutions to your problem? Not necessarily.

What is the downside to inviting only the usual suspects?

Conformity/uniformity in thinking (groupthink), a lack of objectivity or perspective, internal politics or infighting, and a general aversion to risk-taking or radical new ideas are all common pitfalls experienced when the same group of people come together repeatedly to generate ideas.

When participants all work under the same conditions and circumstances, confront the same challenges day in and day out, and repeatedly run into the same limitations or obstacles; when everyone shares the same assumptions about what is or is not possible, options can appear scarce—boxing in the group's thinking abilities.

The power of diversity

Who you invite to your SmartStorming session can have a dramatic impact on your productivity and the session's ultimate success. When you deliberately recruit a diverse group of SmartStormers—an all-star team from different backgrounds, cultures, genders, age, talents, skills, knowledge, expertise, and perspectives—you exponentially increase your group's ability to deliver innovative solutions.

In *Group Genius*, Keith Sawyer also writes, "...when solving complex, non-routine problems, groups are more effective when they're composed of people who have a variety of skills, knowledge, and perspective." He goes on to say, "The reason groups are so effective at generating innovation is that they bring together far more concepts and bodies of knowledge than any one person can. Group genius can happen only if the brains in the team don't contain all the same stuff."[8]

Seven ways to enhance diversity in your groups

1. **Invite a mix of generations.** Baby Boomers, Gen-Xers, Millennials—they each bring a different generational perspective, value, and skill set, plus different cultural reference points, beliefs, attitudes, and archetypes.

2. **Invite a range of expertise, professional backgrounds, and specialties.** Great ideas can come from anywhere. People from any discipline, even one not directly related to the challenge at hand, may offer incredible insights and value. Chances are someone has already solved a problem similar to this one before in a different company, industry, or country.

3. **Balance gender and social orientation.** Just as different generations can provide a variety of perspectives, so can individuals with diverse personal backgrounds.

4. **Invite people from different countries of origin.** Thanks to today's global economy, we are increasingly working side by side with individuals from across the country and across the globe. Capitalize on their diverse world viewpoints and cultural understandings. Cultural fusion is a powerful element of innovation.

5. **Invite right- and left-brain thinkers.** Yes, in the same group! Creative types and linear thinkers, artists and bean counters. You may not think they mix well, but in fact, the yin and yang of linear/analytical versus nonlinear/creative thinkers can be an important element in the creative process.

6. **Invite introverts and extroverts.** Maybe add a dash of Meyers-Briggs personality types. Look for individuals with different ways of perceiving and interpreting: feeling, intuiting, judging, etc. This will add a richer dimension to your group's problem-solving abilities.

7. **Throw in one or two unexpected special guests.** An unexpected participant can stir things up and add a new dynamic into the mix. You can invite customers, clients, suppliers, kids, etc.—anyone who can provide fresh, new perspectives on your challenge.

Who NOT to invite to your SmartStorm

A successful SmartStorming session is a co-created effort, not a competitive sporting event for egos. Group flow can only occur in an environment that feels safe, positive, and fairly governed by established rules and guidelines. Unfortunately, not everyone is interested in or capable of being a team player focused on the greater good. Here are a few of the personality types you might want to avoid inviting to your SmartStorming sessions.

Attention Vampires—They always want to stand out, be in the spotlight, and the center of attention. It's always about them. Attention Vampires can smother a SmartStorming session by dominating the conversation, excessively pushing their ideas and ultimately sucking the life out of the whole group.

Wet Blankets—These are the pessimists who see the flaws in everyone else's ideas. Nothing goes unscathed. Wet Blankets have the unique ability to instantly dampen the enthusiasm level of a session. They are discouraging and depressing, and the majority of their comments don't hold water.

Idea Assassins—These seasoned killers LOVE to shoot down ideas—anyone's and everyone's. Under the pretense of being constructive, they will find flaws, poke holes, and pick apart fledgling ideas until they bleed to death. These are the same people who go to birthday parties and enjoy popping the balloons.

Dictators—They love every idea—as long as it's theirs. These totalitarians believe they are the only ones with good ideas, or good taste, for that matter. Everyone else's contributions need to conform to theirs or risk being shot down. A lot of bosses unknowingly become Dictators in meetings; their role in the company relative to others in the room makes it too easy. Such idea overlords are to be avoided at all costs. Never let them dictate a negative outcome for your group.

Obstructionists—To them, nothing is simple or easy. They overcomplicate conversations and procedures, and bring up extraneous facts or considerations that derail the flow of the group. Obstructionists overthink, overspeak, and single-handedly dead-end otherwise promising sessions.

Social Loafers—These are the people who show up for a brainstorm session, but rarely participate in the generation of new ideas in a meaningful way or contribute much of substance. They usually sit back, appearing bored or aloof, and let others do the heavy lifting.

As you can see, when deciding upon participants to invite to your SmartStorming sessions, it's best to seek out individuals who possess a positive, can-do attitude and collaborative nature.

Rules of the Game

Just hearing the word "rules" is a turnoff for some people. Rules mean they are going to be restricted, limited, or told what they are and are not allowed to do. But rules are essential. Every well-conducted group activity in the world has rules—sports, games, meetings, legal proceedings, medicine, classrooms, even extreme kick-boxing death matches have rules. If a group of people are coming together to accomplish something, there must be rules and guidelines established to ensure that the process runs smoothly and productively. This is precisely why *Robert's Rules of Order* has long been the accepted guidebook for conducting orderly and productive meetings.

Nowhere is this more important than in a group ideation session. As we have already established, this experience can be fraught with perils that can derail a session, including:

Judgment/Negativity/Intimidation—We once knew a company president who started every brainstorm session the same way. He would look around the room—at all the people there who worked for him—and announce, "You know how they say there is no such thing as a bad idea? Well, that's not true. There *are* bad ideas. Ideas so bad they should never be spoken out loud. … Okay, so what have we got?" Needless to say, at that point the creative spirit of the group was effectively hogtied and gagged. No one had the courage to utter even one risky (a.k.a. unconventional, potentially innovative) idea. It doesn't take anywhere near this degree of intimidation to stifle a group's creativity. Even without such a daunting setup, many people will be naturally timid about sharing their thoughts, for fear of being viewed as foolish. Fear of judgment kills more ideation sessions than anything else, except perhaps…

Ego—The overly asserted ego is a surefire idea-squasher. As you've already learned, the ego asserts itself in many guises, with names like The Attention Vampire, The Wet Blanket, and The Idea Assassin. These entities are the antithesis of the fearful participant; they assert their opinion that their own ideas are always golden, and everyone else's are flawed—and they have no qualms about forcefully expressing both of those beliefs. Just one such ego-driven individual in a brainstorming session is enough to make it crash and burn. Put two or more in the room, and you're doomed. Nothing to do then but sit back and watch them battle for dominance.

Outside Distractions—iPhones, BlackBerrys, smart phones, iPads, laptops, and other electronics brought into the session (when not being used for idea generation) almost always lead to distraction, split attention, and attention leaks. Out-of-control robo-texting distracts not only the concentration of fellow participants but also a Pilot's attention. Unfortunately, this phenomenon is something we have all become far too accustomed to in business meetings (and personal get-togethers). The offenders generally laugh off any criticism and chalk it up to multitasking. But in fact, research has shown that the effective multitasker is a myth. The truth is that the more tasks one attempts to accomplish simultaneously, the less effective he or she is at any of them. And nowhere is this more evident than in a brainstorm.

Off-Topic Conversation—Coworkers often take advantage of the opportunity to catch up with each other when they find themselves in a meeting together. Obviously this behavior is not conducive to effective brainstorming once the session is under way. The more time and attention devoted to discussing other projects, the less will be focused on generating breakthrough ideas.

Fortunately, Rules of the Game can eliminate, or at least significantly minimize, such disruptive problems. By establishing a list of rules and guidelines for participation *before the session*, introducing them to the group, and, most important, getting universal agreement from all participants to abide by the rules, you give your SmartStorming sessions a markedly greater chance of achieving super-productivity.

Once you have decided what your session rules will be, write them on a large sheet of paper (or on a whiteboard), then display them prominently in the room before starting the session. Take the group through the rules, one at a time, making sure the meaning and context for each rule are clearly understood by everyone. Ask for verbal agreement. You can also invite the group to contribute any additional rules they might want to suggest and add them to your list.

What happens when someone breaks a rule? We will discuss that in greater depth later; but as a starting point, you will at least have a visual reminder of the rules to refer to, posted on the wall, right there in front of everyone.

Many brainstorming experts have generated their own list of rules. Alex Osborn's original work included four: focus on quantity, withhold criticism, welcome unusual ideas, combine and improve ideas. Tom Kelly, of the renowned design firm IDEO and author of *The Art of Innovation*, adds others, such as "be visual" and "one conversation at a time." Here is our expanded list of some of the best known and most effective Rules of the Game to get you started.

(The Rules of the Game can also be found in Chapter 21. A poster-size version can also be downloaded at http://SmartStormingBook.com/Toolkit.htm.)

Rules of the Game

Suspend all judgment
Criticism and judgment will inhibit participants from sharing ideas; ideas will be evaluated later on during the selection process.

There is no such thing as a bad idea
Hey, you never know. Even the worst-sounding idea can contain the seed of a great idea within it.

Maintain an ego-free zone
In a collaborative group problem-solving effort, the originator of any idea is irrelevant.

Go for quantity, not quality
For every 100 ideas generated, only a few will be truly original ideas with potential.

Embrace wild, audacious ideas
You never know how far you can go until you've gone too far. It's better to push concepts to the edge than be too conservative.

Build upon one another's ideas
A group working collaboratively can generate bigger and better ideas than individuals working alone.

One conversation at a time
Side conversations create distractions and split the participant's focus.

Nothing is impossible
Yesterday's impossible ideas (flying, personal computers, 3-D movies, etc.) are today's realities. Think forward.

No texting or emailing during the session
Multitasking is a myth; texting distracts participants from the goal of generating ideas.

The boss speaks last
When an authority figure participates in a brainstorm, his or her comments and opinions often sway or inhibit a group's exploration of ideas. Ask respectfully that the boss hold comments until all others have shared.

When someone breaks the rules

We are often asked what the Pilot should do when somebody breaks the rules. In order to answer the question, we need to consider three distinct types of rules infractions: negativity (judgment, criticism), self-interest (railroading one's own ideas, attention-seeking, dominating conversation), and distractions (texting/iPads/laptops, excessive clowning around, side conversations, or other distractions).

Managing negativity

It is essential that the Pilot review the Rules of the Game with participants before the session begins.

- Display a large poster listing the Rules in a location where they will be visible to everyone throughout the session.

- Give particular attention to the first rule, "Suspend all judgment." Ask everyone to agree, and then announce a zero-tolerance policy for the session.

- Explain the method of enforcement. If anyone exhibits any type of negative behavior, he or she is to be immediately bombarded mercilessly by the group with crumpled paper balls (foam or squishy balls are even more fun and effective, if you have some). Make it a game. Encourage everyone in the room to participate in order to create a self-policing environment. While it may seem silly, this technique is a playful, good-natured way to remind a culprit of his or her transgression, and allow the group itself to enforce the "No Judgment" rule. Try it. You will be amazed at how quickly it defuses what could be a tense moment and allows you to quickly get your session back on track.

Other tips:
- Before your session, hand out a noisemaker to each participant (whistle, bell, clicker, etc.). Ask your group to act as whistle-blowers and actually blow a whistle (or ring a bell, click a clicker, etc.) every time someone slips and makes a negative comment.

- You can challenge the offender to come up with three better ideas (than the one criticized) on the spot. It's always easier to shoot down ideas than to develop new ones.

- Allow the group to gag the judging culprit with a bandana.

- Make all judging culprits sing the chorus of "Oops! I Did It Again" by Britney Spears.

Managing self-interest

When a participant is dominating the session, and especially when pushing only his or her ideas, the Pilot should immediately remind the group that equal contribution and collaboration is the goal of the session. As we said earlier, "Ten heads are better than one."

Other tips:

- Reinforce the fact that the SmartStorming session is an ego-free zone; the origin of any idea is irrelevant.

- Thank the attention hog for the idea(s); then turn attention to the rest of the group and ask: "What other perspective does someone have to share?"

- Alternatively, redirect the conversation away from the domineering participant by saying, "Thank you. Now let's give the rest of the group a chance to share their ideas."

- Quickly shift gears and introduce a *nonverbal* SmartStorming exercise. For example, ask everyone to silently write down five ideas, and then read their favorite aloud. (See idea-generation techniques in Chapter 20.)

- Break the group up into smaller teams of three people to generate ideas.

It is important to establish clear boundaries with an Attention Vampire right away. The longer you allow the behavior to continue, the more difficult it will be to stop it and get your SmartStorming session back on track.

Managing distractions

In today's high-tech business environment, our constant connection to the outside world is the most common impediment to smooth-flowing sessions, and the one that is most difficult to stop. Many people feel compelled to be continuously reachable and in touch, especially during the workday, and to frequently check and respond to any email messages they receive. The proliferation of texting in our culture only exacerbates the situation.

In order to get the most productivity out of a group ideation session, it is essential that everyone unplug in order to be more fully focused on the task at hand. Therefore, it is crucial that the Pilot ask everyone in the room to agree to the "no smart phones/iPads/laptops" rule. If anyone truly feels they are unable to be out of constant communication for sixty or ninety minutes, then thank them for their interest—and ask them politely to excuse themselves. Of course, welcome them to share any ideas they may have after the session.

Other tips:
- Make an airline-style announcement. Ask the group to turn off all electronic

devices and stow them away safely. Or make a humorous commercial announcement like the ones you see at the movies. (Note: There are a number of these on YouTube. If you have Internet access, you could play one for the group. Just search for "turn off cell phones.")

- Single out any texting culprit and ask, "So, what ideas does your friend on the outside have to offer?"

- Pause the session and have the group stare or make faces at the texting culprit (great peer pressure) until he or she realizes their transgression.

- Make a rule that whenever someone is caught texting or taking a call, they have to take over as Reporter.

- For hard-core smart phone/iPad/laptop addicts, you may want to ask everyone to check their devices at the door upon entering the room. You can lessen the group's withdrawal anxiety by announcing that there will be short breaks during the session when everyone is allowed to use their devices.

Managing the boss

When it comes to rules, the boss presents some unique challenges. In many business environments, people may not be comfortable pelting their superior with crumpled paper or foam balls, or dismissing their efforts to dominate a conversation.

While there is no guaranteed method for avoiding any such issues with the person in charge, there are some things you can try:

- If at all possible, keep the boss out of the session. Assure him or her that you will share any good ideas the group generates afterward. You may also simply tell the truth: that many people may be intimidated by the boss's presence in the room. And since he or she certainly wants the ideation session to be as productive as possible, it may be best if he or she waits to join the group until the end, when ideas have been developed and selected.

- If the boss must be in the session, ask prior to the start that he or she refrain from describing his or her likes and dislikes. Explain respectfully that if he or she were to do so, some participants in the room might become self-conscious about suggesting any idea that might risk criticism.

- When the boss is participating, make every effort to avoid allowing him or her to speak first. This is a surefire way to get others in the room to clam up. However, if the momentum is established by others, there's a greater likelihood the boss will play a supporting role.

- The same guidelines apply to clients or customers. If they are participating in the session, be sure they follow the same rules as the rest of the group.

A great tactic for avoiding the whole issue of rule-breaking is to divide the group into smaller teams of three. Have these subgroups develop ideas, and then have them take turns sharing the best ideas with the whole room. The odds of someone breaking the rules in a smaller, more intimate group are greatly diminished.

Stocking your group's inner creative pond

Innovation is fueled by curiosity, imagination, and inspiration. So are super-productive SmartStorming sessions. And that kind of inspiration can only flow freely when individuals and groups are exposed to a variety of new forms of mental stimuli (such as ideas, concepts, images, words, information, data, sounds, social media, live events, etc.).

The more mental stimuli a group has to play with, the more imaginative and resourceful they become at solving problems. New stimuli spark the brain's power of associative thinking and trigger spontaneous leaps in making new connections. Seeing new connections and combinations between two or more seemingly unrelated things is a hallmark of innovative thinking.

The daily practice of exposing one's mind to new and interesting stimuli to expand one's creative range and depth is called "Stocking the Creative Pond." This is the principle championed by Julia Cameron, the bestselling author of *The Artist's Way*. Cameron uses the metaphor of the mind as a creative reservoir—a kind of well-stocked pond that requires constant replenishment with "new and exotic fish to fry." She writes, "As artists, we must learn to be self-nourishing. We must become alert enough to consciously replenish our creative resources as we draw on them." She later warns, "If we don't give some attention to upkeep, our well [pond] is apt to become depleted, stagnant or blocked."[9]

This principle of continually stocking the pond with new stimuli is especially important for individuals who engage in frequent brainstorming sessions. Over time they run the risk of overfishing their creative reservoirs. Whenever you hear complaints about groups recycling the same old ideas over and over again, never coming up with anything truly new and unique, it's usually a telltale sign this principle of stocking the pond is being neglected or ignored.

How can you and your group keep your creative reservoirs well stocked with sources of new inspiration? We will discuss this important process in more detail in Chapter 8, Generating Ideas! Unleashing Your Group's Creative Genius.

Capturing your group's ideas

There are a number of different ways a group's ideas can be captured during a session. Here is a brief overview of some of the most widely used methods.

Sticky notes—Participants individually write down their ideas on sticky notes (one idea per note). This is one of the most common methods used by brainstorm facilitators because it allows a roomful of participants to "parallel process" (generate a large number of ideas simultaneously).

The benefits of using this method:
- A group of individuals working independently can generate more ideas, more quickly, than a group channeling all its ideas through a single person recording everyone's ideas.

- This method is usually done silently, so introverts can contribute ideas free from self-consciousness, peer pressure, or the intimidation of dominating personalities.

- Participants can select the ideas they wish to share with the group.

- Since each idea is recorded individually, on a single note, they can be physically organized, moved around, or grouped into clusters, based on similarities in theme or attributes.

- Ideas can be submitted for consideration anonymously.

Potential drawbacks of using this method:
- Idea overwhelm—the sheer number of sticky note ideas generated can quickly become unwieldy, especially if a roomful of participants are engaging in multiple rounds of generating ideas.

- Working independently, participants miss out on the opportunity to interact in real time, exchange perspectives, or spontaneously build upon one another's ideas.

- There is less opportunity for the Pilot to actively guide the group to explore a wide range of different problem-solving directions.

Writing ideas on a flipchart or whiteboard—This is another very common method of capturing a group's ideas. Someone from the group is asked to serve as the session Reporter (scribe/idea catcher). His or her job is to listen carefully and record and number all of the ideas presented by a group on a large flipchart or whiteboard.

The benefits of using this method:
- Group genius—Group members get the opportunity to interact in real time, exchange insights, cross-pollinate perspectives, and spontaneously build upon one another's ideas.

- The Pilot is free to actively inspire and guide the group to explore a wide range of different problem-solving directions.

- Ideas listed on the flipchart/whiteboard provide a common reference point for the group. Everyone can see the range of ideas generated and what areas of inquiry still need to be explored.

- The process is focused, orderly, and productive.

- The evaluation and selection process becomes faster and easier, as all of the group's ideas have been numbered and neatly listed in one place.

Potential drawbacks of using this method:
- Speed bump—The speed at which a Reporter writes down ideas can be significantly slower than the rate at which a group can call out ideas. So there's a chance the flow of ideas can get backed up or bottlenecked, and some ideas can get lost in translation.

- Ideas on a flipchart/whiteboard can't be physically moved around or grouped into clusters based on similarities in theme or attributes.

When choosing a volunteer Reporter, it's important to select an individual who possesses strong listening skills, plus the ability to capture and write down a group's ideas quickly and legibly. A skilled volunteer Reporter will make your leadership job easier and capture all the ideas your group has to offer.

Laptop Reporter—Another simple method used to capture the ideas in a session is to have a dedicated Reporter record the ideas generated by a group on a laptop. Once captured, these ideas can be projected in real time on a screen, printed out for participants to discuss, and/or emailed to participants and stakeholders. You can also utilize a laptop Reporter as an adjunct to any of the other idea-capture methods discussed here.

Interactive whiteboards—These devices allow you to digitize the ideas and drawings written on a whiteboard. There are many different types of these products on the market, such as older technologies that feature whiteboards with built-in copier capabilities—with the click of a button, the information on the whiteboard is scanned, printed, or digitized. Other products provide a video capture device and sensor that attach to an ordinary whiteboard to track and record ideas. Newer technologies feature touch-enabled "smart boards" with "digital ink" markers that record ideas and offer a multitude of options for saving and displaying files as screenshots, documents, web pages, etc.

Which idea-capture method is right for you?

As you can see, the options for capturing the ideas generated in a SmartStorming session range from low-tech, low-cost sticky notes and flipchart pads to high-tech, high-cost smart boards using digital ink markers. Deciding which option is right for your session depends upon your resources, budget, and personal preferences.

For the majority of people, the low-tech, low-cost methods of using sticky notes, flipchart pads, and ordinary whiteboards works perfectly well. In fact, many Smart-Storming Pilots, brainstorm facilitators, and participants actually prefer to use low-tech, hands-on methods of writing down ideas. There seems to be something more spontaneous and organic about jotting down ideas quickly on paper.

When we lead SmartStorming sessions for our clients, we tend to use a number of different low-tech methods. For example, we might begin a session by having a volunteer Reporter write down a group's ideas and insights on a large flipchart pad. Then, after an activity or two, we might divide the group into smaller teams and provide each team member with a sticky notepad so they can generate as many ideas as possible individually, then share and build upon one another's ideas collectively.

Many facilitators who lead large groups or important strategic sessions prefer to use a laptop Reporter or a high-tech smart whiteboard device for the ease of capturing, storing, and sharing ideas.

The most important consideration in selecting an idea-capture method is which ones feel the most comfortable for you to lead and your Reporter to manage.

What to remember

- The Six-Step SmartStorming Process provides a proven, systematic structure that addresses each important element necessary for successful brainstorming.

- There are three unique roles in a SmartStorming session: the Pilot, Reporter, and SmartStormers.

- Don't simply invite the usual suspects to your sessions. Strive for diversity of backgrounds, expertise, and experience for fresh, new perspectives.

- Avoid inviting overly judgmental, disruptive, or attention-seeking personalities.

- Establish, post, and enforce Rules of the Game for every SmartStorming session.

- It's important to help your groups stock their inner creative reservoir with a continuous supply of fresh, inspirational stimuli.

- There are a number of ways to capture the ideas generated by a group, including using sticky notes, a flipchart or whiteboard, a laptop, or a high-tech "smart board" device. For the majority of people, low-tech, low-cost sticky notes, flipchart pads, and ordinary whiteboards work perfectly well.

- It's important to select the idea-capture method that feels most comfortable for you to lead and your Reporter to manage.

Part Two
The Six-Step SmartStorming
Process

CHAPTER 5

Step 1—Creating Your Blueprint for Success

YOU ARE HERE

Pre-Session Planning

"Where no plan is laid, where the disposal of time is surrendered merely to the chance of incidence, chaos will soon reign."

—Victor Hugo, author

It is often said that where professionals plan, amateurs wing it.

And as we have already established, innovation (and group idea generation in particular) is too important an endeavor to approach in an amateurish manner and simply leave to chance. The risks of failure are significant, especially over the long term. Clearly, as with any other important business activity, in order to ensure success, brainstorming sessions should be properly planned.

As we discussed earlier, too many brainstorms end in disappointment because they fall short of goals and expectations. And so, unfortunately, since many people have never experienced a genuinely successful and rewarding one, they may not even know what to plan for.

Try to imagine what the perfect brainstorming session would look like. How many people would be there? Who in your organization would you want to be in attendance? How would they behave? What would the overall atmosphere and tone of the session be? Would people enjoy themselves? Would they express fresh, creative ideas freely and stay on track? How would you help the team get off to a fast, strong start? How would you go about inspiring and guiding your group each step of the way to generate the widest variety of fresh, new ideas possible? How many cool, breakthrough ideas would you be harvesting from your session?

If you want to create the kind of experience you are imagining, it is essential that you thoroughly preplan your sessions in a way that will ensure such an outcome. This first SmartStorming step is very often glossed over or omitted completely in traditional brainstorming, and yet, it is not only one of the easiest, it is one of the most critical. In fact, taking this one step alone can have a dramatic impact on the ultimate success of your ideation sessions.

There are three key advantages in preplanning your SmartStorming sessions:

1. **Preplanning helps your session flow more easily and productively from beginning to end.** As the leader, you enter the room with a greater sense of confidence because you have comprehensively mapped out the session your group is about to embark upon. You have clearly predetermined the challenge, goals, and objectives; invited the best crew (knowledge and experience) to help you achieve your goals; preselected the best idea-generation tools and techniques for the challenge; and determined the appropriate set of criteria for efficiently evaluating and selecting ideas. When you preplan your sessions, you minimize the Murphy's Law forces of chaos and entropy that can undermine traditional, loosely structured brainstorming sessions.

2. **Preplanning dramatically increases your group's yield of new ideas.** SmartStorming provides a rich, diverse portfolio of proven group idea-generation tools and techniques that will inspire fresh thinking and new ways to approach problem solving. These tools and techniques can be used individually or in a variety of combinations to eradicate limiting assumptions, explore multiple viewpoints, stimulate the popcorning of ideas, and accomplish specific types of ideation objectives. Preplanning provides you the valuable opportunity to orchestrate the best tools and techniques to ignite your group's imagination and achieve your goal. Doesn't that sound a lot more effective than just improvising what technique to use on the spot? Preplanning can dramatically increase your group's number and range of new ideas.

3. Preplanning frees you up to lead more effectively. Once you have completed your SmartStorming Pre-Session Planner, you will have created a clear, concise overview of how your session will flow from beginning to end. This is your blueprint, which takes all the guesswork out of how to structure your session—what to do or when to do it. It's all there, organized and in sequence. So as the group leader, you can focus on the matter at hand—generating ideas.

The SmartStorming Pre-Session Planner

The SmartStorming Pre-Session Planner makes it easy to plan each element necessary to structure great sessions, each and every time. The planner is simple and methodical. It is designed to stimulate your best thinking and get you highly organized, regardless of how challenged you may be in the organizational department. Creative, right-brained types (like your authors) will find the SmartStorming Pre-Session Planner a surprisingly fun and easy tool to use, and one that will help them stay focused and on track. Logical left-brain thinkers will appreciate the elegant simplicity of the Planner's checklist format.

SmartStorming preplanning requires an investment of just a few minutes of quality time, but guarantees your session will flow more efficiently and more enjoyably, and produce far superior results than traditional brainstorming efforts. Make it a habit to complete your SmartStorming Pre-Session Planner before each session, and you will change forever the way you approach group ideation meetings.

Following is an example of the SmartStorming Pre-Session Planner, which can also be found in Chapter 21, Guides, Planners, and Worksheets, and downloaded in digital format at http://SmartStormingBook.com/Toolkit.htm.

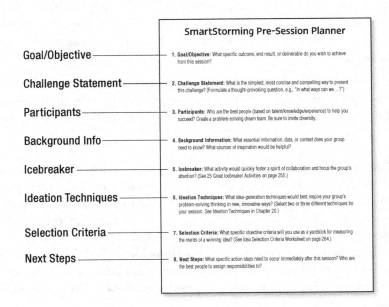

	SmartStorming Pre-Session Planner
Goal/Objective	**1. Goal/Objective:** What specific outcome, end result, or deliverable do you wish to achieve from this session?
Challenge Statement	**2. Challenge Statement:** What is the simplest, most concise and compelling way to present this challenge? (Formulate a thought-provoking question, e.g., "In what ways can we...?")
Participants	**3. Participants:** Who are the best people (based on talent/knowledge/experience) to help you succeed? Create a problem-solving dream team. Be sure to invite diversity.
Background Info	**4. Background Information:** What essential information, data, or context does your group need to know? What sources of inspiration would be helpful?
Icebreaker	**5. Icebreaker:** What activity would quickly foster a spirit of collaboration and focus the group's attention? (See 25 Great Icebreaker Activities on page 255.)
Ideation Techniques	**6. Ideation Techniques:** What idea-generation techniques would best inspire your group's problem-solving thinking in new, innovative ways? (Select two or three different techniques for your session. See Ideation Techniques in Chapter 20.)
Selection Criteria	**7. Selection Criteria:** What specific objective criteria will you use as a yardstick for measuring the merits of a winning idea? (See Idea Selection Criteria Worksheet on page 264.)
Next Steps	**8. Next Steps:** What specific action steps need to occur immediately after this session? Who are the best people to assign responsibilities to?

Here is a brief overview of each part of the Pre-Session Planner:

1. Clarify Your Goals and Objectives (the specific end result you wish to achieve)
It's very difficult to get where you want to go if you don't know where you're going. That's why goals and objectives are so vitally important. The more clearly defined your goals and objectives, the more likely it is your group will achieve them.

Goals and objectives are not the same thing. Goals are broader and more conceptual in nature. Objectives are specific and measurable. And so in a Smart-Storming session, your goal may be to develop strong, executable ideas (marketing strategies, product ideas, process innovations, etc.) that can be used to effectively solve a particular challenge (increase sales, leverage new technological capabilities, improve operational efficiencies, etc.). Your objective might be to generate fifty new ideas, six fresh strategies, or ten new tactics, or to more fully develop an existing idea during the time frame you designated for ideation.

Clarifying your goals and objectives focuses the group's attention and sets a high bar. This first part of the planning process clarifies exactly what you expect your group to achieve.

2. Craft a Compelling Challenge Statement (a clear and provocative description of the issue, challenge, or opportunity being addressed)
It is important to define the specific challenge to be addressed in your session in a simple, concise, and inspiring statement. First, be certain you are clear on precisely what challenge you will be focusing on. Then, express that challenge in a powerful and motivating way by using provocative language that will energize your group.

Make your challenge statement a springboard for the imagination, one that jump-starts your group's creative thinking process. Take the time to craft a compelling statement, and notice how much more innovative your group's ideas will be.

3. Choose Participants (selecting the best people to invite to your session)
You can dramatically increase the quantity and quality of the ideas your group produces by thoughtfully selecting your participants. Choosing individuals with the most appropriate backgrounds, skills, knowledge, and experience for the challenge, instead of simply inviting the usual suspects, is a critically important part of group ideation success. Why not think like a World Series championship team manager and recruit an all-star dream team possessing a diverse range of skills, one that virtually guarantees a positive outcome? This section in the plan-

ning process helps you do just that—evaluate exactly who the best SmartStormers are for your particular ideation challenge. (See Chapter 21 for a Participant Selection Planner.)

4. Provide Background Information (what your group needs to know)
In a typical brainstorming session, participants enter the room with only a vague notion of the task at hand. They may know the general subject, but all too often don't understand the specifics of the challenge. The most effective way to get your sessions off to a fast and productive start is to provide your SmartStormers with all the information they need to succeed—*before* the session takes place.

In this section you will identify the right mix of information and inspiration to jump-start your group's thinking process and fuel their imaginations. Naturally you will want to prepare a thorough brief (summary) of the challenge, the goals and objectives for the session (identified in parts 1 and 2), etc.

But why not also direct your team to interesting websites that contain related information, provide relevant articles, pose a few provocative questions for them to consider before attending the session?

There are many types of information that can make the difference between an abundant yield of new ideas and fallow fields: general background information, competitive information, mental creative stimuli that excite the senses and inspire new associations and connections (as discussed earlier in the section on "Stocking Your Creative Pond"), stimuli such as thought-provoking images, books, magazines, or articles; fieldwork; visiting places of inspiration (nature, movies, performances, lectures, museums, galleries, etc.); and related online resources such as websites, blogs, discussion groups, Pinterest pinboards, YouTube videos, or TED Talks. Be creative! You will reap enormous benefits.

5. Choose Your Icebreaker (create group alignment)
When participants enter the room, chances are they arrive with scattered attention, preoccupied with other concerns. The first job of a good Pilot is to help focus the group on the challenge ahead, free up their attention from outside distractions, break down interpersonal barriers, and galvanize them as a collaborative team aligned toward a common goal. The fastest way to accomplish this is through brief, playful icebreaker activities. Icebreakers are truly like magic. Within a few short minutes, your group will be more fully present, focused, and ready to tackle the challenge. SmartStorming provides a wide range of fun and effective icebreaker exercises for you to choose from; or you can create your own. This section prompts you to select the most appropriate icebreaker to use with your group. (See Chapter 21 for 25 Great Icebreaker Activities.)

6. Select Ideation Techniques (inspire fresh, new thinking)
While every part of a SmartStorming session is important, arguably the most important is the time allotted for actual idea generation. This is where it all finally happens, where creativity emerges and great ideas fly around the room— if you have addressed each of the preceding parts. Simply throwing ideas against the wall is hardly the most effective way to help groups generate an abundance of innovative concepts. There are dozens, if not hundreds, of techniques for stimulating the flow of original thoughts, helping teams expand and enhance the ideas of others and create totally new directions by combining or exploring various aspects of ideas.

The SmartStorming system provides a rich portfolio of proven idea-generation tools and techniques that help you and your group develop a wider depth and breadth of fresh, new ideas session after session. Some techniques are effective for coming up with volumes of ideas in a very short time; others help you drill down beyond limiting assumptions to see new possibilities, and still others can help your group multidimensionalize a problem from a range of different perspectives. This preplanning section helps you decide which tools and techniques will be most appropriate for your challenge and your group in order to ensure outstanding results. (See Chapter 20 for Idea-Generation Techniques.)

7. Establish Selection Criteria (the standards you will use to evaluate ideas)
A productive SmartStorming session can produce literally hundreds of new ideas. Some are great. Some have potential. Some are, well, you know.... How you organize, evaluate, and select the best of the bunch can be a daunting challenge, particularly in the heat of the moment and if you haven't considered your process ahead of time.

SmartStorming helps make this sometimes challenging process quite simple. Your selection criteria will be built directly from your challenge, goals, and objectives established earlier. By predetermining the specific yardstick you will use to measure the merits and effectiveness of potential ideas, you will have a clear, unambiguous process in place, ready to implement. (See Chapter 21 for the Idea Selection Criteria worksheet.)

8. Planning Next Steps and Follow-Through (begin the process of bringing your ideas to life)
Many people believe that a brainstorming session ends once the most promising ideas have been selected. In fact, the end of the idea-selection process actually launches an entirely new process—follow-through. Many people don't even consider this to be part of effective ideation. But even the most innovative ideas are

totally useless unless they are transformed from ethereal concepts into tangible realities.

To bring new ideas to life, next steps and timetables need to be determined, responsibilities assigned, milestones established, and progress meetings scheduled. The eighth and final part of the SmartStorming Pre-session Planning process is to outline ahead of time the follow-through and action steps necessary to quickly catapult your group into productive action. (See Chapter 21 for the 5-As Action Planner.)

That's it. Once you have completed your SmartStorming Pre-session Planner, you are all set! You will feel well organized, buttoned down, and more confident in piloting a great session. Your group will appreciate the difference the new structure and techniques will make in liberating their creativity to more effortlessly achieve success.

Of course, this is just a brief overview of the eight preplanning elements. You will learn more about each of them in later sections of the book.

Other important considerations when planning a session

In addition to blueprinting a great session with your Pre-Session Planner, there are three other important areas of planning that can have an impact on the quality and productivity of your future session.

These considerations are: 1) the duration of the session; 2) the time of day the session is scheduled to take place; and 3) the type of room/environment in which the session will be held.

Here are a few simple tips to help you plan the most comfortable and productive sessions possible.

Length of the session—When deciding how much time to allot for a session, it's important to first consider the specific nature of the challenge you plan to address. Is the issue a single, relatively straightforward challenge that can be handled in a session lasting a few hours or less? Or are you tackling multiple issues (or aspects to a challenge) that will require a full day, or multiple days?

The more challenges there are to address, the greater the number and variety of ideation techniques you will want to plan on using. We recommend using at least two different techniques per challenge. Piloting a group through each ideation technique can take anywhere from fifteen to sixty minutes, depending upon the type of techniques selected. When planning a lengthy session, it's recommended that you schedule short (ten-minute) breaks every seventy-five to ninety minutes.

Another time factor to consider is how many participants are scheduled to attend your session. It's important to appreciate that large groups tend to proceed at a slower pace than smaller, more nimble groups.

A simple formula you can use to ballpark the length of a session is to add up the approximate amount of time each activity in the process might take. For example:

Icebreaker activity = 10 to 15 minutes

Review brainstorming rules = 5 minutes

Introduce challenge, goals, and objectives = 10 minutes

Generate ideas = 15 to 60 minutes per ideation technique

Idea selection = 20 to 30 minutes

Next steps = 10 minutes

Breaks = 10 minutes (every 75 to 90 minutes)

Of course, these example timings can be modified to accommodate the specific challenge(s) at hand, or the time constraints of your group.

Time of day—When scheduling a SmartStorming session, it's wise to plan it for the time of day when people are at their most alert and active. Morning sessions are usually preferable. Avoid scheduling sessions that run over into the lunch hour (especially if you are not providing snacks, lunch, or beverages). Late afternoon sessions are generally less productive than those scheduled earlier in the day.

Session location—Always try to select a room for your session that is large, bright, comfortably furnished, and well ventilated. The type of environment you select will affect your participants' mood and energy level. If the room is small, dark, and stuffy, or the temperature is too hot or cold, participants will become uncomfortable and restless, and lose focus. Also, look for a room that provides ample uncluttered wall space where ideas can be displayed and evaluated.

These may seem like obvious best-practices to consider each time you plan a session. But you would be surprised how few brainstorm facilitators consider how time of day and room environment can affect productivity. Many facilitators simply schedule their sessions at a time that is convenient for them, and reserve whatever room happens to be available.

Now that you know about these important aspects of SmartStorming session planning, we're confident you will make the small, additional investment of time and effort required to design an enjoyable and rewardingly productive session.

What to remember

- Professionals plan for success; amateurs wing it.

- Preplanning your sessions will help them flow more easily, dramatically increase your group's creative yield of new ideas, and free you up to lead more effectively.

- The SmartStorming Pre-Session Planner makes planning your sessions simple.

- Three additional considerations to keep in mind when planning a session are 1) the time of day the session is scheduled; 2) the duration of the session; and 3) the type of environment selected for the session.

- Schedule your SmartStorming sessions for the time of day when people are at their most alert and active. Morning sessions are usually preferable.

- The more challenges there are to address, the greater the number and variety of ideation techniques you will want to plan on using.

- When planning a long session, it's recommended that you schedule short (ten-minute) breaks every seventy-five to ninety minutes.

- Select a room that is large, bright, comfortably furnished, and well ventilated.

CHAPTER 6

Step 2—Aligning Your Group for Collaboration

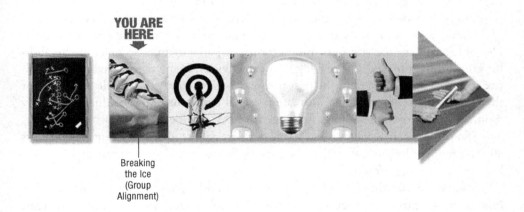

Breaking
the Ice
(Group
Alignment)

"Man is most nearly himself when he achieves the seriousness of a child at play."

—Heraclitus, Greek philosopher

A word about icebreakers

A common complaint about traditional brainstorming is that meetings get off to a slow start, and little, if anything, is done to foster a collaborative spirit or a shared sense of mission. In other words, nothing is done to break the ice (relax social formality) and align the group toward a common purpose and goal.

The deceptively simple, yet brilliant idea of investing the first ten minutes of a meeting engaging in a playful team-building activity to help people relax, break down interpersonal barriers, and foster a safe, open environment for sharing ideas has been around for a long time.

In today's fast-paced and highly distracted business world, few seasoned professionals would argue against the value of starting a brainstorm meeting with an icebreaker activity. The benefits of icebreakers are well known and supported by decades of research indicating that when groups engage in team-building exercises at the start of a meeting, they are significantly more collegial and productive than groups that bypass the process.

Yet, if icebreaker activities are so invaluable, why do so many facilitators forgo their use? It seems that icebreaking activities in general have gotten a bum rap over the years—they are the victim of bad PR, or, more likely, improper application. Many facilitators we've spoken with perceive icebreakers to be little more than trite team-building gestures or a frivolous waste of time. Others believe that engaging in a *playful* activity at the beginning of a meeting sets the wrong tone and detracts from the *serious* nature of their agendas. And then there are those few honest souls who admit to feeling self-conscious about their ability to effectively lead an icebreaker activity.

Brainstorm facilitators are not the only ones who harbor some resistance to the idea of icebreakers; it is not uncommon for participants themselves to let out an audible groan at the prospect of engaging in such activities. Many report having had negative icebreaker experiences in the past because the activities selected felt contrived, or they felt coerced into revealing intimate personal details or had to endure an activity dominated by attention-seeking or competitive personalities.

So while it seems evident that icebreakers are a great idea in concept, the benefits all too often get lost in translation (i.e., the facilitator's choice or execution of an icebreaker activity doesn't work).

But since breaking the ice is an important and necessary step in any effective brainstorming process, SmartStorming helps eliminate common icebreaker missteps. In this chapter, you will learn more about why icebreakers are an indispensable component of the group ideation process, as well as the leadership skills and techniques you will need to pilot engaging and productive group alignment activities in all of your future SmartStorming sessions.

The importance of icebreakers

The first thing an experienced SmartStorming Pilot will do when participants enter the room is to take a moment to read the mood of the group. He or she will observe closely to see if participants are relaxed and interacting with one another in a spontaneous, congenial way, or seem stressed, preoccupied, or standoffish. In the majority of cases, sessions start off with a mixed bag of both.

One of the simplest ways to discern your group members' states of mind is to notice where their individual and collective attention is focused, because that is where their minds are at that moment. A common situation you may face is a phenomenon one of our clients labeled the "bodies in the room, minds elsewhere" syndrome.

What the client was describing is the situation in which some participants show up physically, but their attention is somewhere else, focused on outside concerns or projects. Clearly this is less than ideal when attempting to lead them successfully in a process as involving as group ideation. When you have a group's full, undivided attention, you can easily get them focused on the goal and get your session off to a fast start. But when their attention is stuck on outside concerns, it takes considerably more time and effort to get things off the ground.

An important insight to keep in mind here is that each individual group member joining your SmartStorming session is entering the room from a different personal reality. For example, some participants may be enjoying a day with a comfortable workload; if so, they will have plenty of free attention available for generating ideas. Others, however, may be feeling overwhelmed by the stress of juggling multiple projects and deadlines; in this case, they will show up with exhausted or divided attention.

Personalities also contribute to the mix. Some participants enjoy being creative and look forward to the opportunity to contribute ideas, while others may feel insecure about their creative thinking abilities and slink into the session riddled with insecurities.

Regardless of how your participants show up to your SmartStorming session, it is your job as the Pilot to ground your group in the here and now, free up their attention from outside matters, and transform them from a group of individuals into an aligned team, focused on achieving a common goal.

A well-chosen, well-piloted icebreaker can help you accomplish all of the above in as little as ten minutes. And that's a pretty impressive feat when you think about it!

A word about the nature of attention

Icebreaker activities are an indispensable tool because they help quickly free up your group's attention. Free attention is extremely important because it is the focused mental creative energy that fuels your group's curiosity and imagination. The more free attention a group has available for idea generation, the greater their yield of fresh, new ideas will be. It is as simple as that.

Broadly speaking, attention comes in two basic states: free and stuck.

Free attention is awareness that is fluid, is easy to focus and shift from subject to subject, and can be used to explore any concept that captivates one's imagination.

Stuck attention is awareness that feels fixed on an issue, situation, or problem and cannot be easily freed up or shifted to another subject. Worries, concerns, preoccupation, and seriousness are all forms of stuck attention. When a group's attention feels stuck, it is very difficult for it to focus on or participate in events taking place in the present moment.

Why free attention is so valuable

As we mentioned earlier, the more free attention a SmartStorming group has at their disposal (individually and collectively), the greater their ability will be to explore a wider range of viewpoints, see new connections, make leaps of imagination, and identify promising pathways of opportunity.

The more stuck attention a group experiences, the less open and spontaneous they will be at generating ideas and creative problem solving.

The good news is that when you are able to help free up your group's attention from issues or outside concerns, you can re-channel that attention back into productive idea generation, just what you need for a successful SmartStorming session. And icebreaker activities are the ideal tool for the job.

Transforming a group from "Me" to "We"

A championship sports team can have any number of superstar players on their roster, but when they step foot on the court or field, that group of individual athletes transforms itself into a single-minded, goal-oriented, collaborative team. Winning coaches understand the power of team alignment. So do winning SmartStorming Pilots.

When you begin your SmartStorming session with an icebreaker, you help relax assertive egos and create a playful, noncompetitive environment for sharing ideas. Icebreakers are one of the most reliable ways to transform a room of "ME, ME, ME" into a single, collective "WE."

And that transformation from individual, self-serving egos to a unified group mind is one of the most important ingredients for success. When you shift your group from "Me" to "We," you unlock the power of collective group genius.

How to pilot your icebreaker activity

The keys to piloting a successful icebreaker are preparation and leading your activity with confidence and enthusiasm.

It all begins in the pre-session planning stage, where you select the most appropriate type of icebreaker for your group. Icebreaker activities come in a wide variety of themes and formats, so choosing the right one takes a bit of familiarity with the available options, plus a little good old-fashioned trial and error.

Selecting an appropriate icebreaker

There are two overall approaches you can take when selecting an icebreaker. First, you can choose an activity that relates directly to the session challenge. For example, you can ask participants to quickly compose and read aloud a four-line poem about the benefits of your new product or service. A second, more traditional approach is to select a fun team-building activity totally unrelated to your challenge, such as asking: "What's the fastest way to make a million dollars—without breaking the law?" The choice is yours; both approaches can work very well.

Perhaps a more important consideration when choosing an icebreaker is the makeup of your group (age, gender, cultural diversity, levels of seniority, etc.). Certain icebreakers simply work better for different groups.

For example, an edgy, personally revealing icebreaker like Truth or Dare could be an appealing, fun choice for a younger, hip group of twenty- to thirty-five-year-olds who know each other fairly well. But the same activity might go over like a lead balloon with a group of older, more conservative executives who share no personal relationships.

Conversely, a group of mature Baby Boomers might relish the nostalgic challenge of a round of Trivial Pursuit, while the same activity may be considered way too old-school by a group of Gen-Xers or Millennials.

Also consider the nature of your brainstorming challenge. If the goal of your SmartStorming session is to generate as many new ideas as possible, you may want to choose a fast-paced, free-association icebreaker activity like Idea Sprinting (which will be covered in detail when we get to ideation techniques) to get the creative juices flowing, rather than a low-key, team-building activity.

So in a nutshell, size up the nature of your group and the challenge at hand, then use your intuition to select the most appropriate icebreaker activity to get your session off to a fast, positive start. (See 25 Great Icebreaker Activities on page 255.)

Getting your group into The Zone

In an ideal world, each and every member in your SmartStorming group would show up ready and willing to enthusiastically participate in your icebreaker activity. But in the real world, almost every group contains members who might be a bit shy or introverted by nature, or feel self-conscious about their abilities, or doubt the value of what they have to say or offer. Self-consciousness, fear of judgment, and seriousness are the three biggest impediments to spontaneous participation.

So how can you encourage these reluctant personalities to join in your icebreaker activity?

The secret lies in creating a safe environment for sharing, establishing a fun challenge, and getting them so absorbed in your activity that all sense of time and self-consciousness slips away. In short, you want to get your group into The Zone.

Eight tips for leading successful icebreakers

Here are several proven tips for piloting successful icebreaker activities:

1. **Preplan and rehearse like a pro.**

   While icebreakers by nature are considered a fun activity, it pays to invest the time up front to read over the instructions several times until you are familiar with the activity and comfortable leading it.

   Ever notice how TV game show hosts always make the action appear effortless and spontaneous? Like all professionals, they master their role behind the scenes. For fun, try rehearsing your icebreaker instructions out loud (like your favorite game show host) until communicating each step in the icebreaker activity becomes second nature.

2. **Keep it simple and nonthreatening.**

   Icebreakers are most effective when they are kept simple and are not too personal or embarrassing. You may consider offering participants the option to pass on the activity if they are not comfortable. Also, take the time to be sure your instructions are clear and easy to follow, and confirm with the group that they understand all the directions before beginning. That way you will create a relaxed comfort level right from the start.

3. **Stock up with supplies.**

   Some icebreaker activities require specific supplies (such as writing or arts and crafts supplies, large pads, crayons, markers, modeling clay, etc.) or special props (such as foam balls or toys). Once you have selected your activity, check to make sure you have all the supplies or props you need, in the quantity you need them, prior to your session.

4. **Don't forget the timer.**

   The ideal length for a group icebreaker activity is a speedy ten to fifteen minutes, max. That's it. Anything longer can become a diversion from the real purpose of your SmartStorming session. And as we all know, time flies quickly when you are having fun. It is your job as the leader to make sure your icebreaker begins and ends on schedule. An inexpensive kitchen timer or stopwatch is a very useful tool to have on hand. Even most smartphones come equipped with handy countdown timers.

   Using a timer is easy. Once you have given your group clear instructions, set your timer to ten to fifteen minutes and hit the start button. Be sure to place the timer in plain sight to keep track of the time elapsed.

   It is always recommended to give your group a verbal two-minute warning before time runs out. When the alarm sounds, the activity ends.

5. Before you begin, do the math.

The most successful icebreaker activities are the ones where everyone is encouraged to participate and contribute. To give everyone in the group an equal opportunity, you need to have an idea of how much airtime should be allotted for each person.

Here is a simple formula to help achieve balanced participation: Count the number of participants in your SmartStorming session and divide that number into the total number of minutes you've allotted for your icebreaker. For example, if you have ten participants and allocate ten minutes for your ice-breaker, each person will have one minute in the spotlight. If you have only five participants, then each will have two minutes.

It is helpful to announce how much time each person has to participate so they know what to expect and can plan ahead. Naturally, some participants will lose track of time and take more than their share allotted. That is to be expected, but should be quickly corrected.

A good Pilot keeps one eye on the time and the other eye on moving the activity forward to conclude on schedule. If a participant does go on and on and on, you will need to remind the person that time is short and others are awaiting their turn.

6. Keep your enthusiasm level HIGH!

When piloting your icebreaker activity, it is important to do so in a spirit of confidence and positive enthusiasm. We refer to this as keeping your vibrational level high. Why is it so important to keep a high, positive energy level when leading your activity? Because your group will (consciously or unconsciously) match your level of energy.

If you lead your activity in a flat, low-energy, monotone manner, your group's energy level will drop down to match your low vibrational frequency. A low energy level seldom inspires energetic participation. Whenever you hear complaints about boring icebreakers that seem to drag on for an eternity, chances are the Pilot's vibrational level was too low. By contrast, your positive energy and enthusiasm (high vibrational level) will quickly elevate a group's energy level to match. High vibrational energy, combined with a light, fun attitude, will help draw participants out of self-consciousness or seriousness.

7. Keep it fresh.

They say that variety is the spice of life. So try experimenting with a different icebreaker activity at each new SmartStorming session. Don't become a one-trick pony. Good Pilots build up a personal portfolio of ten to twenty favorite activities they can use on any occasion. This book includes twenty-five proven icebreakers, and with a little research, you can find hundreds more new and different icebreaker techniques on the Internet.

8. Have fun!

Icebreakers are meant to be both enjoyable and engaging. The more fun you have piloting your icebreaker activity, the more fun your group will have participating. Think of icebreakers as "play with purpose!"

As your icebreaker activity works its magic, just watch the egos fade into the distance, interpersonal barriers come down, attention become freer from issues and outside concerns, and your group come together as a collaborative team, ready to tackle any challenge you define.

The twenty-five proven icebreaker activities on pages 255–258 will help get a group's creative juices flowing and your sessions off to a fast start. You can also download the icebreaker instructions in digital format at http://SmartStormingBook.com/Toolkit.htm.

What to remember

- Icebreakers are a very effective way to help participants relax, break down interpersonal barriers, and foster a safe, open environment for sharing.

- A well-chosen icebreaker helps ground participants in the here and now, free up their attention from outside matters, and transform them from a group of individuals into an aligned team, focused on achieving a common goal.

- Icebreakers help release stuck (fixed) attention and relax egos.

- When piloting an icebreaker activity, it is important to do so in a spirit of confidence and positive enthusiasm. Keep your vibrational level high!

- Do the math: Be sure to count the number of participants in your session and divide that number into the total number of minutes you've allotted for your icebreaker. For example, if you have ten participants and allocate ten minutes for your activity, each person will have one minute in the spotlight. Don't let your icebreaker activity exceed the time limit you set.

- Above all else, icebreakers should be FUN!

CHAPTER 7

Step 3—Creating a Springboard for the Imagination

YOU ARE HERE

Statement of
Challenge, Goal,
and Objectives

*"Of all the things I've done, the most vital is coordinating
those who work with me and aiming their efforts at a certain goal."*

—Walt Disney

When properly prepared and aligned, your SmartStormers will work hard to solve the problem you present to them. Defining the challenge and your group's goals and objectives not only provides direction but also clarifies your expectations for the end result you would like to achieve in the session. How clearly and compellingly you state the group's challenge has a direct impact on the quantity and quality of the ideas they will generate.

To ensure a successful outcome, it is the SmartStorming Pilot's job to establish the following criteria for the session:

1. Clearly define the group's goals and objectives for the session.

2. Accurately identify the specific issue, challenge, or opportunity to be addressed and present it in a compelling and thought-provoking manner.

3. Set an ambitious but achievable expectation for deliverables—the specific quantity and types of ideas, solutions, strategies, or tactics you want your group to generate by the end of the session.

One, two, three—simple, clear, and easy to understand.

Defining your group's goals and objectives

There is an old saying, "If you don't know where you're going, you will probably end up somewhere else." In the context of brainstorming, ending up somewhere else usually translates into a session that has veered off course (off purpose) and has failed to deliver the desired quality or quantity of useful ideas.

The two most common mistakes traditional brainstorm facilitators make are: 1) not clearly defining the goals and objectives for their sessions; and 2) sending their groups off to tackle the wrong challenge. Often this is caused by focusing efforts on a *symptom* of a problem rather than addressing the actual *source* of the problem.

Let's look at these two issues more closely.

Poorly defined goals and objectives

Goals can become hazy when too little information is provided, or there is a gross oversimplification of the problem. Conversely, goals can lose their clarity when overshadowed by too much data, information, or layers of complexity, or divided among too many objectives.

It is important to avoid the extremes of information understatement and information overload when stating the goals and objectives for your session. Presenting your goals with the right balance of relevant information and specificity helps your group's understanding and gets their efforts off on solid footing.

Types of challenges

It is important to recognize that there are a variety of types of challenges that groups may need to address. Often we are faced with an actual problem that must be solved. In this case, when we refer to a problem, we mean something that is wrong and presents us with less than optimal circumstances, or something that creates doubt, uncertainty, or difficulty.

But not all challenges are problems. Sometimes we are presented with new opportu-

nities, and our challenge is to identify the most effective ways of capitalizing on the potential of the situation. There are challenges related to simply improving or optimizing the
status quo—something that currently isn't necessarily a *problem*, but that can be made
better. Sometimes we simply have to come up with a new product name or company
slogan.

By being clear on the type of challenge you face, you will be more likely to generate the most appropriate solutions.

For any type of challenge, it is crucial to simplify it by breaking it down into the
most specific areas of exploration possible, rather than trying to address overly broad
and complex situations. For example, if you are searching for ways to add greater value
to an existing product or service, try identifying key areas of exploration—e.g., process
improvement, better internal and external communication, better pricing models—
and then generate ideas on each area separately, rather than tackling everything at once.
If some new market condition presents an unexpected opportunity (such as a competitor suddenly announcing that he's going out of business), first identify a variety of
areas on which you can capitalize—attracting their legacy customers, leveraging your
superior business strength in your marketing messages, negotiating better prices with
your suppliers, etc.—and then ideate on each one separately.

By narrowing your focus, you will find you are able to generate more, better ideas
than by trying to think in too many directions at once.

Solving the wrong problem

Real problems, those potentially negative issues or situations, present an additional consideration: ensuring that you are addressing the underlying cause rather than
merely masking obvious symptoms. Determining the root cause of a problem may not
always be as straightforward or easy as it might appear on the surface. So it is important to spend sufficient time and energy probing the different facets of a challenge
before committing to one specific problem-solving approach.

If a challenge defies your group's best attempts to solve it, chances are their efforts
are focused on eliminating a *symptom* of the problem rather than the actual *source* of the
problem itself.

Symptom vs. source

What is the distinction between the *symptom* of a problem and the *source* of a
problem? A *symptom* is a sign, issue, circumstance, or disorder that indicates the existence of something wrong somewhere. The *source* of a problem is its underlying cause,
the specific reason the problem (symptom) is occurring in the first place. For example,
a sharp pain in the lower left side of one's back would be a *symptom* of a problem; the
underlying *source* of the pain in this case might be kidney stones.

In a business context, symptoms present themselves as negative events, situations, outcomes, impressions, or feedback, such as a decline in sales, loss of customers, or a decline in product quality, service, or reputation. It is common for organizations to spring into corrective action as soon as the symptoms of a problem trigger warning bells.

For example, a company's product sales drop dramatically; the company might react to the problem by throwing its resources (time, money, and manpower) into strategizing new ways to fight the competition. They might hire a new advertising agency to develop a provocative ad campaign, increase the size of their sales force, or aggressively slash prices to stimulate demand for their product to boost market share.

Any of those problem-solving approaches might be effective *if* the source of the problem is strictly a marketing or sales issue.

However, the decline in sales could be a symptom of a much deeper problem. If the company probes beyond the obvious symptom, they might discover that its product has grown outdated in light of newer, more innovative competitive products. Battling the competition in the marketing and sales arena would do little to address the underlying source of the company's problem—the lack of product innovation.

Learning to discern the source of a problem is imperative for effective problem solving.

Five ways to discern the source of a problem

1. State and restate the problem

Begin by asking, "What is the problem?" Does it have more than one aspect to it? If so, identify what those other aspects are. Strive to create a written description of the problem in the clearest manner possible. Be sure to write your problem statement in your own words; avoid using any kind of jargon or business-speak that can muddle comprehension or communication.

Once you have written a problem statement that seems to hit the mark, take a few minutes to push for further clarity. Restate the problem in different words or, better yet, in a number of entirely different ways until the true nature of your challenge reveals itself.

2. Explore diverse viewpoints

Ask a wide range of people familiar with the situation (team members, customers, suppliers, consultants, etc.) to contribute their insights, perspectives, and opinions on the cause of the problem. Identify recurring or overlapping issues. Also ask people with no firsthand knowledge of the issue or problem if they have ever heard about or experienced anything similar.

3. Challenge assumptions

When problems occur, people often make a lot of assumptions. Many of those assumptions can be erroneous and obscure the true nature of things. To achieve greater objectivity, list all of the assumptions you (and your group) may have about the situation and the cause of the problem. Next, challenge each assumption by asking, "Is this belief true?" "Is it always true?" "How do we know it's true?" "What would happen if we looked at it from the opposite/reverse point of view?" This kind of exploration can lead to new insights about your challenge.

4. **Inside-Out and Before and After**
   Inside: List all the internal forces or possible ways your organization's culture, systems, or processes could be contributing to or causing the problem. This process is not always easy, but if you step back and stay objective, it could reveal some important insights.
   Outside: List all of the external forces (marketplace, competition, economic climate, shifting customer behaviors, etc.) that could be contributing to or causing the problem.
   Before and After: Look at the situation (and activities) *before* the problem occurred. Next, list all of the things that changed just before and after the problem arose. What was the "tipping point" where the greatest amount of negative change occurred?

5. **Be an investigator: Who? What? When? Where? Why? How?**
   Asking questions is a very effective way to drill down to the source of a problem. You can do this exercise solo or with your group. To explore the possible causes of a problem, ask yourself/your group each of these six journalistic questions:

   "*Who* would best know the cause of this problem?"
   "*What* are the possible causes of this problem?"
   "*Where* is the origin point of this problem?"
   "*Why* did this problem occur/develop?"
   "*When* did this problem occur/develop?"
   "*How* did this problem occur/develop?"

Symptoms lead to solutions

Every good physician knows the importance of taking the time necessary to diagnose the specific cause of a patient's ailment before rushing in to solve the problem. Symptoms, when observed objectively, are actually helpful signals that alert us to the fact that a more serious, underlying problem or issue exists. By accurately identifying symptoms, you can follow the path (the chain of causes and effects) down to the actual root cause of the problem.

Clarifying the focus

All highly productive SmartStorming sessions begin with a well-crafted problem statement or challenge. In his book *The Art of Innovation*, author Tom Kelley, of the renowned innovative design firm IDEO, reveals his company's secret recipe for launching super-productive group idea-generating sessions—they "sharpen the focus" before launching into an ideation session. Kelley writes, "Good brainstormers start with a well-honed statement of the problem. This can be as simple as a question. Edgy is better than fuzzy. The session will get off to a better start—and you can bring people back to the main topic more easily—if you have a well-articulated description of the problem at just the right level of specificity." He goes on to say, "We've also found that the best topic statements focus *outward* on specific customer needs or service enhancements rather than focusing *inward* on some organizational goal."[10]

For example, a group of pharmaceutical sales executives might begin their brainstorming session with a challenge statement like: "What are some new ways we can communicate our drug's benefits to doctors?" A more powerful, thought-provoking challenge statement might ask, "What makes our drug's effectiveness and safety meaningful and relevant to the lives of doctors and their patients?"

Did you notice how much clearer and more compelling the customer-focused question was compared to the more mundane, inwardly focused organizational goal?

Common challenge statement mistakes to avoid

Mastering the skill of crafting a simple, clear, and compelling challenge statement that can ignite your group's passion and imagination requires a bit of trial and error. But with practice it will become second nature.

To help flatten your learning curve, we have provided a few examples of the most common mistakes untrained brainstorm facilitators make when setting up a challenge. Notice how each of these approaches could potentially handicap a group's comprehension and productivity.

"Overly complex" challenge statement—Providing too much data and information can overwhelm a group and obscure the big picture; also trying to solve multiple problems at once can scatter attention and exhaust attention. For example: "How can we increase distribution efficiency, leverage vendor relationships, and optimize the effectiveness of our sales teams in order to increase revenues?" Can you see how ponderous challenge statements can get?

"Understated complexity" challenge statement—Oversimplifying the complexity of a problem or omitting intrinsically important information can obscure the true nature of the problem, making effective problem solving difficult. For example: "What can we do to get more new customers?"

"Off-strategy" challenge statement—Focusing on solving symptoms rather than the source (cause) of a problem can only lead to wasted efforts and ineffective solutions. For example: "How can we increase employee retention?" (Notice there is no effort to address the underlying source of the problem issues within the organization, causing a high rate of employee turnover.)

"Closed-ended" challenge statement—Pointing a group down a too specific or narrowly defined path can limit their ability to explore fresh, new directions or imagine alternative solutions to the problem. For example: "We need to change our image in order to be perceived as more contemporary by our customers. What celebrity can we hire to endorse our product who will project a hip, modern image?" By phrasing the statement in such a way, you are automatically closing off the exploration of other potential solutions other than using a celebrity spokesperson.

"Too open-ended" challenge statement—Providing a group with too broad a challenge can perpetuate false starts, sidetrack efforts in off-strategy pursuits, or lead down dead-end streets. For example: "Where should we be taking the company in the future?"

Providing your group with the right balance of information and specificity about the challenge is critical for keeping their exploration of ideas focused and productive.

Crafting a powerful challenge statement

When you introduce a challenge statement to your SmartStormers, it should be a compelling call to action, a statement that ignites the group's enthusiasm and catapults them beyond traditional thinking—into the realm of the imagination.

The most powerful and effective challenge statements contain these characteristics:

- **Concise:** It is simple, direct, clear, and easy to understand.

- **Intentional:** It provides the group's *raison d'être* (inspired purpose and goal).

- **Directive:** It creates a sense of urgency by stating an immediate call to action.

- **Provocative:** It sparks the imagination and inspires new associations and connections.

- **Open-ended:** It encourages exploration and the discovery of a range of new possibilities.

When crafting your challenge statement, remember that simplicity is key. Get rid of unnecessary complexity and clutter. The clearer and more concise your statement is, the easier it will be for your SmartStormers to understand. The more emotionally compelling and edgy, the greater its potential to ignite your group's passion and sense of mission. For example, here is a typical, "plain vanilla" marketing-related challenge statement:

"How can we increase brand loyalty among eighteen- to twenty-four-year-olds?"

Now a more compelling and thought-provoking challenge statement approach:
"In what ways can we super-please our customers and inspire them to become our brand evangelists?"

A process-related challenge might typically be expressed in this way:
"How can we streamline our internal communications processes?"

A more inspirational approach:
"In what ways can we make it easier for our colleagues to access and share information?"

And product- or service-related challenges often sound like this:
"How can we increase the perceived value of our product/service without increasing costs?"

As opposed to:
"In what ways can we delight our customers by delivering greater value, at the same or lower prices?"

Creating a launchpad for your group's imagination

The most powerful challenge statements ask a simple, provocative question. They begin with an open-ended phrase that immediately ignites spontaneous associative thinking. Some good "point-of-departure" opening phrases include:

"In what ways can we…?"

"What if…?"

"What are the possibilities…?"

"Let's list all the ways…"

"If we had no limitations whatsoever, what could we do…?"

"If we knew we couldn't fail, what would/could we do…?"

Set the creative bar HIGH

The final step after defining the challenge, goals, and objectives is to provide your group with an ambitious, but achievable target for the number (and types) of ideas you expect them to generate by the end of the session.

A word of caution: If this is done in a heavy-handed or overly demanding way, it could be intimidating to a group. But if you communicate it as a playful challenge, it actually injects a sporting spirit of fun into your group's efforts.

Winning sports coaches understand the benefits of setting ambitious goals for a team; doing so motivates them to higher levels of performance. By establishing a yardstick for success in your session, you infuse your SmartStormers with a positive form of tension that will quickly focus their attention, get the adrenaline flowing, and maximize their performance. A highly energized, highly focused, goal-driven team is a far more powerful creative force than one with a vague or open-ended agenda.

So instead of passively settling for whatever number of ideas your group happens to end up with, you can proactively motivate your group to hit (or better yet, surpass) the ambitious target number of ideas you have set for them.

Piloting tip: You can provide your group with a single, ambitious target goal for the session. For example, "Let's shoot for three hundred new ideas by the end of today's session!" Or you can give your group a number of smaller targets to achieve during the session, such as, "Our goal for this activity is thirty new ideas in fifteen minutes!"

How to set a high bar for your group

Here's the simple formula for motivating your group to deliver a greater number and range of fresh ideas in your sessions. First, give them a specific number (or range) of ideas you would like them to achieve (the target).

Next, give them a tight, but realistic deadline in which to achieve that goal (Target number of ideas x Tight time frame = Higher yield of ideas).

For example:

"Let's shoot for fifty new ideas in the next twenty minutes."

"Let's come up with six new strategies by end of session."

"Let's identify ten new market opportunities in the next fifteen minutes."

"Let's outline four different plans in the next ten minutes."

"Let's identify fifteen emerging trends before our next break."

"Let's identify ten new product ideas in the next forty-five minutes."

How many IPMs (Ideas Per Minute) can you realistically expect from your group? In our experience, a highly focused and motivated group can conjure up between five and eight new ideas per minute (when the goal of the exercise is quantity, rather than developing or fleshing out existing ideas). Why not find out what your group is capable of achieving? Try this simple Idea Sprint exercise with your next group.

1. Present a compelling issue or problem to address.

2. Challenge your group to deliver fifteen (or more) new ideas in three minutes.

3. Set your timer, say, "GO!" and watch the ideas flow.

It works! You can also challenge your group to come up with twenty-five ideas in five minutes.

Match your group's abilities to the challenge

You can dramatically improve your group's odds for achieving (or exceeding) the target you set by matching the skills, knowledge, and experience of the participants you invite to the specific nature of the challenge at hand.

Does your challenge require special expertise? If so, recruit a dream team with the background necessary to confidently tackle the subject at hand. They will perform at higher levels than a ragtag group with disparate levels of understanding or experience.

A resourceful SmartStorming Pilot always handpicks the most knowledgeable, experienced, and motivated team of participants when faced with a tough problem-solving challenge.

Worksheet: Determining Your Challenge, Goals, and Objectives

This simple step-by-step worksheet can help you gain greater clarity about a challenge, determine your goal(s) and objective(s), develop a compelling challenge statement, and determine the target number (and types) of ideas you wish your group to achieve.

1. What is the specific issue, challenge, or opportunity to be addressed?

2. What is/are the most likely, specific underlying cause(s) of this issue, challenge, or opportunity (its point of origin)?

3. What would need to change in order for this issue, challenge, or opportunity to be permanently solved/addressed?

4. What are the specific goal(s) and objective(s) of your SmartStorming session?

5. What is the most concise and compelling way to state this issue, challenge, or opportunity? (Challenge Statement)

6. What deliverables (the target number and type[s] of ideas) do you want your group to generate in your session?

What to remember

- It's important to accurately define your session goal(s) and objective(s) and to be clear on the type of challenge you face and the most appropriate types of solutions.

- Define the specific problem/challenge/opportunity for the team in a compelling and thought-provoking manner, and set ambitious, but achievable goals for the session in terms of quantity and type of ideas to be generated.

- Effective challenge statements should be neither too detailed and complex nor too loose and general.

- The best challenge statements are concise, intentional, directive, provocative, and open-ended.

- Like a winning sports coach, a good Pilot always challenges (motivates) the group by setting ambitious goals.

- Set a high bar for your group by identifying a specific number of ideas to shoot for within a limited time frame.

CHAPTER 8

Step 4—Generating Ideas!
Unleashing Your Group's Creative Genius

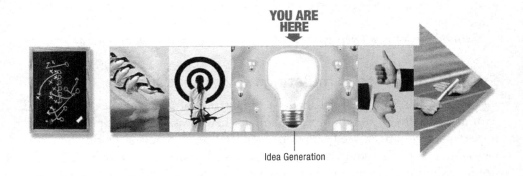

Idea Generation

"Logic will get you from point A to B. Imagination will take you everywhere."

—Albert Einstein

Innovation is an ongoing process of change that is fueled by a constant flow of fresh, new ideas. No new ideas, no innovation.

In this chapter, you will learn some of the key concepts related to effective idea generation, and we will introduce you to an array of proven idea-generation techniques you can use to inspire and unleash a group's fullest creative problem-solving potential. Each of the techniques presented features its own unique mechanism of action, designed to engage and stimulate a group's thinking in new and different ways—freeing it from old, habitual patterns.

A brief word about the ideation process

Have you ever considered what an *idea* actually is or how one comes into being?

Generally speaking, an idea is a mental impression (an image, thought, notion, or concept) in the mind, triggered by the discovery of *a new connection*. In other words, an "Aha!" moment of new insight.

An idea might suggest the solution to a problem, the next evolutionary step in a process or product, the creation of something completely new that has never existed before, the formulation of a plan, or a new path of opportunity.

Ideas can appear out of the blue, as a sudden "Eureka!" flash of insight triggered by a thought, sight, sound, or experience. Or they may germinate for hours, days, weeks, months, or even years in the deep recesses of our subconscious mind. Or, of course, ideas can be generated on demand, as needed, in vast quantities—which is the whole point of brainstorming.

For our purposes, it's not really important to understand how ideas come into being; what *is* important to appreciate is that every individual possesses the innate creativity and imagination to make novel new connections that can lead to a breakthrough idea.

In other words, *a huge, game-changing idea can come from anyone, at any time!*

Stimuli: the key to stimulating new connections

In Chapter 4, you learned about the importance of "stocking the creative pond" with new and diverse stimuli before fishing for new ideas. This principle is especially important for groups charged with thinking outside the box and generating innovative new concepts. To this point, Steve Jobs was quoted as saying, "Creativity is just connecting things. When you ask creative people how they did something, they feel a little guilty because they didn't really do it, they just saw something. It seemed obvious to them after a while. That's because they were able to connect experiences they've had and synthesize new things."[11]

The greater the variety of mental stimuli (ideas, concepts, impressions, images, words, information, data, sounds, experiences, etc.) participants are exposed to prior to the ideation process, the more inspired, resourceful, and productive they become at making novel new connections. Stimuli are the catalyst that ignites a group's associative thinking abilities and triggers bold leaps of imagination.

Without new stimuli to stock the creative pond, it's common for a group's thinking to grow stagnant, get bogged down in ruts of habitual patterns, or default to recycling familiar old ideas. Fortunately, you can reinvigorate even the most frustrated or lackluster group by exposing them to new sources of inspiration.

Stock the creative pond with new stimuli

How can you and your group keep your creative reservoirs well stocked with sources of new inspiration? The answer is surprisingly simple—just open up your eyes and all your senses. Inspiring stimuli are everywhere!

We are literally immersed in a rich, planetary media-sphere of ideas, images, videos, stories, information, data, history, music, performances, lectures, online resources, etc. In fact, there are so many different forms of stimuli bombarding our psyches each day that our brains have adapted mental filters to avoid experiencing overload. But with a little practice, you and your group can tune in to the kind of stimuli that piques your interest…and fuels your imagination.

Where to start? Why not begin with what has become the single most popular and comprehensive source of inspiration on the planet? The Internet, of course. Thanks to the World Wide Web, everyone can feel just like Alice through the looking glass, following his or her curiosity down the rabbit hole of mankind's accumulated knowledge, wisdom, inspiration, and culture—the collective genius and creativity of the world—available to you 24/7/365.

And search engines like Google are the perfect vehicle for triggering associative leaps and serendipitous new connections on any subject imaginable, which can lead to unexpected discoveries or solutions.

Other rich sources of creative stimuli include television, radio, books, magazines, movies, theater, games, concerts, performances, museums, galleries, schools and universities, shopping, cooking, dining, sports, social media, affinity groups, travel, and even nature itself (Isaac Newton's "Law of Gravity" was inspired by the stimulus of a falling apple).

Nature also inspired George de Mestral, the Swiss inventor of Velcro. After a nature hike with his dog, de Mestral became intrigued by the burrs that clung tenaciously to his pants. Under a microscope, he observed how the small "hooks" on the burrs interlocked with the tiny loops in the fabric of his pants. That new insight inspired him to invent a two-sided fastener, one side with stiff hooks like the burrs, and the other side with soft loops like the fabric of his clothes. He called his invention "Velcro," which is a combination of the words "velour" and "crochet."

By developing our sense of curiosity and perception, we can nourish our minds each and every day—creating an automatic restocking system to keep our internal creative reservoirs brimming with all kinds of new exotic fish.

Opening your mind to different types of stimuli

People often ask if they should stock up on stimuli specifically related to the challenge they are tackling, or if it is valuable to seek out unrelated or inspirational stimuli. The short answer is: All new forms of stimuli are helpful in stimulating new connections.

For example, let's say you and your group were charged with developing concepts for the next generation of electric car. It would make sense to seek out stimuli specifically relating to the challenge such as case studies, technical data, emerging automotive design trends, technologies, products, materials and designs, advances in battery technology, manufacturing processes, and consumer research as well as test-driving every electric car on the market.

Inspiration abounds with firsthand experience.

So in many cases, the more directly relevant the stimuli, the better; it's no secret that a large percentage of innovative advances are really adaptations, in one form or another, of previously existing ideas that have been evolved, modified, or repurposed.

On the other hand, you and your group can also get imaginative and seek out stimuli *indirectly* related to your subject, such as information about electricity itself, lightning, solar power, fireflies, electric eels, nanotechnology, etc. You might play with wind-up toys, visit a science museum, exchange ideas with a group of five-year-olds, and watch science fiction movies about the future.

The key is to follow your curiosity to discover any type of new stimuli that can inspire and spark your imagination. Why not ask your group members to establish a daily habit to replenish their creative reservoirs? It's easy; just ask them to dedicate fifteen minutes each day to observing, learning, or doing something new and interesting. They can also keep an "inspiration journal," where they can write down or sketch any new insights or inspired ideas, as well as paste images of inspiring people, places, or things they come across.

Ten ways to stock the pond before a session

1. **Get knowledgeable:** Provide the group with the issue or challenge, plus the session goals and objectives, in advance. Include any background information or materials relevant to the issue. Encourage your group to read up and become knowledgeable. Once they've prepared, encourage them to shift their attention to other unrelated activities to allow the new stimuli to percolate in their subconscious minds.

2. **Get curious:** Invite participants to indulge their curiosity about any aspect of the issue or subject, and follow wherever it may lead. Encourage spontaneous, free association and investigation with note taking. The more intuitive connections they can make about the topic, the better. Web surfing is a great way to follow spontaneous associations and make new connections. Just search for various aspects/characteristics about the challenge, then explore the results for possible solutions.

3. **Think outside the box:** Ask everyone to pre-storm three wild or audacious ideas they can bring to the session to serve as discussion starters. The more unconventional and novel the ideas, the better. Why start off a session with conventional or predictable ideas?

4. **Show and tell:** Another good option is to encourage everyone to bring in some form of thought-provoking stimuli (i.e., pictures, objects, articles, stories, analogies, anecdotes, trivia, or facts) related to, or inspired by, the challenge to help spark new ideas.

5. **Harvest the wisdom of others:** Ask participants to tap into the power of their social networks to gather insights and information, explore perspectives, and exchange new sources of inspiration. Networks such as Facebook, LinkedIn, and Twitter are ideally suited to use as a sounding board for ideas, to solicit suggestions for improving or building upon ideas, or to harvest the ideas of others.

6. **Get firsthand experience:** Encourage everyone to gain some firsthand, real-world experience. If the subject of your SmartStorming session is to identify innovative ways to market a new brand of ice cream, ask participants to visit ice cream parlors to sample different types of ice cream and to observe the way customers browse, sample flavors, and make selections. They can also conduct informal interviews with ice cream lovers, store owners, supermarket managers, and even the person who stocks the ice cream refrigerators in a supermarket. Of course, a group field trip to the Ben & Jerry's ice cream factory in Vermont may be a fun and informative way to stock the creative pond, too.

7. **Consult with history:** There is a high probability that a similar challenge has been successfully solved in the past in some other field or industry. Challenge your group to do a little investigative work to find out how they did it.

8. **Think visually:** It's been said that a picture is worth a thousand words. So instead of thinking and writing down ideas as words, try stocking the pond with rich visual stimuli, such as pictures, images, videos, graphics, icons, diagrams, and symbols. Visual stimuli are everywhere—in magazines, books, advertisements, galleries, movies, theaters, television, videos, and of course, on the Internet. Photo/video sharing and stock photography websites such as Pinterest (www.pinterest.com), Flickr (www.flickr.com), Getty Images (www.gettyimages.com), and YouTube (www.youtube.com) are just a few of the visual resources that can help stimulate new ways of seeing and thinking.

9. **Consult with genius:** Your group can tap into the inspiration of innovative thinkers such as Einstein, Edison, Walt Disney, Mark Zuckerberg, or Steve Jobs. Simply imagine how each of them might have approached the challenge at hand.

10. **Play with new combinations:** Invite your group to play around with combining seemingly unrelated ideas, objects, ingredients, parts, technologies, functions, products, or services from different fields or industries. For example, what elements from the airline, fast-food, and/or retailing industries can

be mixed and matched or applied to the challenge? Random combinatory play can lead to some very interesting new possibilities.

Once a group's creative reservoirs have been richly stocked with fresh, new stimuli, the stage is set for generating a wealth of new, innovative ideas.

Understanding divergent and convergent thinking

The secret to leading successful, highly productive idea-generation sessions lies in understanding the distinction between *divergent thinking* and *convergent thinking*.

Divergent thinking is the thought process used to spontaneously generate as many different ideas as possible in the time allotted. During this freewheeling, anything-goes process, all critical judgment is suspended; a group is encouraged to shoot for quantity of ideas rather than quality. Wild, even audacious ideas are encouraged.

The purpose of the divergent thought process is to free up a group's creative-thinking abilities (curiosity, imagination, and intuition) from any sense of limitation so it can net the widest range of ideas to address the challenge. The Rules of the Game (described in Chapter 4), such as "Suspend all judgment," "There's no such thing as a bad idea," and "Nothing is impossible," are designed to help establish a judgment-free, fertile atmosphere for exploring possibilities.

Once the divergent-thinking part of a session is completed, those ideas can then be organized, evaluated, and judged using convergent thinking.

Convergent thinking can be thought of as the opposite of divergent thinking. Its purpose is to analyze and judge ideas, with the goal of narrowing down a range of ideas to the fewest that meet the selection criteria.

As a simple rule, use divergent thinking when the goal is to generate ideas; use convergent thinking afterward to evaluate, judge, and select ideas. It's vitally important to keep these two modes of thinking completely separate during the course of a session. We'll discuss this subject in more detail in Chapter 12: Managing Divergent and Convergent Thinking.

The importance of using idea-generation techniques

Ideation techniques are, quite simply, novel, thought-provoking activities designed to help groups tackle challenges in ways they might not otherwise consider. Some make it easier for groups to view issues from fresh perspectives; others provide engaging processes to help stimulate the imagination, make new connections, identify opportunities, overcome shyness, facilitate collaboration, encourage idea-building, and much more.

In short, ideation techniques make it possible for groups to generate a greater breadth and depth of ideas (i.e., more, better ideas).

Anyone who takes a moment to Google "ideation techniques" will quickly learn that there are hundreds in existence. Some are well known and extensively documented and used; others, less so.

We recently conducted an informal online survey to find out just where people stand on ideation techniques—which ones they know, which ones they use in brainstorms, and what they think about them. The results are interesting, if not completely surprising.

When asked whether they believe knowing and using different types of ideation techniques would be beneficial to brainstorming, the answer was a resounding "Yes!" Many respondents also suggested that knowing and understanding a variety of techniques is critical to group brainstorming success.

However, when respondents were provided with a list of well-known ideation techniques, they were relatively familiar with only one technique—Mind Mapping—followed by Edward de Bono's Six Thinking Hats and the ubiquitous SWOT Analysis. All others listed had little to no familiarity for the respondents.

It is important to note that this survey was conducted among our network of readers, presumably an audience that is more tuned in to brainstorming and ideation techniques than the average businessperson. And yet, it is clear that even among this group, very few know, understand, and use a range of ideation techniques.

Again, this result isn't entirely surprising. In our own ongoing research, we find that less than 10 percent of individuals in any industry (even creativity-focused businesses like advertising, marketing, and product design) typically know only one or two ideation techniques.

And so it would appear that while we understand and acknowledge the value of having a library of proven ideation techniques at our disposal, few of us have made the time or effort to identify and learn those techniques.

To survive and thrive in today's innovation-driven economy, it is important to educate oneself in a variety of ideation techniques—and to master those techniques to lead groups to higher levels of creative problem-solving success.

Different approaches to creative problem solving

There are a number of ideation approaches a SmartStorming Pilot can utilize to help free his or her group from old habitual ways of thinking and engage its imagination and problem-solving abilities in new and different ways.

Here is a brief overview of some of the best known approaches:

Adaptive Thinking

These techniques are based on the philosophy that everything new is really an adaptation of something else that already exists or has existed. By using this problem-solving approach, groups can play with new and different ways to adapt, modify, evolve, and rearrange the characteristics of a product, process, or service in order to stimulate fresh, new ideas.

Analogy/Metaphor

Sometimes the best way to understand a real-world problem or challenge is by looking at it imaginatively through the context of an analogy or metaphor. Analogies and metaphors can provide valuable reference points for understanding the nature of something that seems unclear (or unknown) by comparing it to something familiar that we do understand.

By using imagery, stories, fables, objects, or situations, we are able to identify and compare two things that share common properties or characteristics: for example, a human heart and a mechanical pump.

Associative Thinking

Our brain's thinking process is wired by nature to work associatively, meaning that one idea spontaneously triggers another, which triggers another, which triggers another, and so on. Unfortunately, this innate approach to creative problem solving is often ignored in favor of the rote, linear style of thinking most of us are taught in school. Associative thinking techniques such as Mind Mapping help free individuals and groups to generate, structure, and analyze ideas in the spontaneous, creative ways our minds were meant to work.

Challenging Conventions

One of the biggest impediments a group or organization can face in their problem-solving efforts are their assumptions (preconceived notions or limiting beliefs) about the way things are, or what may or may not be possible. These self-limiting assumptions can create blind spots that "box in" thinking. Idea-generation techniques that question assumptions (and the status quo) enable groups to explore ideas and points of view outside of their comfort zone of habitual thinking.

Counterintuitive/180-Degree Thinking

A trait shared by many innovative thinkers is the ability to think in a counterintuitive or opposite direction from the status quo. Quite often the most radical or worst-sounding idea can contain the seeds of a game-changing idea. Counterintuitive thinking techniques are designed to turn a group's rational thinking approach around 180 degrees, thereby allowing the group to explore new avenues of opportunity in the opposite direction of what is expected.

Empathy-Based Insights

Empathy is the ability to compassionately understand the emotional state (thoughts, feelings, needs, wants, etc.) another person is experiencing, within the frame of reference of that other person.

Gaining deeper understanding into the emotional drivers that motivate individuals or groups can be an essential component for effective problem solving.

Empathy-based techniques help groups develop greater awareness and emotional understanding of the issues that affect a target audience, insights that can be valuable in developing meaningful and effective solutions.

Exploring Viewpoints

As Dr. Wayne Dyer says, "When you change the way you look at things, the things you look at change." This perspective is especially relevant when it comes to innovative thinking and creative problem solving.

The ability to explore an issue or challenge from a wide range of different viewpoints empowers a group to understand the issues involved in a broader, deeper, ultimately more holistic way, and to illuminate blind spots and identify new pathways of opportunities.

Forced Associations

Forced association is a well-known ideation method that challenges a group to solve a problem or tackle a challenge in unexpected ways by provoking new associations between two (or more) unrelated or random objects, subjects, or properties (e.g., What do you get when you cross a riding lawnmower with an espresso machine?). Forcing associations between two, three, or more different things helps override our logical thought process and stimulates new creative connections.

High-Velocity Thinking

High-velocity thinking involves rapid-paced, beat-the-clock idea-generation activities that challenge a group to achieve an ambitious number of ideas within a tight deadline; these activities are extremely effective in helping groups get off to a fast start, overcome self-consciousness, and generate a large volume of new ideas very quickly.

20 proven idea-generation techniques

We have included twenty of our favorite idea-generation techniques in this book, each of which has been used extensively in SmartStorming sessions and has proven to be extremely effective at helping groups generate more fresh, innovative ideas. Each technique features its own unique mechanism of action that will push your group's thinking beyond the kind of habitual, day-to-day patterns that can hinder creativity. No matter what issue or challenge your group faces, you will find the right ideation power tool here, one that will help you and your group more innovatively solve the issue, problem, or challenge, or take full advantage of a new opportunity.

The following is a brief overview of the twenty techniques. You will find detailed, easy-to-follow instructions for each of them in Chapter 20.

1-4-All (Individual and collaborative idea generation)

This simple, yet powerful, triple-strength creative problem-solving approach helps compound and amplify the collaborative genius of individuals, small teams, and the entire group—in a single activity.

1-4-All is a three-part technique that begins with individual participants developing their own unique ideas to address the challenge. Next, they join forces with three other participants to form a small ideation team, to share and build upon one another's ideas. And in the third step, the small teams share their best ideas with the group, after which all participants join forces to build upon the ideas presented.

Bad2Good (Counterintuitive idea generation)

Bad2Good is a provocative technique based on the premise that often, bad-sounding, counterintuitive ideas can actually contain the seeds of an innovative, game-changing idea if effectively turned around.

If you wonder how seemingly bad ideas can lead to good ideas, consider this example. Suppose you were brainstorming ideas for how to keep football players more comfortable, cool, and dry during a game. What could be a worse idea than suggesting, "Let's have football players wear women's lingerie"? But that is essentially the "bad idea" that helped launch an innovative, billion-dollar sports apparel brand called Under Armour. Under Armour founder Kevin Plank envisioned using a special fabric (used in woman's lingerie) to create a base-layer T-shirt that would be more comfortable than cotton and would more effectively wick moisture away from the skin—an ideal fabric for helping to keep athletes cooler and drier.

See how good a bad idea can be? This highly entertaining, 180-degree thinking technique helps free a group's imagination from the confines of conventional thinking.

Brainwriting (Silent, collaborative-writing technique)

Brainwriting is an enjoyable, silent, collaborative-writing technique that begins with individual problem solving and then grows exponentially to involve every member of the group. Participants begin by writing down a single idea. Ideas are passed around from person to person and built upon until the process comes full circle, and everyone has contributed to each of the original ideas.

In addition to helping a group generate a large number of ideas in a relatively short time, this simple technique is also an excellent contribution equalizer. Because it is performed nonverbally, Brainwriting creates a safe, nonjudgmental environment for those quiet or self-conscious Silent Thinkers in your group, making it much more comfortable for them to contribute ideas. It also effectively silences intimidating, opinionated, or dominating personalities and levels the playing field when the boss, senior-ranking executives, or outside influencers (clients, customers, external partners, etc.) are participating in the session.

With Brainwriting, you are guaranteed the fullest contribution of ideas from everyone in your session.

Channeling Genius (Exploring viewpoints technique)

This imagination-driven ideation technique asks a group to select a ground-breaking visionary, innovator, inventor, artist, or performer (living or legend), such as Steve Jobs, Albert Einstein, Walt Disney, or Oprah Winfrey; or a fictional character, such as Sherlock Holmes, MacGyver, or the Terminator, to serve as its problem-solving inspiration.

The objective is to develop a range of new ideas to solve or address a challenge in the same style and manner (creative thought process) as one of the chosen innovators in their field might have approached it. For example, "In what ways might Walt Disney have solved our public relations issue?"

Escaping the Box (Challenging conventions)

When people say they need to "think outside the box," what they really mean is that they need to think outside of their current limiting assumptions and beliefs.

The more preconceived notions an individual, group, or organization has about an issue or challenge, the more limited their options can appear. That is why limiting assumptions are such a huge impediment to innovative thinking.

Escaping the Box is a powerful technique that helps a group identify and successfully challenge the status quo and move beyond any perceived limitations or barriers. By doing so, the group is empowered to imagine bold new solutions never before thought possible.

Frankensteining (Forced-association idea generation)

Frankensteining is an engaging idea-generation technique that challenges participants to discover ways of combining two (or more) seemingly unrelated ideas to create a distinctly new and unique product, service, process, or thing.

This combinatory-play approach of merging different ideas, ingredients, features, functions, attributes, or characteristics to create something altogether new is a hallmark of the innovation process. For example, someone once combined a telephone and a photocopier to create the fax machine.

Frankensteining encourages participants to switch off their logic-based thinking and enjoy the process of creatively tinkering and experimenting like a mad scientist at play to discover new, unexpected possibilities.

Group Graffiti (Collaborative wall-writing activity)

Group Graffiti is a highly interactive technique that gets participants up out of their seats and thinking quickly on their feet.

As its name implies, Group Graffiti is a collaborative writing and drawing activity in which participants walk back and forth along a blank "concept wall" and fill it by writing down new ideas. Participants are encouraged to spontaneously build upon one another's ideas until the entire graffiti wall is filled. This enjoyable process stimulates the cross-pollination of ideas in a fun, interactive physical activity.

Group Graffiti is a great technique to use as a group pick-me-up if the energy level in a session becomes low.

Idea Mashup (Forced-association idea generation)

This popular problem-solving approach takes advantage of the mind's amazing ability to link two or more disparate items—words, images, objects, subject, and ideas—and then to use the associations generated to develop new, unexpected solutions.

Forced associations help override a group's linear thought processes; using random external triggers forces participants to make new connections between the challenge at hand and the trigger. These triggers prompt participants to really stretch their imaginations and think outside their comfort zones.

Idea Speed Dating (Rapid collaborative idea generation)

This fun, collaborative idea-building technique was inspired by the social networking concept of speed dating. Participants first work individually to generate some initial ideas for how to solve an issue or challenge. Next, participants meet one-on-one with other SmartStormers in a series of brief, round-robin, idea-building sessions that last only ten to fifteen minutes each.

During each mini session, idea partners share their ideas and exchange insights for how to improve and develop or build upon one another's ideas. The tight time limit keeps the collaborative idea-generation activity energized, focused, and highly productive.

Idea Sprinting (High-velocity idea generation)

Idea Sprinting is a fast-paced, beat-the-clock idea-generation technique. It's specifically designed to help a group generate a large quantity of new ideas over a short period of time. For example, "Let's shoot for twenty-five new ideas in the next five minutes!" The group is challenged to meet (or better yet, exceed) the number of ideas requested within the time frame defined.

This high-velocity activity gets participants' attention focused and the creative juices flowing; there is no time for inhibitions or self-consciousness. Idea Sprinting can help your group generate dozens, if not hundreds, of new ideas. It's a surefire way to get your session off to a roaring fast start.

In Their Shoes (Empathy-based idea generation)

Empathy is the ability to compassionately appreciate the emotional state (feelings, thoughts, needs, desires, etc.) another person is experiencing within the frame of reference of that other person's reality.

This empathy-based, idea-generation technique is designed to help a group develop deeper understanding and insight into the *emotional drivers* (desires, needs, resistances, etc.) that influence or motivate a person, group, or target audience.

Whether a group's challenge is to find effective new ways to engage teenagers via social media, improve the quality of a customer's shopping experience, or motivate aging Baby Boomers with a medical condition to see their doctors, have your group imagine (in as vivid detail as possible) what a typical day (or a specific situation or condition) in the life of that person, group, or audience would feel like. The group will gain valuable new insights that can be used to develop meaningful and effective solutions, as well as identify new opportunities.

Mind Mapping (Visual associative thinking)

As we mentioned earlier, Mind Mapping is among the most well-known and widely used idea-generation techniques. It's a visual planning and problem-solving process that mimics the brain's natural process of making spontaneous associations.

The technique begins with a single key word or symbol (representing the topic or issue) written in the center of a sheet of paper. Participants then spontaneously write down any associations (ideas) triggered by the key word or symbol. Lines are drawn to connect these new associations with the central topic. Next, building off of the new associations, participants branch out into subassociations. This process is repeated a number of times until the Mind Map is filled with divergent associations, all connecting back to the central topic. On paper, these ideas (radiating out in all directions) resemble the branches of a tree, a root system, or even a spider's web.

Mind Mapping is a powerful tool for fully exploring a topic in a visual manner. It helps identify, connect, and organize a broad range of information. The technique can be used for many types of challenges, such as solving complex problems, identifying and developing new business opportunities, setting goals, etc.

Mind Maps can be created by an individual, a team, or even a large group.

Pre-Storming (Pre-session idea generation)

One of the simplest and most effective ways to gain a large number of new ideas very quickly is to ask participants to show up to the session with three initial ideas ready to share. Think of these as the ticket for admission into the session.

Asking participants to pre-storm ideas prior to the session accomplishes two positive things: first, it motivates participants to familiarize themselves with the challenge, goal, and objectives, and second, it allows insights and ideas time to percolate in the unconscious mind for several days—often resulting in new and unexpected connections.

What's impressive about Pre-Storming is that if you have ten SmartStormers scheduled to attend your session, and each brings three ideas—that's thirty new ideas in the bank *before* your session even begins!

This foolproof process may seem so obvious that it's barely worth mentioning as a technique. However, you might be surprised by how few brainstorm facilitators actually take advantage of Pre-Storming.

Pump Up the Value (Adaptive idea generation)

Thanks to the Internet and global competition, customers have become more savvy and demanding than ever before. And what do they demand? More and better value in the products or services they purchase.

Value can be defined as the perceived worth, merit, or importance of a product, service, or process based on price/cost. In other words, does it meet or exceed expectations for what it should be or do? Is it worth the price?

This innovative technique helps a group imagine new ways to pump up the value proposition in its products, services, or processes—new ways to make it better, simpler, faster, cheaper, easier to use, more reliable, more satisfying, more beautifully designed, or even more emotionally endearing.

To help a group succeed, we provide a versatile reference tool called the "Value Compass." This compass points to a variety of different directions (ways) in which your group can drive innovation by adding or providing greater value.

Reimagine It! (Analogy/metaphor idea generation)

One of the most powerful approaches for gaining a fresh perspective on an issue or challenge is by exploring it through the context of an analogy (a similarity between two things that share common features or characteristics), a metaphor (something representational or symbolic of something else), or a fictional characterization (ascribing human attributes, traits, or characteristics to an animal, object, subject, issue, or situation).

This imagination-fueled technique uses creative visualization, imagery, storytelling, or fictional characterizations to help participants grasp the essential nature of a challenge in new, visceral ways. It's a great way to free up a group from old linear thinking patterns.

SCAMPER (Adaptive idea generation)

SCAMPER is another well-known idea-generation technique based on the theory that every new, innovative product, service, or process is really (in one way or another) an adaptation of something else that already exists or has existed in the past.

Each letter of the SCAMPER acronym represents a different way a group can play with, adapt, or change the characteristics of a product, service, or process to stimulate fresh, new ideas:

S = Substitute
C = Combine
A = Adapt
M = Magnify
P = Put to Other Uses
E = Eliminate (or Simplify)
R = Rearrange (or Reverse)

SCAMPER is versatile, thought-provoking, and easy to lead, and can be done as a verbal, written, or visual activity.

SmartSWOT (Exploring multiple viewpoints)

The SWOT analysis is one of the most widely used strategic planning tools. Utilized by organizations and businesses around the world, SWOT helps groups identify, highlight, and evaluate the **S**trengths, **W**eaknesses, **O**pportunities, and **T**hreats involved in pursuing a specific project, launching a new venture, or achieving a desired goal.

SmartStorming's SmartSWOT technique adds several new and thought-provoking dimensions for a group to explore in order to gain even greater insight and ultimately identify new strategies and tactics for achieving success.

SmartSWOT helps groups understand any issue or challenge in a more comprehensive and holistic way.

Think Much, Much Bigger (Idea expansion process)

Contrary to popular belief, most organizations do *not* suffer from a lack of new ideas. But in today's innovation-driven world, a *good* idea just isn't good enough! This idea-building technique is an effective way to take the most promising ideas previously generated in a SmartStorming session and push or expand them to an exponentially bigger/larger realm for significantly greater potential. In other words, Think Much, Much Bigger helps you transform good ideas into much, much bigger, game-changing concepts.

Vision Boards (Visual inspiration and idea generation)

It has often been said that a picture is worth a thousand words. Images possess the power to inspire a wealth of fresh, innovative ideas. Also known as mood boards or inspiration boards, these visual collages are used often by creative professionals like designers and architects to explore new ways of approaching a project and previsualizing future realities. Why? Because images can quickly provoke strong emotional responses and inspire new insights, often much more effectively than words alone.

When tackling a project or challenge or exploring new opportunities, Vision Boards can very quickly help a group develop a clear understanding of what they find appealing, what is possible, what works, and what doesn't. Vision Boards can act as inspirational stimuli (stocking the creative pond) for idea generation.

Plus, they're fun! Searching online for interesting, inspirational images, or even combing through magazines, catalogs, and books allows your imagination to run wild.

What If…? (Challenging conventions)

There's a saying, "You never know how far you can go until you've gone too far." It is always easier to pull an audacious idea back from the edge than it is to make a safe, conventional idea more innovative.

Real, game-changing innovation is driven by bold, visionary ideas—ideas with the power to break through the barriers of conventional thinking and redefine what's possible.

This thought-provoking technique is designed to help your group challenge the status quo by encouraging it to think as far outside the box as possible—to shoot for the most ambitious, forward-thinking, and disruptive *What if...?* ideas imaginable. Afterward, the most intriguing ideas are reevaluated to determine how they can be adapted or modified to become practical, real-world opportunities or solutions.

How to choose the best techniques for your challenge

With so many different and effective idea-generation techniques in your Smart-Storming toolbox to choose from, you might be wondering how to determine the best ones to use for the challenge at hand.

The short answer is, there really are no wrong choices. All of these proven techniques will help a group achieve superior results generating ideas. That said, some techniques might be better suited to certain types of challenges than others.

We encourage you to read over and test-drive each of the techniques described here. (Full instructions for all twenty techniques can be found in Chapter 20: Idea-Generation Techniques and Tools.) As you become familiar with the results they produce, you will develop a strong intuitive sense for the best ones to use for specific challenges, and how to mix and match different techniques in a session. Certain ideation techniques can also be used when needed, to jump-start or improve a group's performance.

To help you gain an understanding of the techniques and how they can be applied, we have provided a guide on the next page with suggestions for which techniques to use for specific types of challenges.

Guide for determining when to use different techniques

When planning your SmartStorming sessions, we recommend you select two to three different ideation techniques to use during the course of the session. By employing a variety of different techniques, you will not only keep your group highly engaged but also achieve a greater depth and range of fresh, new ideas and insights.

You will find easy-to-follow instructions for all twenty idea-generation techniques in Chapter 20.

Goal/Objective	Appropriate Technique(s)
To help a group think up new, bigger, and better ideas	Channeling Genius What If...? Think Much, Much Bigger
To help a group think outside its comfort zone	Bad2Good Escaping the Box
To help energize a group and fuel its idea-generation momentum	Group Graffiti Idea Speed Dating Idea Sprinting
To help liberate a group from old, habitual thinking patterns	Channeling Genius Frankensteining Idea Mashup Mind Mapping Reimagine It! SCAMPER What If...?
To help a group explore new and different perspectives about a challenge	In Their Shoes Mind Mapping SmartSWOT
To help a group find new ways to improve or innovate a product, process, or service	Pump Up the Value SCAMPER What If...?
To help make sure everyone in the group is contributing ideas	1-4-All Brainwriting Group Graffiti Pre-Storming
To help silence dominating or attention-seeking personalities	Brainwriting Group Graffiti

What to remember

- An *idea* is a mental impression (an image, thought, notion, or concept) triggered by the discovery of *a new connection.*

- Every individual possesses the innate creativity and imagination necessary to make new connections that can lead to a big, game-changing idea.

- Stocking the mental pond with new and diverse stimuli (e.g., concepts, images, videos, information, data, music) before fishing for ideas is the key to sparking new connections.

- The secret to leading successful sessions lies in understanding the distinction between *divergent thinking* and *convergent thinking.* As a simple rule, use divergent thinking when your goal is to generate ideas; use convergent thinking afterward to evaluate, judge, and select ideas.

- There are a variety of proven, highly effective idea-generation techniques that can help engage a group's thinking in new and different ways, and help them generate more fresh, innovative ideas and solutions.

- In Chapter 20: Idea-Generation Techniques and Tools, you will find instructions for twenty proven idea-generation techniques you can use in your Smart-Storming sessions.

CHAPTER 9

Step 5—Harvesting Your Group's Most Innovative Ideas

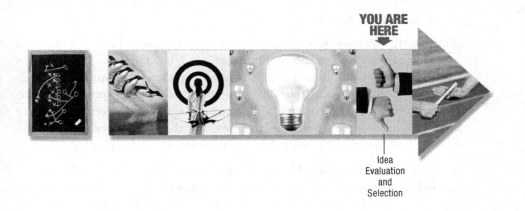

YOU ARE HERE

Idea
Evaluation
and
Selection

*"A new idea is delicate. It can be killed by a sneer or a yawn;
it can be stabbed to death by a quip and worried to death
by a frown on the right man's brow."*

—Ovid, Roman poet

SmartStorming sessions can easily generate dozens, if not hundreds, of new ideas. Of course, only a handful might successfully address the challenge, and even fewer will be great ideas. So how do you effectively separate the wheat from the chaff, identify the diamonds in the rough, and discern between the false glitter of fool's gold and a genuine goldmine of an idea?

In this chapter, you will learn a highly effective, step-by-step process for harvesting the very best ideas generated by your group, including how to use a simple diagnostic tool designed to help you objectively determine which ideas possess the right stuff and which ones fall short.

But before you learn more, it is worth examining some of the issues and dynamics that can make the evaluation and selection process so challenging.

Common challenges in the idea-selection process

Idea overwhelm—Inevitably, once the freewheeling, whirlwind idea-generation phase has ended, a brainstorming group will find itself staring at a sprawling paper jungle of ideas—a sea of concepts hastily scribbled down on flipchart paper, sticky notes, or whiteboards.

The prospect of sorting through, deciphering, and evaluating such a large volume of ideas can seem daunting and unmanageable. Unfortunately, in many instances, that proves to be the case.

Dominating personalities—If a group doesn't have an objective evaluation process in place *before* the selection process begins, it can devolve into a contest where promising ideas live or die based on the assertions of dominating personalities or the thumbs-up or thumbs-down whims of executive privilege. A surprising number of brainstorming sessions conclude when the boss (or the most senior-ranking group member) unilaterally selects the ideas he or she determines to be the best (which more often than not translates into "the ones I like most").

Lack of selection criteria—The importance of establishing a set of selection criteria *before* beginning a brainstorming session cannot be overemphasized. Objective criteria provide the essential benchmarks necessary for a fair and orderly evaluation process by establishing a set of common reference points for all participants to use when considering the merits of each idea.

Without objective criteria, most selection processes quickly deteriorate into a subjective debate based on the personal preferences (and prejudices) of participants. If you have ever experienced a contentious idea-selection process in a brainstorm session, there is a good chance there were few, if any, evaluation criteria established ahead of time.

Aversion to selecting risky ideas—While most organizations today tout the value they place on bold, innovative thinking, in reality, not every executive or manager possesses the fortitude and strength of character required to champion risky new ideas.

This kind of risk-averse mindset can cause groups to shrink away from radically new or different types of solutions, or to search for ways to water down concepts that push the organization's culture outside its comfort zone. Risk-averse organizations find it extremely difficult to innovate.

As you can see, there are a number of different dynamics that can affect a group's idea evaluation and selection process. How many of these situations have you encountered in your experience?

Fortunately, the process you will learn in this chapter will help you avoid these kinds of pitfalls and provide you with the skills and techniques you'll need to pilot a smooth-running idea evaluation and selection process, session after session.

Emotion vs. reason: A word about how we make decisions

It's no secret that many of the decisions made by individuals or groups are somewhat less than rational. Marketers and advertisers have long understood that while people may spend significant time and effort considering information (facts, data, criteria, reviews, and testimonials), their actual buying decision is based primarily on emotion. All of those facts and figures simply help to rationalize their emotional decision.

Supreme Court Justice William O. Douglas, a keen observer of human nature, once stated, "Ninety percent of any decision is emotional. The rational part of us supplies the reasons for supporting our predilections."

This same emotional decision-making dynamic also comes into play when a group of brainstormers is tasked with evaluating and selecting ideas.

In fact, influencers such as feelings, personal preferences, assumptions, beliefs, gut feelings, peer pressure, and of course, ego play such a significant role in the way we evaluate decisions that it is difficult to avoid the inevitable clash of conflicting, subjective preferences or prejudices.

In an ideal world, our decision-making process would fairly balance both the *emotional* and *rational* parts of our brains; it would take into consideration the strengths of our innate emotional intelligence (instincts, intuition, etc.) and balance them with the rational analysis of objective selection criteria.

The SmartStorming idea-selection process was designed to help you and your groups achieve the best possible balance between emotional and rational decision making. As you will see, it accomplishes this feat by first asking participants to use their subjective intuition and reasoning abilities to narrow a large number of ideas down to a short list of the most appealing and promising. Then participants (or a separate selection committee) are instructed to evaluate the merits of each of those ideas against a predetermined set of objective selection criteria. You will learn more about this process later in this chapter.

Switching from divergent to convergent thinking

The evaluation and selection step of your SmartStorming session is the official crossover point where you, as the Pilot, redirect your group's thinking from spontaneous, 360-degree, anything goes idea generation (divergent thinking) to the narrowing, discerning focus of the evaluation and selection process (convergent thinking).

If divergent thinking is casting the widest net possible to capture new ideas, then convergent thinking can be thought of as harvesting the very best of the catch. Like a funnel, convergent thinking narrows down a large number of ideas through the process of analyzing, judging, and selecting. We use convergent thinking to gain clarity, draw conclusions, determine the bottom line, and select the best, strongest ideas.

How do you shift your group from divergent thinking to convergent thinking?

Simply inform your group that the idea generation part of the session has officially ended; the new task at hand is to focus exclusively on narrowing down the number of ideas so that only those that best address the issue or challenge remain.

Be mindful that participants don't slip back into divergent thinking (brainstorming) to fix or improve ideas. Flip-flopping back and forth between convergent and divergent thinking will disrupt the flow of your session and sidetrack the selection process.

Who should be selecting ideas?

A question we are often asked during our workshops is *"Who* should be involved in evaluating and selecting ideas?" Should the entire group who generated the ideas be included? Should a few senior or specialized members of the group handle the task? Or would it be better to enlist the help of a separate, carefully chosen selection committee to evaluate ideas after the session is over?

The answer depends on the specific situation or challenge you have addressed, and who possesses the specific knowledge, understanding, expertise, and authority to identify the most promising idea options. In addition, those responsible should also possess a healthy degree of objectivity and a willingness to embrace innovative or unconventional concepts, and ultimately be a stakeholder in successfully addressing the challenge at hand.

If the group generating the ideas has knowledge, expertise, and a stake in the outcome, it would be appropriate to have them participate in evaluating and selecting ideas.

If the group size is large (more than eight people), then it would be wise to identify a smaller team of the most senior or experienced and knowledgeable members to evaluate and select ideas. If a large group is composed of representatives from different departments, divisions, or areas of specialty, you may want to select one or two members from each to serve on a smaller selection committee.

In some cases, it may make sense to have one group generate ideas, then have a separate group or committee take on idea selection.

Deciding who will be responsible for evaluating and selecting ideas should always be done *prior* to the session, during the pre-session planning process.

The SmartStorming evaluation and selection process

The following process will help you avoid the most common pitfalls that many groups face when attempting to evaluate ideas, and more confidently guide your group through a fair, conflict-free idea-selection phase.

Here is a brief overview of how it works:

Step 1: Before your session—Predetermine a set of objective selection criteria for evaluating the merits of your group's ideas.

Step 2: While generating ideas—Harvest the most valuable ideas as you go along, after each idea-generation activity. Transfer those ideas to your Idea Bank.

Step 3: For final idea selection—Narrow down the number of ideas in your Idea Bank using your objective selection criteria as a yardstick.

(Optional) Step 4: Use the SmartStorming Idea Selection Diagnostic Matrix to identify the specific strengths and weaknesses of your best ideas.

Step 1: Before your session—Predetermine a set of objective selection criteria for evaluating the merits of ideas.

The SmartStorming idea-selection process actually begins during the pre-session planning process. As you may recall, an important step on the SmartStorming Pre-Session Planner asks you to list the specific set of selection criteria that will be used as your yardstick for evaluating the merits of ideas. This can be done by you alone or in collaboration with other stakeholders.

Determining your selection criteria

Your selection criteria will serve as the objective benchmarks (reference points) a group needs to help identify those specific characteristics, attributes, or benefits a winning idea must possess in order to successfully address the challenge at hand.

In his best-seller, *7 Habits of Highly Effective People*, Dr. Steven Covey writes that a key principle for achieving success with any goal is to "begin with the end in mind."[12]

This same principle applies to determining the set of criteria you will use to evaluate and select your group's best ideas. Try to visualize as clearly as possible what the perfect solution or end result would look like.

For example, if you were developing a set of criteria for a marketing program to promote a new product, you would first visualize the end result you want—perhaps a highly successful media campaign that is simple, distinctive, memorable, persuasive, and most importantly, convinces customers to purchase the product.

Based on this vision, you can extrapolate the *must have* characteristics, attributes, or benefits a winning idea would need to possess. For example:

- **Simple**—clear, concise, easy to understand

- **Distinctive**—differentiating, stands out from the competition
- **Memorable**—"sticky" makes a lasting, positive impression
- **Persuasive**—drives customers to take action
- **Increases sales**—attracts new customers, entices current customers to buy more, more often

Here's another example. If your group were challenged to develop ideas for an innovative new product to bring to market, you could extrapolate the *must have* characteristics, traits, or attributes a winning idea would need to possess in order to ensure a highly successful product introduction, such as:

- **Innovative**—new, uniquely different, and better than other products
- **Defining**—what we want our company/organization to be known for
- **Desirable**—speaks directly to or satisfies an unmet customer need or want
- **Value-adding**—provides more benefits and features than the competition
- **Differentiating**—looks and feels different from the competition

Or, if your group were developing ideas to improve or streamline a process, you could extrapolate the *must have* characteristics:

- **Simple**—easy to understand, communicate, and implement
- **Efficient**—saves time, effort, money, material, and resources
- **Improves productivity**—fewer steps, increases quality and capacity
- **Flexible**—can easily adapt to increased volume, use, or demand
- **Cost-effective**—within budget to implement, significant return on investment

As you can see, once you have developed a clear vision for the end results you want your ideas to achieve, you can extrapolate a useful set of objective criteria to use as a yardstick for measuring the merits of your group's ideas.

We recommend that you limit the number of selection criteria to a manageable, easy-to-remember short list of five or six items. Too many criteria can bog down your selection process and make it feel unwieldy.

Once you have identified your list of criteria, do your best to describe each one in the simplest, most concise way possible. A good format to follow is to distill the essence of each criterion down to one key word, usually an adjective or verb, followed by a concise, one-sentence descriptive definition (as illustrated in the examples above). Here's a simple formula you can follow:

(Key word) + (Simple, concise description of meaning) = Criterion

For example:

Innovative—new, uniquely different, and better than other products

Step 2: While generating ideas—Harvest the most valuable ideas as you go along, after each idea-generation activity. Transfer those ideas to your Idea Bank.

The simplest, most effective way to avoid the dilemma of "idea overwhelm" (the prospect of facing an overwhelming number of ideas to evaluate at the end of an ideation process) is to cull out the most valuable ideas after each round of idea generation. We refer to this process as harvesting ideas.

As we mentioned in earlier chapters, it is recommended that you plan to use a variety of ideation techniques, perhaps two or three (or more) during the course of a single SmartStorming session. Then you and your group can harvest the most promising ideas after each of the different techniques (using intuition and the group's best reasoning abilities as your guide).

These ideas are extremely valuable, so be sure to have the session Reporter transfer them to the Idea Bank for safekeeping until the final selection process.

How to set up and manage your session Idea Bank

Think of your Idea Bank as a kind of safety deposit box where you store your group's most valuable ideas harvested after each round of generating ideas. Your Idea Bank begins as a series of large sheets of paper posted prominently on the wall or some other safe area (on a whiteboard, for example) where everyone can see them.

We recommend one large sheet of paper for each ideation technique you plan to use in your session. For example, if you plan to pilot your group through Idea Sprinting, Bad2Good, and Group Graffiti activities, you would post three large sheets of paper in a row.

IDEA BANK		
Idea Sprinting	Bad2Good	Group Graffiti

How it works: Harvesting ideas as you go along

Continuing with our example, let's say your first ideation technique was Idea Sprinting, and that your group came up with thirty-five ideas during the allotted time.

Next, you would instruct your group to *quickly* evaluate (in five minutes or less) all the ideas generated, and then narrow down the number of ideas to a short list of the most promising solutions to the challenge.

This short list of selected ideas should be read out loud so the Reporter can transcribe them onto the first sheet of the Idea Bank.

IDEA BANK		
Idea Sprinting	*Bad2Good*	*Group Graffiti*
1) Butterfly Effect 2) Minimal Chic 3) Zero Gravity 4) Pop-Up Store 5) Coveted Luxury 6) Future Human 7) Elite Membership		

Next, you would pilot your group through the second ideation technique, Bad2Good. Let's say your group came up with twenty ideas during this exercise. Again, you would instruct the group to narrow the number of new ideas down to a short list, and the Reporter would then transcribe this second round of ideas onto the second sheet.

IDEA BANK		
Idea Sprinting	*Bad2Good*	*Group Graffiti*
1) Butterfly Effect 2) Minimal Chic 3) Zero Gravity 4) Pop-Up Store 5) Coveted Luxury 6) Future Human 7) Elite Membership	1) Virtual Bliss 2) Paris Calling 3) New Attitude 4) Extreme Relaxation 5) Exclusivity	

Finally you would lead your group through the third ideation technique you've chosen, Group Graffiti. Imagine forty-two ideas were generated. You would go through the same harvesting process a third time.

IDEA BANK

Idea Sprinting	Bad2Good	Group Graffiti
1) Butterfly Effect	1) Virtual Bliss	1) Solar Soda
2) Minimal Chic	2) Paris Calling	2) The Next Apple
3) Zero Gravity	3) New Attitude	3) Plug-N-Play
4) Pop-Up Store	4) Extreme Relaxation	4) Nano-Tech
5) Coveted Luxury	5) Exclusivity	5) Wish List
6) Future Human		6) Clash Match
7) Elite Membership		7) Celebrity Power
		8) Space Design
		9) Peer Envy

As you can see, at the end of your idea-generation process, you will have an easy-to-manage short list of the most valuable ideas—rather than an overwhelming volume of ideas to sift through and evaluate.

(Note: If participants are generating ideas on sticky notes, the Reporter can simply place the selected sticky note ideas themselves on the Idea Bank in each round instead of transcribing the ideas as a list.)

Step 3: For final idea selection—Narrow down the number of ideas in your Idea Bank using your objective selection criteria as a yardstick.

Once a group has completed rounds of generating ideas and harvesting the most promising ones, the time has come for the final selection process. This is where you will narrow down the number of ideas in the Idea Bank, resulting in a short list of ideas that will most effectively address the challenge.

Up to this point, you and your group have been harvesting ideas using your (subjective) intuition and best reasoning abilities. But now the time has come to inject a measure of objectivity, and evaluate ideas based on how effectively they will address the challenge. You do this by introducing the selection criteria you created during the pre-planning process. These criteria will serve as the yardstick by which the group (or a smaller selection committee) will measure the merits of each idea; the criteria will help define a good or "winning" idea.

How to pilot
Before the final selection process begins

1) Begin by posting a large copy of the selection criteria in the room where all can clearly read it.

   Take a few minutes to review the set of selection criteria with the group—one criterion at a time—to make sure everyone understands the meaning of each. It is best to make sure no criterion is left too vague or open to interpretation.

   This step will create group alignment and, more importantly, establish a common framework for evaluating and selecting ideas. The more aligned a group is in understanding the criteria, the smoother your selection process will be.

   Next, provide each person with a strip of colorful peel-and-stick dots for voting. We recommend limiting the number of dots given to each individual (five to seven) so that each participant becomes as selective as possible in casting his or her vote.

When you are ready to begin the selection process

2) Ask group members to walk up to the Idea Bank and carefully consider each of the ideas posted. Remind everyone to use the selection criteria posted nearby when evaluating ideas.

3) Instruct participants to *silently* cast their votes by placing one colored dot next to each of the ideas in the Idea Bank they feel most successfully addresses the challenge and meets the selection criteria.

   Note: If you find this method to be a challenge with a group, instead of using dots for voting, you can try other effective voting methods, including using a secret ballot (provide each participant with a numbered list of the ideas, ask them to circle the numbers of the ideas they think best address the challenge, then tally the ballots to identify the winning selections); show of hands (majority wins); Yes/No or Green/Red voting cards; or even electronic, handheld audience response polling devices.

   If the boss (or other influential person of stature) is participating in the voting process, politely ask him or her to kindly postpone voting until everyone else has finished. This will help minimize the chance of his or her opinion swaying the group.

4) When the voting is completed, the ideas that have received the largest number of dots (or votes using another polling method) are the group's selected ideas.

5) The final step is to assess your short list of selected ideas (or set of sticky notes) to determine if any can be combined with other ideas based on similarity in

theme or attributes. If so, then combine those ideas and eliminate any duplicate or redundant ideas from the list.

IDEA BANK

Idea Sprinting	Bad2Good	Group Graffiti
1) Butterfly Effect ●●	1) Virtual Bliss ●●●	1) Solar Soda ●●
2) Minimal Chic ●	2) Paris Calling ●●●●●	2) The Next Apple
3) Zero Gravity	3) New Attitude	3) Plug-N-Play
4) Pop-Up Store ●●●●●	4) Extreme Relaxation ●●	4) Nano-Tech ●●●●●
5) Coveted Luxury	5) Exclusivity ●	5) Wish List ●
6) Future Human ●●		6) Clash Match
7) Elite Membership		7) Celebrity Power ●●
		8) Space Design
		9) Peer Envy ●●●●●

If you (and your group or selection committee) are confident that you have identified and selected the best ideas possible to address your issue, challenge, or opportunity, you can end your selection process here.

However, if you would like a greater degree of assurance that the ideas selected really do measure up to the objective criteria, you can run those ideas through an optional diagnostic step.

(Optional) Step 4: Use the SmartStorming Idea Selection Diagnostic Matrix to identify the specific strengths and weaknesses of your best ideas.

The SmartStorming Idea Selection Diagnostic Matrix is a simple, highly effective tool that helps clearly identify the inherent strengths and weaknesses of each promising idea selected, in a way that minimizes personal subjectivity. Using the matrix will neatly resolve any disagreements or points of contention about the merits of an idea. It will also quickly reveal precisely where an idea needs work.

When might you choose to take this extra step? Generally, when you need to be as confident as possible that your selected ideas are strong (e.g., when the stakes are high and you are working on especially important challenges, with little room for error; when there is not enough time to engage in multiple rounds of brainstorming; when you will be called upon to justify the merits of ideas you have selected to superiors or outside decision makers; when you would like a more detailed analysis of your ideas so that you can more easily revisit and improve them; etc.).

How it works

The Idea Selection Diagnostic Matrix is a simple grid on which you have written your objective selection criteria and your best ideas. The criteria are placed across the top of the grid (as key words, one each above a vertical column), and the final selected ideas are written down the left-hand side of the grid. (See example below.)

In order to fit your ideas in the space allotted, each idea should be distilled down to a short, concise, one- to three-word description or label that captures the essence of the idea. For example: "Minimal Chic," "Pop-Up Store," "Solar Soda," etc.

Once your criteria and ideas are written on the grid, it is time to determine whether or not each idea meets each of the objective selection criteria.

See how the most promising ideas measure up

Begin with the first idea at the top of the list. Moving from left to right, one box at a time, the Pilot asks the group, "Does this idea meet the first criterion?" If the group consensus is that the idea does meet the criterion, a check mark is put in the intersecting box. If the idea fails to meet the criterion, the box is left blank.

On occasion, a group may find itself divided or deadlocked as to whether an idea meets one of the criteria or not. In these cases, simply place a question mark (?) in the box, then move on to the next criterion.

The Pilot continues evaluating the first idea until all of the criteria have been considered, then moves down to the next idea on the list. The same diagnostic process is repeated for each idea listed.

Once you and the group have finished running all of the ideas through the diagnostic process, it should be apparent which ideas are objective winners (in the example below, ideas #2 and #5 meet every criterion), which ideas have weak spots or gaps, and which ideas should be eliminated (idea #3).

The beauty of this objective diagnostic approach is that it simplifies the evaluation process by creating just three categories of ideas:

1) Strong ideas that meet *all* of the criteria (solid winners with check marks in every box);

2) Ideas that meet *most* of the criteria, but have discernible gaps or weaknesses (these ideas may be set aside for further development); and

3) Ideas that fall short in three or more areas (these ideas should be eliminated).

	Innovative	Relevant	Compelling	Adaptable	On Strategy	Doable
1) Minimal Chic	✔		✔	✔		✔
2) French-Mex Restaurant	✔	✔	✔	✔	✔	✔
3) Pop-Up Store		✔	✔			
4) Solar Soda	✔	✔	?	✔	✔	
5) Personalized Paradise	✔	✔	✔	✔	✔	✔
6) Musical DNA	✔		✔	✔	✔	✔

As you can see, the SmartStorming Idea Selection Diagnostic Matrix is a simple, yet highly effective tool. This final, optional step in the idea selection process will provide you with greater confidence that the ideas you have selected really do possess the qualities necessary for successfully addressing your challenge or opportunity.

Putting it all together

The diagram below illustrates how the steps in the SmartStorming selection process flow together from Step 1, the preplanning stage where you determine the selection criteria for your session; to Step 2, the harvesting of ideas throughout the idea-generation session; to Step 3, the group's pick of ideas based on the selection criteria; and to the optional Step 4, where the leading ideas are run through the MRI-like litmus test of the Idea Selection Diagnostic Matrix.

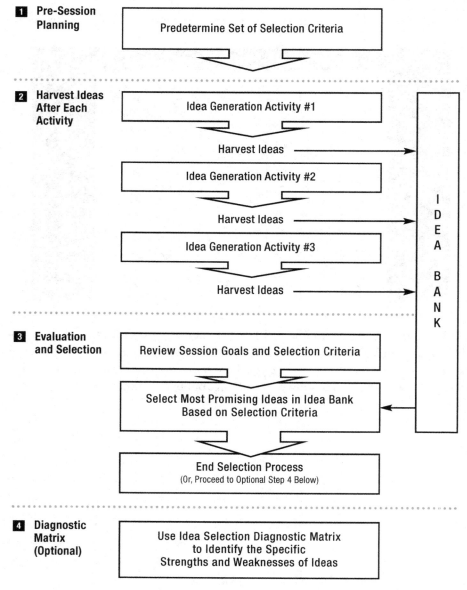

1 Pre-Session Planning

Predetermine Set of Selection Criteria

2 Harvest Ideas After Each Activity

Idea Generation Activity #1

Harvest Ideas

Idea Generation Activity #2

Harvest Ideas

Idea Generation Activity #3

Harvest Ideas

IDEA BANK

3 Evaluation and Selection

Review Session Goals and Selection Criteria

Select Most Promising Ideas in Idea Bank Based on Selection Criteria

End Selection Process
(Or, Proceed to Optional Step 4 Below)

4 Diagnostic Matrix (Optional)

Use Idea Selection Diagnostic Matrix to Identify the Specific Strengths and Weaknesses of Ideas

Tips for managing the idea-selection process

Get everyone on the same page *before* the final round of idea selection.
Reviewing the session goals, objectives, and selection criteria before starting the final selection process helps frame the context for what the group set out to achieve, and fosters group alignment by establishing a common set of benchmarks for evaluating the merits of ideas.

Keep discussions unconditionally constructive and free of conflicts.
An important part of leading a group through the evaluation process is fostering an atmosphere that is collegial and focused on the task of narrowing down the number of ideas. A good Pilot continually monitors the room to make sure the group is working collaboratively through the selection process. Whenever participants disagree (or become argumentative), shift the conversation away from the area of disagreement and toward other aspects of the idea they can agree on.

Keep discussions on a convergent path while narrowing down ideas.
As we mentioned earlier in the chapter, it is easy for groups to wander off topic during discussions, or drift back into blue sky, divergent thinking to fix or improve ideas they are evaluating (*"Hey, what if we took this idea and…"*). A SmartStorming Pilot should be aware of which direction his or her group's thinking is flowing and keep it focused and moving forward on a convergent path, narrowing down the number of ideas to a short list of best possible solutions.

Don't stop the selection process to fix ideas.
It's fairly common for a group or selection committee to identify a weak spot or flaw in the most promising ideas during the evaluation process. As tempting as it might be to simply stop everything to fix the defect or to make a good idea even better, doing so might sidetrack your selection process completely. Brainstorming ways to fix or improve ideas will shift a group out of analytical-mode convergent thinking and launch it back into imagination-fueled, "What if…" divergent thinking. It's far more efficient to stay in the convergent mindset. Simply select those ideas, quickly note where they might need to be improved, and then set them aside for discussion at a later time. There are benefits to having everyone sleep on it for an evening and then revisit those ideas with a fresh eye.

Preserve your session's Idea Bank for future evaluation.
We recommend you (and project stakeholders) retain the Idea Bank from each SmartStorming session. There's always a possibility that a few seeds of other good ideas may have been overlooked.

Rules for the idea-selection process

Just as there are rules of the game for the idea-generation stage of a SmartStorming session, there are a few rules that help foster group alignment in the evaluation and selection process. We recommend sharing these rules with your group or committee before evaluating ideas:

Keep discussions convergent
The goal of the selection process is to narrow down the number of ideas to a short list that best addresses the challenge.

Respect differences of opinion
All points of view are valuable to hear and consider. If differences of opinion arise, focus upon those points the group does agree on.

Radical ideas should not be dismissed
Even the wildest, most audacious idea can contain the seeds of an innovative, game-changing idea.

Select ideas first, improve ideas later
Don't stop the selection process to fix ideas. Select them now; then schedule a meeting to improve ideas at a later time.

Combine ideas where possible
Eliminate redundancy; look for ways to combine ideas that share similar themes, approaches, traits, or attributes.

The boss votes last
When an authority figure participates in the selection process, his or her opinions can often sway a group's evaluation of ideas. Ask the boss to hold comments until all others have discussed the merits of each idea.

What to remember

- The evaluation and selection phase of a SmartStorming session is the official crossover point from expansive, anything goes divergent thinking to the narrowing discernment of convergent thinking.

- Most decision making is based on emotion, not reason. People use information (facts, data, criteria, reviews, and testimonials) to *rationalize* their decisions, but at the moment a person actually makes their decision, it is based primarily on emotion.

- You can achieve a more balanced selection process between emotions and reason by having participants use their intuition and best reasoning abilities to narrow down the overall number of ideas; then evaluate the merits of the remaining ideas against a predetermined set of objective selection criteria.

- You can avoid the prospect of "idea overwhelm" by harvesting ideas as you go, and transferring your selections to an Idea Bank after each round of idea generation.

The SmartStorming evaluation and selection process:

- Step 1: Before your session—Predetermine a set of objective selection criteria for evaluating the merits of your group's ideas.

- Step 2: While generating ideas—Harvest the most valuable ideas as you go along, after each idea-generation activity. Transfer those ideas to your Idea Bank.

- Step 3: For final idea selection—Narrow down the number of ideas in your Idea Bank using your objective selection criteria as a yardstick.

- (Optional) Step 4: Use the SmartStorming Idea Selection Diagnostic Matrix to identify the specific strengths and weaknesses of your best ideas.

Note: There are a number of different methods a group can use to vote for ideas, including colorful, peel-and-stick dots, a secret ballot, a show of hands (majority wins), Yes/No or Green/Red voting cards, or electronic handheld audience response polling devices.

CHAPTER 10

Step 6—Transforming Ideas into New Realities

YOU ARE HERE

Next Steps
and
Follow-Through

"Thinking is easy, acting is difficult, and to put one's thoughts into action is the most difficult thing in the world."

—Johann von Goethe, poet, novelist

How many times have you participated in a brainstorm in which the group was able to generate some great ideas—but those ideas were never carried forward? A common complaint we hear about traditional brainstorming is the lack of follow-through. Even when worthwhile ideas are generated, all too often they are soon forgotten. Everyone leaves the room, never to hear of their great ideas again.

In short, those good ideas wither on the vine.

Besides the obvious problem—that potentially game-changing ideas with real potential never see the light of day—an added consequence is that when this situation

115

becomes a consistent pattern, people lose enthusiasm for participating in brainstorms at all. No one wants to waste their valuable time generating ideas that are never carried through to completion.

In the first five SmartStorming Steps, you learned how to generate a wealth of innovative new ideas, in terms of not just quantity, but quality. But a brainstorm shouldn't end with the generation and selection of ideas. A brainstorm is not the completion of a process—it is just the beginning.

While it is true that innovation is fueled by ideas, it is *realized* by action. Only by taking meaningful action can the idea ever become a reality. Seeds are worth nothing if they are not planted, fed, and watered. And even the most powerful and life-changing ideas are worth nothing if they are never executed.

SmartStorming addresses this challenge by providing a simple, but effective method for determining and assigning next steps—before leaving the session. We call it the SmartStorming 5-As Idea Implementation Process. When you and your team go through each step, in sequence, you will significantly increase the odds that your best and most exciting ideas will actually come to life.

As a reminder, identifying Next Steps is an important part of your SmartStorming preplanning process. If you have considered ahead of time, when completing your Pre-Session Planner, what action steps need to occur immediately after your session, and who the best people are to assign responsibilities to, you will be well on your way to successfully applying the 5-As Idea Implementation Process.

The CEO's dilemma

A recent Accenture survey of *Chief Executive* magazine readers found that two-thirds of the CEOs surveyed recognized innovation as a key factor necessary for success and competitive advantage.

Yet that same survey revealed that most companies are ultimately able to commercialize fewer than 20 percent of their best ideas. And just one in eight executives felt strongly that their companies excelled at implementing innovative ideas.[13]

How is this possible? In a business environment focused so heavily on innovation as a key measurement of success, why is there such an obvious disconnect between the generation of ideas and their ultimate realization?

While it is not the goal of this book to address the many organizational challenges that can make it difficult, or even impossible, to implement ideas, we do believe there are some positive steps that can be taken by SmartStorming Pilots and their teams—as an integral part of the brainstorming process—to help ensure that ideas survive the short, but sometimes arduous journey from the ideation session to those all-important next steps.

The SmartStorming 5-As Idea Implementation Process

The 5-As Idea Implementation Process is an effective, top-line approach for ensuring that your ideas move forward in a positive and productive way, to become reality. The five steps are: Act, Assess, Assign, Agree, and Activate.

Step 1: Act—Proactively foster an action-oriented attitude.

Daily distractions, too many demands on time and attention, procrastination, overcomplication, ineffective communication, and bureaucracy are all organizational shortcomings that contribute to the delay or death of good ideas. But in many cases, most of these unproductive behavior patterns are simply undesirable habits that have become, over time, acceptable within a team or organization.

Individuals and teams may have the best of intentions, and actually view themselves as action-oriented. But in reality, the demands of ongoing obligations often get in the way of proactively developing new ideas and initiatives. However, just as an individual (or a team, or an organization) can, over time, develop a habit of inaction, so can they just as effectively nurture a culture committed to taking action. In his excellent book *Making Ideas Happen,* author Scott Belsky refers to this as living and working with "a bias toward action."[14]

As a leader (and Idea Champion), it is your job to proactively and enthusiastically model a "do it now" attitude for your team and to nurture this mindset in them. Create a sense of urgency and a "forward leaning" attitude when a project is ready to be carried forward. Acknowledge and reward those who take action—and actively coach those who do not to help them improve.

When filling roles or positions on your team, look for dynamic individuals who will serve as catalysts for action. If there are people who are particularly strong at follow-through, utilize them and their skills. If possible, assign them the most critical and time-sensitive tasks.

Plan regular (weekly, semiweekly) status update meetings to ensure that everyone is on task and projects are moving forward.

Make "action taking" a highly valued quality among your team—and observe the impact it has on productivity.

Step 2: Assess—Size up the big picture, then break it down into action steps.

As quickly as possible, assess how big, time-consuming, and complex the task of bringing your ideas to life will be:

- How many people, and who, specifically, will be required to carry it forward?

- What other day-to-day activities, projects, or obligations might compete for stakeholders' time and attention?

- What adjustments need to be made to ensure adequate time and attention can be allocated to bringing the new idea to fruition? (Note: You can always revise your assessment as the project progresses—but start the process now.)

Next, break large projects down into smaller, more manageable steps. You know the old expression that states you eat an elephant one bite at a time? Many important projects, when viewed in their entirety, can seem too big to conquer. Even if this isn't the case, when you don't bother to break a project down into its smaller, more manageable components, often people don't really know where or how to start.

Determine first what major subprojects will be part of your overall initiative. Next, break each of those subprojects down, first into major milestones and finally, specific sequential tasks required to reach each milestone. Be as specific and detailed as possible. The more granular your assessment, the clearer the path to completion will be.

Maintain reasonable, but motivating pressure on the team. Carefully consider the time it will take to move the project to the next level—and strive to keep your timeline as tight as is reasonable.

Why would we recommend setting ambitious timelines? Because nothing will sap enthusiasm and hinder productivity more than too much time.

In *Making Ideas Happen*, Belsky points out a direct correlation between time and enthusiasm.[15] When an idea is new and a project is fresh, everyone is excited and motivated. But the more time passes without a project reaching a conclusion, the less enthusiastic the team becomes. The pressures and demands of ongoing, day-to-day responsibilities take precedence. Other new projects pop up. More immediate needs become priorities, demanding valuable time, attention, and resources. And your once-exciting idea has devolved into a vague memory.

Don't be afraid to challenge your team. You may have observed that when someone has two weeks to accomplish a task, they will most often take two weeks. Ask for the same task to be completed in ten days, and they will do it in ten days. It is human nature to attempt to answer the challenge—but not necessarily to exceed expectations. So keep timelines realistic, but optimistic. Think of shorter timelines as a way of turning up the heat! Things start cooking much faster.

Step 3: Assign—Establish specific roles, responsibilities, and deliverables.

Once you have assessed the needs of the task, it's time to decide who will do what. Identify the best person/people for each task. Consider the talents, skills, and expertise of each member of your team—who is self-igniting, goal-oriented, resourceful, dependable, has good organizational skills, etc.—and assign roles to the most appropriate person. Try to create an A-Team that can overcome any challenge!

Step 4: Agree—Create team alignment and personal accountability.

If the stakeholders were participants in your SmartStorming session, make every effort to assign initial responsibilities and get their agreement to specific timelines and deliverables *before* leaving the room. If the necessary people are not present, determine how to best assign tasks to them. If the project is particularly large or complex, it may not be feasible to assign all tasks at this time. Just make sure you set the process in motion, and get agreement from those involved on how it will continue to move forward most efficiently.

An additional component to establishing Agreement is Accountability. What are the consequences to someone on the team not delivering as he or she promised? It is important to determine how team members will be held accountable, and what actions to take if there is a breakdown in the process. If you step over this important issue, you are setting yourself up for your project to stall or, in some cases, fail completely.

Establishing agreement on specific roles, responsibilities, accountability, and consequences helps eliminate ambiguity and creates team alignment toward achieving a shared goal.

Step 5: Activate—Pull the trigger; make it happen!

Once you have quickly and efficiently gone through the first four steps, it's time to press the start button. If you have thoroughly considered Next Steps in your pre-planning and have now taken the time to go through each of the previous steps, everyone in the room should be in agreement. If at all possible, try to complete this process before you end your session. If that is not feasible, do it as soon after as possible.

Remember, the longer you wait to put the implementation process in motion, the greater the risk your project will never see the light of day (like the 80 percent referred to in the Accenture survey) or, at the very least, that its quality will suffer due to a lack of time and enthusiasm.

Is this brainstorming?

Although much of this sounds like the job of a project manager, we believe that it is imperative for effective SmartStorming Pilots to inspire their groups, not only in the generation of ideas, but also in their execution. Depending on your industry or field, organizational culture, specific projects, and goals, most of the actual implementation of a project may not fall on your shoulders. But the more aware you are of the necessary elements and the better you are at helping to inspire and ensure their application, the greater the chance your group's creative genius will not go to waste!

SmartStorming 5-As Idea Implementation Process Planner

The 5-As Idea Implementation Process is an effective, top-line approach to ensuring that your ideas move forward in a positive and productive way to become reality. This planner will help you identify the five steps in the process: Act, Assess, Assign, Agree, and Activate.

Step 1: Act—Proactively foster an action-oriented attitude. (List three things to do today to ensure your team is enthused and motivated to take action. What can you do to inspire them?)

Step 2: Assess—Size up the big picture, then break it down into action steps. (Define the scope of the project in terms of time, complexity, and resources. What skills/capabilities are necessary?)

Next, break down the overall project into manageable chunks. What subprojects make up the overall project? Identify the major milestones, then individual tasks, required for each subproject.

Step 3: Assign—Establish specific roles, responsibilities, and deliverables. (Who is the very best, most reliable person to assign to each task based on their talents, skills, and individual traits? Do they have the necessary time and resources to deliver the job?

Step 4: Agree—Create team alignment and personal accountability. (What will you do to establish agreement about specific timelines and deliverables *before* participants leave the room? How will you assign tasks and establish agreement with team members not in the room?

Step 5: Activate—Pull the trigger; make it happen! (What are the most immediate steps necessary to get the project under way?

What to remember

- A brainstorm is not the end of a process—it is just the beginning. While it is true that innovation is fueled by ideas, it is *realized* by action.

- The 5-As Idea Implementation Process is an effective, top-line approach to help ensure that your projects move forward in a positive and productive way.

  Step 1: Act—Proactively foster an action-oriented attitude.

  Step 2: Assess—Size up the big picture, then break it down into action steps.

  Step 3: Assign—Establish specific roles, responsibilities, and deliverables.

  Step 4: Agree—Create team alignment and personal accountability.

  Step 5: Activate—Pull the trigger; make it happen!

- Make every effort to assign initial responsibilities and get agreement to specific timelines and deliverables *before* leaving the room.

Part Three
SmartStorming
Leadership Skills

CHAPTER 11

Inspiring and Guiding Your Group to Greatness

"The task of leadership is not to put greatness into humanity,
but to elicit it, for the greatness is already there."

—John Buchan, Scottish politician

As you are probably beginning to appreciate, successful SmartStorming sessions do not occur by chance. They are carefully planned and skillfully led. There are numerous principles and skills you'll need to learn in order to pilot highly productive sessions. These skills will help make your sessions easier to manage and flow more smoothly, and help you inspire and guide your group to produce a greater range and depth of fresh, new ideas than ever before.

We encourage you to reread the chapters in this section several times to become familiar with these leadership principles so you can apply them with confidence in your future SmartStorming sessions.

The Pilot's presence

"Confidence is contagious. So is lack of confidence."

—Vince Lombardi

When traveling by plane, have you ever found yourself glancing into the cockpit upon entering the cabin to get a glimpse of who is piloting your flight? Did the pilot look experienced? Did he or she appear to have the right stuff to get you to your destination safely with minimum delay or turbulence?

When the pilot made an announcement over the intercom, did the sound of his or her voice communicate a reassuring sense of being in control? If so, you were probably better able to settle back, relax, and enjoy the flight, knowing you were in good hands.

Interestingly, we have observed a similar situation that occurs when participants first enter a brainstorming session. They instinctively size up the facilitator, based on his or her demeanor, to get a sense of whether they are in competent hands or not. Does the facilitator appear confident? Does he or she seem to have the right stuff to inspire and lead the group through a productive and rewarding session?

While participants may not be risking life and limb during a brainstorming session, they are risking other things—the possibility of wasting valuable time and effort in a futile exercise that produces few, if any, worthwhile ideas.

A SmartStorming Pilot's presence can be an important asset. When a Pilot shows up confident, well prepared, and focused on achieving the goal, the group will immediately sense that they are in good hands and will willingly follow his or her lead. By contrast, if a Pilot is perceived as being underprepared or lacking the confidence, skills, or tools to lead a productive session, the group will feel a sense of apprehension about the task before them.

So what kinds of leadership skills and attitudes should one cultivate in order to become an inspiring and effective SmartStorming Pilot? Here are eight characteristics that are shared by the most successful session leaders:

The characteristics of an inspiring SmartStorming Pilot

Confident—has a commanding presence, knows where he or she is going and how to get there

Prepared—has a well-thought-out, step-by-step game plan for the session

Enthusiastic—projects a positive, can-do attitude and energy that is contagious

Motivational—inspires the group to stretch beyond their comfort zone

Appreciative—for the unique contributions each and every participant can bring to the process

Fair—inspires full participation, eliminates negativity and judgments, and maintains an ego-free zone

Goal-Oriented—sets ambitious goals for the group; keeps conversations on target

Light—keeps the problem-solving process playful and spontaneous

The key to radiating a confident Pilot presence is to be well prepared, enthusiastic, and have your full attention focused *outside* of yourself on your group (rather than self-consciously focused inward). Making continual eye contact is the secret ingredient in creating a warm, meaningful connection with group members. It takes a little practice to maintain an outward focus on others, but when you do, you will feel more engaged with your group, less self-conscious, and more confident. Your group members will appreciate your attention and strive to please you with their performance.

Developing "situational awareness"

In addition to projecting a confident, capable presence, a seasoned SmartStorming Pilot will also possess a heightened sense of awareness (or an intuitive, sixth-sense ability) to read where the group's thinking process is flowing in each moment, and how events are unfolding in the session.

For example, an aware Pilot is able to clearly recognize whether the group is generating ideas spontaneously and quickly or getting bogged down in too much discussion. Is the group moving in the direction of achieving its goal or veering off course on unproductive tangents? Is everyone in the group contributing ideas? Or is the session being dominated by a few strong personalities?

This ability to accurately discern your group's state of mind, performance, and progress as your session unfolds is an invaluable leadership skill—a skill that will allow you to make whatever real-time adjustments are necessary to keep your group on track, fully engaged, and effortlessly generating ideas.

The key to cultivating this skill is to understand and apply the principles of "situational awareness." The term is used widely in the aviation industry. It refers to an aircraft pilot's ability to observe, in real time, what is happening around him or her and to understand how the information (speed, altitude, aircraft performance), events (weather, ground terrain, air traffic), and the crew's own actions are affecting flight progress and safety.

In the simplest of terms, situational awareness refers to being vigilantly aware in any given moment of what is occurring and making the real-time adjustments necessary to achieve your goal or reach your destination.

Cultivating situational awareness is a three-step process:

1. **Perceiving** what is actually going on, moment by moment, in your session

2. **Discerning** how unfolding group dynamics will affect the group's ability to achieve the goals and objectives for the session

3. **Extrapolating** what adjustments or action steps need to occur in order to keep your group fully engaged and its ideation momentum high

Perceiving (seeing), discerning (understanding), and extrapolating (forecasting) are innate abilities we all possess. If developing greater situational awareness sounds complicated, it's not. It is the same skill set we use while driving a car, playing a sport, or outsmarting a computer game. In each of those activities, we observe what is going on, understand where the course of events is leading, and decide what actions need to be taken to achieve our goal. Once we have mastered an activity, these steps become second nature. We are able to read any situation occurring within the activity we are engaged in—and respond accordingly—often without even being consciously aware that we are doing so.

Why is heightened situational awareness such an important skill for you to develop? Because brainstorming is not a linear, straightforward (autopilot) process; it is a dynamic creative process that requires active, hands-on leadership. Without such awareness on the part of the Pilot, a session can quickly veer off course, encounter interpersonal turbulence, or run out of momentum.

Situational awareness in action

Here are some examples of the most common counterproductive group dynamics that can occur in a SmartStorming session, as well as some simple corrective tips for getting your group back on track quickly.

Situation: The group loses focus

What you will notice: The group's discussions have meandered off the subject or issue, or are veering off on an unproductive tangent.

Corrective action: Redirect the group by repeating the challenge statement, or ask them a refocusing question like, "This area of discussion sounds interesting; in what ways can it relate or apply more specifically to the challenge at hand?"

Situation: Negativity or judgment has crept into the session

What you will notice: Some participants begin to criticize or shoot down the ideas of others. When the atmosphere in a session becomes emotionally charged with negativity or judgment, individuals will stop sharing their ideas for fear of being judged. Long periods of uncomfortable silence are a telltale sign that judgment has crept into the session.

Corrective action: Intervene at the very first sign of judgment or negativity. Remind your group about the rules of the session. Rule number one is "Suspend All Judgment!" There will be plenty of opportunity to discuss the merits of ideas later on in the session, during the evaluation and selection process. For now, during the idea-generation stage, ALL ideas are welcome, and there is no such thing as a bad idea. Remember, even the worst-sounding idea can contain the seeds of a great idea.

Situation: The group's enthusiasm and energy level drops

What you will notice: When the idea-generation process begins to lose steam, participants begin to show signs of boredom, seem spaced out, or become fidgety. Sometimes they will start texting, doodling, or engaging in unrelated side conversations.

Corrective action: As soon as you sense a dip in your group's energy level, immediately shift to a new line of provocative questioning; change directions every few minutes to help keep your group engaged and on their toes. Another good technique is to call on participants individually and ask if they have any ideas they might like to share. People tend to pay a lot more attention if there's a chance they will be called upon to contribute.

Situation: Dominating personalities hijack the session

What you will notice: A few strong personalities have begun to seize control of the session, dominating conversations, asserting the superiority of their own ideas, oversharing, shooting holes in the ideas of others, and competing for attention, recognition, or applause.

Corrective action: Politely, but with authority, redirect the conversation away from the domineering participant by saying something like, "Great ideas, John/Jen. Thank you. Now let's give the rest of the group a chance to share some of theirs." With the right emphasis, the offending parties should get the message, as will others in the group, who will see that the way has been cleared for them to begin sharing again.

Another highly effective approach for regaining control and leveling the playing field is to introduce a *nonverbal* SmartStorming activity. For example, ask everyone to silently write down five ideas, and then read their favorite ones aloud. Or break the group up into smaller teams of three or four; have them generate ideas, and then have each team share its best ideas with the entire group.

Situation: Side conversations or "splinter groups" disrupt the session

What you will notice: Two or more group members have begun to engage in their own private side conversation, gossiping, joking, etc., often distracting other group members from focusing on the challenge at hand.

Corrective Action: Remind the group of the rule "No side conversations." Address the culprits directly by asking, in a lighthearted tone, "So, what ideas did you two (or three) come up with in your little private SmartStorming session? Would you share them with the group?" Or, you can pause the session and silently gesture to the rest of the group to playfully stare (or make faces) at the preoccupied offenders; good-natured peer pressure can be a very effective rule enforcement tool.

Situation: The group gets stuck in a rut and starts recycling old, familiar ideas

What you will notice: The group begins to reintroduce the same old ideas, strategies, or tactics over and over again.

Corrective Action: Break the cycle. Ask your group a series of new thought-provoking questions to get them out of their thinking rut and into exploring new territory.

For example:

> "How can we take that old idea and give it a provocative new twist?"
> "What is the most outrageous new idea we can think of?"
> "What new ideas haven't we considered or thought of yet?"
> "If all limitations were taken away, what would we do or say?"

Brainstorm facilitators who are oblivious of this principle of situational awareness tend to be "in their heads" and lead their sessions by rote or reaction.

In contrast, as a skilled SmartStorming Pilot, you can now understand the importance of proactively monitoring your group's attention and energy levels and making any real-time adjustments that may be needed to keep your group in The Zone.

What to remember

- A confident presence is an important asset for a SmartStorming Pilot to possess. Showing up in your session as a well-prepared and enthusiastic leader can have a significant positive impact on the productivity of your group.

- It is important for a Pilot to develop his or her situational awareness skills, because the brainstorming process by nature is not linear. It is a dynamic, creative process that has ups and downs, unexpected twists and turns, and moments of turbulence. The process demands active, hands-on leadership.

- Situational awareness means *being vigilantly aware in any given moment of what is occurring, and making the necessary real-time adjustments to achieve your goal/objective.*

- Situational awareness is a three-step process:

  1. Perceiving what is actually going on, moment by moment

  2. Discerning how unfolding group dynamics will affect the group's ability to achieve the goals/objectives for the session

  3. Extrapolating what adjustments or action steps need to occur in order to keep your group fully engaged and its ideation momentum high

CHAPTER 12

Managing Divergent and Convergent Thinking

*"We cannot solve our problems with the same thinking
we used when we created them."*

—Albert Einstein

Another key principle to understand is that *the quantity and quality of ideas a group generates will be directly proportionate to the leader's ability to inspire and guide them.*

In other words, as the Pilot, it is up to you to actively engage your group's imaginations and manage their idea-generation process. This guiding presence is what separates a good SmartStorming Pilot from a so-so brainstorm facilitator.

When a group becomes deeply absorbed in their problem-solving activity, a very interesting phenomenon occurs: individual egos drop away, interpersonal boundaries relax, and a spontaneous, collaborative spirit of sharing insights and building ideas begins to flow among participants.

This cross-pollination of knowledge, perceptions, and experiences sparks a higher level of collective understanding and creativity within the group. People often refer to this mind-linking phenomenon as "group mind" or "unity consciousness."

When group mind occurs, it becomes easier for you to guide your group's exploration in any direction with a light touch.

More about divergent vs. convergent thinking directions

As we discussed earlier in Chapter 8, one of the most valuable skills a Smart-Storming Pilot can develop is the ability to read the direction in which the group's thoughts are flowing. Just like the ebbing and flowing tides of an ocean, collaborative thinking flows in two very distinct directions: 1) it can diverge outward, in a broad, 360-degree, blue sky exploration of ideas; or 2) it can converge inward, narrowing focus in an effort to judge and select ideas.

Divergent thinking opens the imagination to all possibilities, while convergent thinking analyzes, discerns, and selects from among those possibilities. In a sense, divergent and convergent thinking are the yin and yang of creative problem solving. Neither is superior to the other—one is simply more appropriate for the specific task at hand. Both processes are essential to the ultimate success of any group idea-generation session.

So it is important to understand the benefits of both, to identify when and under what circumstances each type of thinking is taking place, and to learn how to guide the group back to the most appropriate and effective method of thinking.

The benefits of divergent thinking: unrestricted imagination

Divergent thinking allows a group to generate as many fresh, new ideas as possible in a short time frame. During this process all judgment is suspended, and the group is encouraged to go for quantity of ideas (rather than quality), spontaneously build on one another's ideas, and push the boundaries of the imagination to make novel connections. Even wild, crazy, audacious ideas are welcome. The motto for divergent thinking is "Everything is possible!" There is no such thing as a bad idea (because even the worst-sounding ideas can have the seeds of a great idea).

This is the type of thinking most people think of as the *brainstorming* part of brainstorming.

The benefits of convergent thinking: judgment and selection

If divergent thinking is casting the widest net possible to capture new ideas, then convergent thinking can be thought of as harvesting the very best of the catch. Just as a funnel decreases the scope of a substance so that it fits through a narrower opening, convergent thinking narrows down a large number of ideas through the process of analyzing, judging, and selecting.

This is the type of thinking most people think of as the *evaluation and selection process* in a brainstorming session.

How to manage both types of thinking for success

As we mentioned earlier, both thinking directions are essential—but at different times during the brainstorming process. To keep your SmartStorming sessions productive and flowing smoothly from beginning to end, it is important to ensure that each is used in the right place and at the right time—divergent thinking in the idea-generation stage, convergent thinking for selection process—and to keep each of these different thinking processes from interfering with the other. Like matter and antimatter, if divergent and convergent thinking processes are mixed together, the effects can be highly disruptive to your session!

Why? Because convergent thinking will quickly shut down the safe, spontaneous, anything goes atmosphere of blue sky divergent thinking with judgments and criticisms. Conversely, divergent thinking will derail the narrowing, analytical convergent thinking process by stimulating the generation of more new ideas. (While this might not seem like a bad thing, at some point, you must stop generating ideas and start evaluating and selecting. Otherwise, your session goals will never be achieved.)

As a guiding principle, simply remember that the idea-generation portion of your SmartStorming session should be dedicated exclusively to blue sky divergent thinking to maximize your group's yield of fresh, new ideas.

When your group is completely finished generating ideas and you are ready to move on to the evaluation and selection process, only then do you switch their thinking process over to convergent thinking, to evaluate and narrow down the number of ideas generated.

Understanding the distinction between these two thinking processes will easily resolve a number of fundamental issues that negatively influence many brainstorming sessions.

Tips for managing divergent and convergent thinking

To keep the divergent thinking process free of judgment/criticism:

- Post the rules for your SmartStorming session on a large sheet of flipchart paper (or on a whiteboard) at the front of the room where everyone can see them. (See list of SmartStorming Rules of the Game on page 253.)

- Take a few minutes to review and discuss the rules; emphasize those rules regarding criticism and judgment, such as:
    Suspend all judgment
    There's no such thing as a bad idea

Go for quantity over quality
Embrace wild, audacious ideas

- During the idea-generation process, any and all ideas are welcome; instruct your group to save any criticisms or judgments of ideas for later during the selection process.

- Encourage your group to be self-enforcing against any negativity and judgment. Ask everyone to crumple up a piece of paper and keep it close at hand. Give the group permission to pelt any fellow group members who utter a negative word or voice criticism about an idea.

- Be sure to intervene immediately at the first sign of negativity or judgment. Create heightened group awareness about maintaining a judgment-free zone while generating ideas.

To keep convergent thinking on track during the idea-selection process:

- Dedicate the idea-selection process to the single goal of identifying the most innovative or promising ideas generated during the session—those ideas that best meet the selection criteria.

- Be vigilant to make sure the group does not lapse back into brainstorming ways to fix or improve ideas. It is better to simply note those promising ideas that need work, and then schedule a follow-up session dedicated to the purpose of improving any ideas that need further development.

What to remember

- The quantity and quality of the ideas your group generates in your sessions will be directly proportionate to your ability to inspire and guide them.

- When a group becomes deeply absorbed in the activity of problem solving together, individual egos drop away, interpersonal boundaries relax, and a spontaneous, collaborative spirit of idea-building emerges.

- Divergent thinking is for generating ideas; convergent thinking is for judging and selecting ideas.

- Don't allow the two thinking processes to mix. Convergent thinking will shut down spontaneous, blue sky divergent thinking with judgments and criticisms. Conversely, divergent thinking will sidetrack the analytical evaluation and selection process by stimulating the generation of new ideas.

CHAPTER 13

The Art of Asking Powerful Questions

"Successful people ask better questions, and as a result, they get better answers."

—Tony Robbins

SmartStorming piloting, at its essence, is the art of asking great questions. The more thought-provoking the questions you ask, the more insightful or imaginative the answers will be. Innovative thinking, the kind that solves challenges and creates game-changing products, services, and processes, is often sparked by simple, but powerful questions that begin with the words *What if...?*

A Pilot skilled in the art of questioning can positively influence the direction in which the group's attention flows, what it focuses on, how deeply, and ultimately, how many new ideas it generates.

A good metaphor for understanding this concept is to imagine a group's collective, focused attention as a kind of powerful light source that can be adjusted to be either a broad floodlight to illuminate wide areas of inquiry, or focused like a narrow, penetrating spotlight to illuminate deeper aspects of the subject.

Each time you ask a question, you redirect this floodlight or spotlight of collective curiosity in a new direction.

For example, if you want your group to explore a broad range of blue sky ideas, you can steer its thinking into the realm of the imagination by asking a question like, "What types of new and different kinds of products can we create for next year's holiday season?"

If you want to shift direction and have your group narrow its focus to discern the underlying source of a problem, you could ask a probing question like, "Where precisely has the downturn in the economy hurt our sales most?"

Notice how the type of question you ask can direct, or redirect, the thinking orientation of a group. This principle of actively steering a group's focus is a very important concept, because once you understand the principle and can skillfully apply it, you will be better able to guide a group in exploring a wider range of new directions and, ultimately, net a greater range of new ideas.

The ability to influence a group's thinking process is a skill that should be used wisely and judiciously; a good Pilot always allows the group to take the lead by following its intuition and curiosity.

Asking questions is a very powerful tool for group discovery. Questions possess the power to transform the unknown into new understanding, simplify complex issues, stimulate leaps in imagination, shift a group out of the doldrums, and quickly refocus efforts that have veered off on tangents.

In this section you will learn how to use questioning tools and techniques to dramatically increase your group's breadth and depth of new ideas.

Types of piloting questions

There are many different types of questions you can use to inspire and guide your group to increase its yield of new ideas. This leads us to our next SmartStorming piloting principle: *The type of question you ask determines the type of response(s) you get in return.*

In this chapter, you will learn the eight most common types of piloting questions: Thought-provoking, Informational, Option, Associative, Probing, Motivational, Focusing, and Journalistic. Together, they make up a versatile and highly effective set of leadership tools. We encourage you to become familiar with each type and make them all a part of your Pilot's toolkit. Let's explore each type of question in more detail.

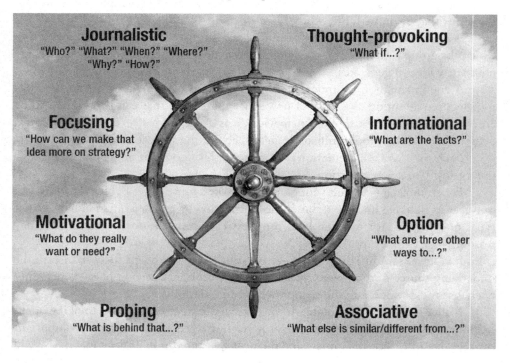

Journalistic
"Who?" "What?" "When?" "Where?"
"Why?" "How?"

Thought-provoking
"What if...?"

Focusing
"How can we make that idea more on strategy?"

Informational
"What are the facts?"

Motivational
"What do they really want or need?"

Option
"What are three other ways to...?"

Probing
"What is behind that...?"

Associative
"What else is similar/different from...?"

Thought-provoking questions

Thought-provoking questions can shift a group out of automatic (or default) thinking patterns, raise awareness, and most importantly, stimulate the group's imagination to explore new possibilities.

Our imagination is a powerful source of innovative ideas because it is completely unhindered by the realities of life, or even the laws of the physical universe. It is also capable of filling in any blanks in understanding, identifying patterns, and making novel, new connections among seemingly unrelated ideas, concepts, data, things, people, places, or events. Thought-provoking questions are perfect for igniting blue sky conceptual thinking that can lead to innovative solutions and breakthroughs.

Examples of thought-provoking questions:

What if…?

In what ways can we…?

If we had no limitations whatsoever, what would we do?

If we knew we couldn't fail, what could/would we do?

What is the most audacious thing we could do/say/imagine?

What would Apple/Nike/Google do in this situation?

When to use:

- When you want to shift a group from habitual thinking patterns into the realm of blue sky imagining.

- When you want your group to question assumptions that can hinder innovative thinking.

- When you want to inject fresh, new energy into your session, or build momentum.

Informational questions

Informational questions are designed to elicit or uncover the known facts about an issue, problem, situation, challenge, or opportunity. They are helpful in discerning what information is available, and what information may be needed or is missing. They are extremely effective when separating out concrete facts from subjective assumptions, speculations, and opinions. Informational questions help anchor problem-solving explorations on solid ground, clarify issues, and create group alignment and consensus.

Examples of informational questions:

What are the facts about this issue/situation?

What specific insights do the information/data/figures reveal?

What facts does the hard evidence support or disprove?

What other information or data do we need to succeed in this challenge?

What facts do we know?

What are we assuming or speculating to be true?

What is unknown about this situation?

When to use:

- When a group needs greater clarity about key facts or issues involved in the challenge.
- When a group is having difficulty comprehending aspects of the challenge.
- When a group has difficulty separating facts from subjective assumptions, speculations, and opinions.

Option questions

Option questions are very useful for identifying and exploring a wider range of problem-solving choices, alternatives, variations, opportunities, or courses of action.

Examples of option questions:

What are three other ways to look at this challenge?

What else can we add or eliminate?

What ideas/features/parts can we combine to…?

What other options or directions haven't we explored yet?

How many different variations on this idea can we develop?

What are some imaginative ways to change/improve/solve/fix this?

When to use:

- When you want a group to explore a wider range of options for a solution.
- When you want a group to investigate different courses of action.
- When a group gets stuck in a rut, recycling old ideas.

Associative questions

Associative questions help stimulate a group to make spontaneous connections between different ideas, notions, concepts, subjects, and pieces of information or data. In associative thinking, one idea triggers an association, which triggers another idea, and so on.

Associative questioning is especially good for liberating a group's thinking from the limitations of habitual linear thinking, for exploring the similarities and differences between different things, and for identifying new relationships between seemingly dissimilar ideas/objects/things. Many "Aha!" moments of insight are triggered by associative thinking.

Examples of associative questions:

What does this/that remind us of?

What else is similar to/different from this/that?

How can we put these pieces together in a new and different way?

What solutions immediately come to mind to solve this problem/challenge?

What patterns or connections can we see/discern?

Where have we seen a similar problem/solution/opportunity?

When to use:

- When a group is having difficulty generating a broad enough range of new ideas.
- When you want to help a group make new associations and connections.
- When you want to stimulate greater collaborative idea-building among group members.
- When a group needs help finding new areas or directions to explore.

Probing questions

Probing questions help groups explore deeper levels of inquiry. They are usually not a single question, but a multilayered line of questioning that helps peel away superficial layers of perceptions to reveal the hidden source of a problem, issue, or challenge. In other words, probing questions can help groups distinguish between the *symptoms* of a problem and the underlying *cause* of the problem.

Examples of probing questions:

If we dug down deeper, what would we find?

What is the single most important thing we should focus on?

What is the source of the problem?

What is the simplest solution to this problem?

What are some opportunities we haven't taken advantage of yet?

What important things aren't we seeing or considering about this challenge?

When to use:

- When a group is generating too many superficial or predictable ideas.
- When a group has trouble zeroing in on the real, underlying source of a problem/issue.
- When a group feels stuck or thwarted by some aspect of the challenge.

Motivational questions

Motivational questions help groups explore and understand the emotional drivers (feelings) behind human behavior, such as desires and resistances, needs, wants, and instincts for survival. Motivational questions can help illuminate a group's understanding about the emotional, psychological, or sociological needs for acceptance, belonging, independence, individuality, safety, security, love, connection, status, etc.

Examples of motivational questions:

What do our customers really want, need, or desire?

What would make our product/service irresistible?

Where is there an unmet need we can fulfill?

What would make our customers feel more satisfied about _____?

In what new ways can we capture the hearts and minds of our customers?

How do we/they feel about _____?

When to use:

- When a group requires greater emotional insight (or empathy) regarding the motivations of a target audience, market, customer, or competitor.

- When your group needs to understand the emotional factors (implications and consequences) involved in a challenge.

- When a group is approaching an emotional issue too intellectually.

Focusing questions

Focusing questions help clarify or redirect a group's attention to align with the session's goal/objectives. They are a valuable tool for grounding or reorienting a group that has lost focus or meandered off topic.

Examples of focusing questions:

What is the most important thing to focus on here?

In what ways does this area of discussion relate to our challenge?

Are we on track for achieving our goal/objective?

How can we adapt this/that idea to solve our specific problem/need/situation?

How can this/that ambitious idea be executed for the budget/resources we have?

In what ways can we make that idea more relevant/meaningful to our customer?

When to use:

- When a group has trouble staying focused on the goal of the session.
- When a group meanders into unproductive diversions or goes off on tangents.
- When the group's ideas seem impractical or overly grandiose.

Journalistic questions: Who? What? When? Where? Why? How?

As the name implies, journalistic questions are the type of investigative questions used by seasoned journalists to gain greater understanding and insight about a person, organization, issue, problem, process, situation, or event, and to ensure that objective viewpoints have been explored for fair and accurate balance.

You can ask different types of journalistic questions (Who? What? When? Where? Why? How?) one at a time, or mix and match them to suit your needs. As you will see, each type of question examines an issue or challenge from a different perspective:

Who: Focuses on a person, persons, group, or organization involved

What: Pieces together data, insights, or bits and pieces of evidence

When: Examines timing and/or timetables of events

Where: Explores the physical location or geography involved

Why: Clarifies causes and effects, symptoms, source, or motivation(s)

How: Uncovers the method, plan, or chain of events involved

Examples of each type of journalistic question:
"Who" questions
Who is doing/using/causing _____?
Who is the target customer for _____?
Who is the foremost thought leader in _____?

"What" questions
What is the problem/issue with _____?
What individual parts/steps make up _____?
What will it take to fix/solve/address/create _____?

"When" questions
When did _____ happen?
When should/could _____ occur?
When is the best/worst time to _____?

"Where" questions
Where is _____ taking place/going to take place?
Where is the source of this problem/issue?
Where does _____ come from/go to/belong?

"Why" questions

Why is _____ happening/not happening?

Why does this pattern of _____ keep occurring?

Why would _____ happen so quickly/slowly?

"How" questions

How are they going to do _____?

How is _____ done/accomplished?

How does _____ work/happen/occur?

Journalistic questions can be used with most challenges. Give them a try; you never know when some interesting new insight or idea will emerge. Journalistic questions can also help reveal where there are gaps in your information or understanding.

When to use:

- When a group is experiencing gaps in information or understanding, or is seeking to understand deeper aspects about the challenge.
- When a group needs to explore a challenge's causes and effects.
- When you want to stimulate your group's sense of curiosity and discovery.

Tips for successful questioning

Here are some simple strategies to help you master the art of asking powerful questions:

Keep your questions simple.

Good questions are simple, concise, and easy to understand; they are also intentionally provocative to prompt a group to think, imagine, reflect, and challenge any limiting assumptions, beliefs, and conventional thinking.

Questions that are concise and to the point are easier to understand and land with greater impact; they also get better responses than long-winded questions. If a question meanders or contains too much detailed information, your group may get lost.

Try to give each question a single focus—avoid the temptation of cramming two or more areas of inquiry into one question. If you have a specific line of questioning to explore, it is better to ask a series of short questions than to attempt to string everything together into a multitier inquiry.

By the way, if you ever encounter a sea of blank faces staring back at you after asking a question, chances are it was overly complex or too obtuse for easy comprehension. Simply rephrase it again as a shorter, simpler question. With a little practice, you will learn how to craft questions with just the right balance of specificity and brevity—neither too broad nor too narrow.

Most of all, a good line of questioning should be open-ended and provide a group ample opportunity to discover its own insights and answers. Try to avoid leading your group down a narrow path or toward a specific conclusion.

Create a cheat sheet of questions to ask in your session.

Preparing a list of provocative questions before a session can significantly improve a Pilot's leadership performance level. A question cheat sheet will not only provide you with greater peace of mind, but will also help keep the momentum of your session flowing strong. With a series of prepared questions at the ready, you will never be at a loss for a question to ask. It is no secret that news reporters and TV interviewers regularly use a prepared list of questions to ask their subjects.

For your convenience, we have included a valuable questioning tool, 25 Piloting Questions for Any Challenge, in this chapter. We encourage you to make a copy of this handy resource and bring it to your next SmartStorming session.

Vary the types of questions you ask.

Variety is the spice of life, so mixing up the types of questions you ask your group will help keep participants engaged and discussions fresh and productive.

Be creative and resourceful. If a line of questioning is not getting a satisfactory response, switch to a new type of question. For example, if you are asking a series of probing questions and participants stare back at you blankly, switch tactics and ask a thought-provoking, "What if…?" question. Or if participants are suddenly unable to respond to a line of informational questions, shift them out of a linear mode of thinking into a state of feeling with some motivational questions.

Peppering your SmartStorming session with a wide range of question types helps keep your group mentally stimulated and engaged.

Keep your group focused on achieving your session goals.

Left to their own devices, groups have a tendency to bounce from one area of discussion to another. Spontaneous, undirected discussion can be a productive way to explore a challenge, if the territory being brainstormed is relevant and rich with potential. But if it proves to be unproductive, you can get your group back to more fertile territory by asking a focusing question. For example: "This area of exploration is very interesting. How can it be applied to our problem at hand?" "This idea is very edgy. How can we make it more applicable to our customer?" "How can we adapt this/that idea to solve our specific problem/challenge?"

Don't settle for the first or most obvious ideas.
When a group first begins to brainstorm, it will usually begin with top-of-mind ideas. More often than not, the first round (or two, or three) of ideas generated will be fairly obvious or predictable. A good analogy for this phenomenon is what happens when you turn on an old faucet that has not been used in a long time. At first, only cloudy, rust-colored water comes trickling out. But once the water has had the opportunity to run for a while, fresher, clearer water begins to flow. So press on!

A good line of questioning can help accelerate this clarifying process:

What's the most obvious solution to this challenge?

What other similar types of solutions come to mind?

What are some unexpected ways to solve this challenge?

Keep your group drilling down deeper and deeper into the problem or challenge them until new "Aha!" moments of insight begin to occur.

Become a master in the art of questioning.
The ability to ask provocative questions is a skill few, if any, of us learn in school. To develop your own personal questioning style, we encourage you to become a student of this verbal art form. Though it takes a little time to master this skill, once you do, you will feel more confident—inspiring and guiding your groups to higher levels of productivity. Here are a few ways to begin strengthening your abilities:

- **Be curious**—Learn as much as you can about the art of questioning and the different types of questions (via websites, books, articles, etc.).

- **Watch well-known interviewers on television**—Pay close attention to the types of questions the host or reporter asks, and how he or she directs and redirects the conversation to cover different areas of inquiry.

- **Collaborate with others**—Sit down with other team members to compile a list of provocative questions you can use as a questioning guide in your next session.

- **Practice your delivery**—Rehearse asking your list of questions out loud in front of a mirror (or for an appreciative audience) to perfect your verbal delivery.

- **Memorize ten to fifteen questions**—It's very helpful to cultivate an inner repository of go-to questions you can ask in any situation.

25 Piloting Questions for Any Challenge

Here are twenty-five effective questions you can ask in regard to any challenge to stimulate your group's imagination and problem-solving ability:

What is the simplest, most obvious solution to this challenge?

What are three other ways to solve/address this challenge?

If all limitations were taken away, what would we do or say?

If we knew we couldn't fail, what would we do, try, or pursue?

Let's quickly free-associate all the things that __(subject)__ reminds us of.

What else is similar to/different from this/that?

What is the most audacious thing we can do, say, or imagine?

What would Apple, Google, or Nike do in this situation?

What haven't we thought of yet?

What's the most important thing to focus on here?

What are some radically new or different ways to approach this challenge?

What idea(s) can we push further?

What possibilities have we missed or not considered yet?

What if we…?

What can we simplify, combine, reverse, modify, or eliminate?

If we dug down deeper, what would we discover?

How would a five-year-old solve this challenge?

What opportunities haven't we seen or taken advantage of yet?

Where is there an unmet need we can fulfill?

How would they solve this challenge fifty years in the future?

What are some of the worst ideas we can think of? (Wait for bad ideas to be offered, then ask…) How can we reverse them to find the seeds of a good idea?

How can we take this wild idea and make it more practical/applicable?

What do our customers really want, need, or desire?

What would an insanely great idea or solution look like?

In what ways can we turn this challenge into a golden opportunity?

The 25 Piloting Questions for Any Challenge can also be found in Chapter 21, and downloaded in digital format at http://SmartStormingBook.com/Toolkit.htm.

What to remember

- Piloting is the art of asking great questions. Skillful questioning can influence the directions in which a group's attention flows, what it focuses on and how deeply, and ultimately how many new ideas it generates.

- Powerful questioning can illuminate the darkness of the unknown, simplify complex issues, stimulate leaps of imagination when linear thinking hits a dead end, refocus a group's efforts when it has veered off purpose, and open doors to a wider range of inquiry.

- The type of questions you ask determines the type of responses you get. This chapter focuses on eight types of piloting questions, including: Thought-provoking, Informational, Option, Associations, Probing, Motivational, Focusing, and Journalistic questions.

- Preparing a question cheat sheet before a session can provide you with a greater sense of confidence and a valuable tool for keeping your group's productivity high throughout the session.

- Vary the types of questions you ask; a wide range will help keep your group mentally stimulated and engaged in contributing ideas.

CHAPTER 14

Escaping the Box—The Power of Challenging Assumptions

"A truly creative person rids him or herself of all self-imposed limitations."

—Gerald Jampolsky, psychologist

As the waves of innovation-driven change sweep across every industry and field, it's never been more important for each of us to develop the discernment and skills necessary to question and challenge prevailing conventions—especially when those attitudes impose any kind of limitation on what new ideas might be possible.

While the idea-generation tools and techniques provided in this book can help dramatically improve the *quality* and *quantity* of ideas a group generates, they become far more effective if you take the initiative, before using them, to free your group from hidden influences that can undermine their problem-solving efforts—hidden influences that can prevent the group from thinking outside the box.

The importance of challenging assumptions

"There is no reason why anyone would want a computer in their home."

—Ken Olsen, Founder of Digital Equipment Corp., 1977

An assumption is a preconceived notion, belief, or idea about the way something *is*, or the way something *should be*. They are largely unexamined beliefs we perceive to be true, something we take for granted, often with little or no evidence or proof. A common phrase that demonstrates this mindset is, *"That's just the way things are."*

Unexamined assumptions can limit an individual's or a group's curiosity and sense of discovery by framing its perception with a false sense of limitations. More often fiction than fact, these beliefs can undermine your group's best critical-thinking and problem-solving abilities. The more preconceived notions an individual, group, or organization operates under, the more limited the possibilities can appear to be.

Whenever you hear someone say, "We need to think outside the box!" what they really mean to say is, "We need to think outside our limiting beliefs and assumptions!"

A brief history of erroneous assumptions

History books are filled with erroneous assumptions (often voiced in the form of negating beliefs) that illustrate the conflict between bold, new ideas and the prevailing conventional thinking of the times. Here are a few well-known historical examples of dubious beliefs that went unquestioned.

"The American colonies have little stomach for revolution."
—King George II, King of England, 1773

"This 'telephone' has too many shortcomings to be seriously considered as a means of communication."
—Western Union internal memo, 1876

"People will soon get tired of staring at a plywood box every night."
—Darryl F. Zanuck, movie producer, commenting about television, 1946

"We don't like their sound, and guitar music is on the way out."
—Decca Recording Co. rejecting the Beatles, 1962

"By the turn of the century, we will live in a paperless society."
—Roger Smith, Chairman of General Motors, 1986

"The concept is interesting and well-formed, but in order to get better than a 'C,' the idea must be feasible."
—Yale professor's response to Fred Smith's paper proposing a reliable overnight delivery service (Smith later founded Federal Express Corp.)

"The fundamentals of our nation's economy are strong."
—Former President George W. Bush, 2007 (a year before the great 2008 financial crisis)

Four ways assumptions can undermine innovative thinking

1. Assumptions operate outside a group's awareness. In the same way that fish are oblivious to the water they swim in, individuals, groups, and organizations tend to be unaware of the myriad of beliefs that can bias their thinking process. Because they often *sound* true or plausible, or are endorsed by "experts," assumptions can quickly gain acceptance without being objectively scrutinized. Once they are adopted, assumptions become the unseen filters that frame discussions and the criteria used to evaluate ideas. If a new idea with merit runs counter to the prevailing beliefs operating within a group or organization, there is a good chance the idea will be challenged, resisted, or rejected.

2. **Assumptions impose a false sense of limitations.** Assumptions can box in consciousness by creating a false impression of limitations where none really exist, such as a belief about what *is* possible and what *is not*; what is *acceptable* and what *is not*; or what *can be* changed and what *cannot*. An assumption can also make a situation appear rigid: "*That's just the way things are.*" In short, they often make it difficult to challenge the status quo.

3. **Assumptions skew the true nature of reality.** Some beliefs become so pervasive that they shape the way people (or a society) perceive and interpret the world. For example, back in the days of Columbus, a significant number of Europeans and seafaring explorers believed that the world was flat. They assumed that the distant horizon was the edge of the world. This flat-world paradigm was perpetuated by believers asking one another flat-world questions like, "What happens if a ship reaches the edge of the world? Will it fall off?" Or, "Are there people on the other side of the world? If so, is their world upside down?" For those operating under this belief that the world was flat, it was difficult, if not impossible, to imagine *round-world* possibilities. In modern times, Christopher Columbus is celebrated for discovering America (and proving that the world is round), but in fact, his boldest accomplishment is that he dared to sail beyond the prevailing assumptions and limiting beliefs of his day.

4. **Assumptions can undermine your group's confidence.** Henry Ford once said, "If you think you can do a thing or think you can't do a thing—you're right." Assumptions can have a profoundly disempowering effect on a group's enthusiasm, especially if the group is operating under a pessimistic assumption that solving a given challenge is going to be difficult or time-consuming, or that the boss/client/customer has doubts about its ability to succeed. Pessimistic beliefs create an atmosphere of *seriousness* that can fill a group with doubt or trepidation. So instead of approaching a challenge from a place of can-do enthusiasm, the group is hindered by the looming pressure of possible failure.

Common assumptions that can undermine a group

There are many ways assumptions can work to undermine a group's efforts. Here are some of the limiting beliefs we hear most often in working with individuals, groups, and organizations:

Assumptions about difficulty:
"Solving this issue/challenge is going to be difficult and time-consuming!"

Assumptions about limitations:
"We've exhausted every possible option."

Assumptions about complexity:
"There's no simple solution to this problem/challenge."

Assumptions about judgment:
"The boss/client/customer will probably hate this idea."

Assumptions about viability:
"There's no market for that."

Assumptions about roles/responsibility:
"That is not for us to decide."

Assumptions about the status quo:
"We can't change that; it's just the way things are."

Assumptions about resources:
"We don't have the people/budget/time/resources we need to…"

Assumptions about assumptions:
"Let's just assume we have all the information we need to…"

Moving beyond assumptions

You now have valuable insight into why so many traditional brainstorming sessions fail to result in truly innovative thinking. It is because the participants are unaware that they are immersed in limiting beliefs about what is possible and what is not, or the way something should or shouldn't be.

The key to liberating a group's creative problem-solving abilities is to first identify any and all assumptions or limiting beliefs group members may be harboring in regard to the issue or challenge, and then to question the validity of those assumptions. This process can be quite liberating, as one limitation after another dissolves under the discerning light of objective scrutiny.

But once the constraints of limiting beliefs are lifted, a group will feel a renewed sense of purpose, energy, and enthusiasm. The most innovative companies in the world are those that boldly challenge the status quo and push beyond any assumptions that can limit innovative thinking.

When you are ready to acquire the knowledge and skills to challenge assumptions, read the "Escaping the Box" technique on page 196.

What to remember

- An assumption is a preconceived notion, belief, or idea about the way something *is*, or the way something *should be*. They are largely unexamined beliefs we perceive to be true, something we take for granted, often with little or no evidence or proof.

- Assumptions and limiting beliefs create a false sense of limitation that can "box in" a group's perspective.

- To liberate a group's creative problem-solving abilities, first identify any assumptions or limiting beliefs they may harbor in regard to the challenge, and then question the validity of those assumptions. Many assumptions sound true on the surface, but will unravel, crumble, or dissolve under the scrutiny of objective analysis.

- Identifying and eliminating assumptions and limiting beliefs before the ideation process will dramatically improve the quality and range of fresh, new ideas a group can produce.

- The more preconceived notions an individual, group, or organization operates under, the more limited possibilities can appear to be.

- See full instructions for the "Escaping the Box" technique on page 196.

CHAPTER 15

Maximizing Your Group's Productivity

*"Productivity is being able to do things that you
were never able to do before."*

—Franz Kafka, novelist

Your ability to inspire and guide a group's exploration of ideas is an invaluable
skill that will dramatically improve the quality of the sessions you lead. When that skill
is combined with proven methodologies for unlocking a group's fullest productivity
potential, it can increase a session's yield of new ideas dramatically.

In this chapter, you will learn proven strategies and methods for how to get a group
off to a fast start, keep its idea-generation momentum at peak performance levels, engage
shy or introverted group members to share their ideas, and confidently manage groups of
any size (S, M, L, and XL) to achieve the highest level of participation possible.

Fueling your group's idea-generation momentum

"If you do not change direction, you may end up where you are heading."

—Lao Tzu

There are discernible ebbs and flows of momentum that naturally occur during
a group ideation session.

In his book *The Art of Innovation*, Tom Kelley describes this phenomenon. "High-
energy brainstormers tend to follow a series of steep 'power' curves, in which momentum
builds slowly, then intensifies, then starts to plateau." He goes on to say, "The best facilitators can nurture an emerging conversation with a light touch in the first phase and know

enough to let ideas flow during the steep part of the ideation curve. It's when energy fades on a line of discussion that the facilitator really earns his or her keep."[16]

When discussions do begin to taper off, Kelley suggests a facilitator switch gears by redirecting his or her group to build on existing ideas, or by making a "jump" transition to a new line of questioning to spark the next power curve.

This cycle of rising and falling ideation momentum that Kelley describes can be visualized as a wave pattern—ideation momentum rising to a crest and then falling (see illustration below). It's a pattern that often repeats itself many times during the course of generating ideas.

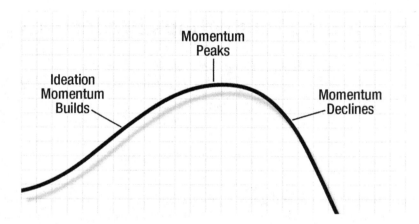

Riding the waves

Once you witness this phenomenon a few times, it won't take long until you develop the situational awareness necessary to read the rhythms of these waves and are able to strategize ways to keep your group ahead of the curve.

Here are a few tips to keep in mind.

- As a group's idea-generation momentum begins to rise, help fuel the momentum by peppering the conversation with provocative questions. Do this until the group becomes self-igniting, generating ideas quickly and easily on its own.

- When the group's efforts begin to lose momentum, change directions and make a jump to a different line of questioning. This will spark the next wave of new ideas.

- A word of caution: It's not wise to allow a group's energy level to dip too low for too long. It can take considerable time and energy to get it back on the upswing. So make it a goal in every session to maximize your group's creative problem-solving momentum, keeping it at high levels for as long as possible, while minimizing the dips.

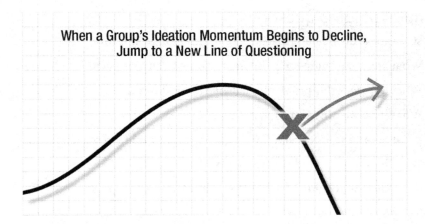

When a Group's Ideation Momentum Begins to Decline, Jump to a New Line of Questioning

Making the jump

One of the best ways to monitor your group's momentum (productivity) is to pay close attention to any visual, verbal, and nonverbal clues they give you (i.e., facial expressions, body language, tone, and tempo of discussions). Tuning in to their energy level and interactions will reveal when your group is deeply absorbed in generating ideas and when it's losing steam (and you should move to a new line of inquiry).

Here are some telltale signs that it's time to make a jump:

- The group's energy level begins to noticeably dip
- Group members appear unfocused or bored
- Group members' body language appears restless or fidgety
- There is a significant decrease in the number of ideas being generated
- Ideas begin to sound repetitive, or old ideas are recycled
- Group members begin texting, checking emails, or engaging in conversations
- Long, awkward periods of silence

How to make a questioning jump

1. Fan red-hot areas of discussion.

2. When the group's energy level begins to dip and the contribution of ideas begins to slow down, pick a new direction, subject, or area of interest.

3. Ask a provocative "jump" question to redirect your group to a completely new line of discussion.

4. Repeat this process as often as necessary to keep your group's idea-generation momentum riding high.

Examples of jump questions

What ideas do we have that we can build upon or improve?

What are some completely different ways we can approach this challenge?

What else does this problem/challenge remind us of?

What have we missed or not considered yet?

What is the absolutely simplest solution to this problem/challenge?

What is an unexpected way to look at this/that?

If we knew we couldn't fail, what would we do, try, or pursue?

CHAPTER 16

Getting Your Group Off to a Fast Start

"I've always found that the speed of the boss is the speed of the team."

—Lee Iacocca

The goal of every SmartStorming session is to generate the greatest number of fresh, new ideas possible during the idea-generation phase of the session. To that end, a Pilot should strive to get the group off to a fast start. The more quickly a group becomes fully absorbed in its problem-solving activity, the more productive and stimulating the session will be for everyone.

There are several effective tools, techniques, and tricks you can use to quickly focus your group's attention, get its creative juices flowing, and fast-track the collaborative idea-generation process.

If this sounds similar to psyching up a sports team for a championship game, you are not far off the mark. Coaches in every team sport understand the competitive advantages of hitting the ground running.

Fast-tracking your group into the "productivity zone" will dramatically increase their output of fresh, new ideas as well as inject energy and excitement into your session.

Here are some simple, yet effective ways to get your group off to a fast start before and during your SmartStorming session.

What to do before the session

- **Get your group members up to speed.** Send participants a copy of the challenge statement, goals, and objectives a few days *before* the session begins. Be sure to include any relevant background information or reference materials the group will need.

- **Ask participants to do a little homework** or informal research to better understand the issue, subject, or challenge.

- **Allow ideas to percolate.** Advise participants to let the issue or challenge *percolate* in the back of their minds while they are engaged in other activities. This allows the unconscious mind to play and make new connections.

- **Go where the action is.** Encourage all participants to get out and do some firsthand field research. If you are planning to design and market a new line of yoga clothes, take yoga classes at a number of different yoga studios, talk to yoga instructors and fellow students, and test-drive prototypes of your yoga garments, as well as those of your competitors. Whatever type of challenge you will be tackling, apply these principles. Dig deep and experience firsthand what's happening in the real world.

- **Stock the creative pond.** Ask participants to surf the web, browse magazine stands, go to the movies or to an art gallery or museum for inspiration. The goal is for each participant to fill his or her internal creative reservoirs with fresh, new stimuli *before* fishing for ideas.

- **Request that your group pre-storm ideas.** Request ahead of time that each participant show up to the session with three preliminary ideas (three ideas x ten participants = thirty ideas...that's thirty new ideas walking in the door *before* the session even begins). Tell your group that three ideas is their ticket to enter the session.

What to do during the session

- **Hit the ground running.** Don't delay the start of your session. Get going as close to your scheduled start time as possible. Begin your session with a fast-paced type of icebreaker exercise to get the creative juices flowing. (See 25 Great Icebreaker Activities on page 255.)

- **Use Pre-Storming to kick off your session.** Request ahead of time that each participant bring three initial ideas. Have participants quickly take turns describing their ideas. Select the most interesting ideas and challenge the group to find ways to transform those concepts into much bigger, better ideas.

- **Pick up the pace.** Establish a quick, rapid-fire tempo of questioning and answering in your session. Pivot and change questioning directions every few minutes. Explore opposites, similarities, and variations.

- **Play beat-the-clock.** Use a high-velocity idea-generation technique like Idea Sprinting, which sets a tight deadline for achieving an ambitious goal. "Let's shoot for fifteen new ideas in three minutes!" or "Let's shoot for twenty-five new ideas in five minutes!" (See Idea-Generation Techniques in Chapter 20.)

- **Encourage idea-building.** Instruct your group to build and add on each other's ideas. Many people think the only worthwhile contribution in a brainstorm is a new, unique idea. But just as valuable is enhancing and improving the ideas of others. This is how big ideas are developed.

- **Create friendly competition.** Divide the group into small teams of three to five participants. Encourage competition by stating that the team that develops the most ideas within a certain time frame wins bragging rights. Reshuffle group members after each round, creating new team combinations, then repeat. Creating new teams after each round keeps participants engaged and the ideas they generate fresh.

- **Use high-yield idea-generation techniques.** Engaging techniques like Idea Sprinting, Brainwriting, and Group Graffiti will help your group generate a prodigious number of ideas in a relatively short amount of time. (See Idea-Generation Techniques in Chapter 20.)

The benefits of creating dynamic tension

One of the reasons many traditional brainstorming efforts get off to a painfully slow start is that there is little to no sense of urgency or dynamic tension injected into the process. Slow starts make it difficult for participants to loosen up, spontaneously share ideas, or become absorbed in the problem-solving challenge at hand.

Without some form of constructive dynamic tension (new stimuli, challenging deadlines, friendly competition, etc.), there are few compelling reasons for your group to make an ambitious effort. The tips, tools, and techniques mentioned above will infuse your sessions with just the right amount of dynamic tension (and sense of competitive fun) to inspire your group to superior levels of performance.

What to remember

- The goal of every SmartStorming session is to generate the greatest number of fresh, new ideas possible. The faster a group becomes fully absorbed in its problem-solving activity, the more productive the session.

- There are a number of things a Pilot can do to boost a group's productivity, including asking them to pre-storm ideas prior to the session, starting with a fast-paced icebreaker activity, establishing a rapid tempo of questioning, and using a high-yield ideation activity (like Idea Sprinting).

- Injecting dynamic tension (challenging deadlines, friendly competition, etc.) into your sessions will create an atmosphere of competitive fun and inspire your group to superior levels of performance.

CHAPTER 17

Engaging the "Silent Thinkers"

"If you do not speak up when it matters, when would it matter that you speak?"

—Jim Hightower, activist

Generally speaking, there seem to be three different personality types that emerge in group ideation sessions. The first is the self-confident, outgoing personality who fully engages in the activities and contributes ideas throughout the session. The second type is somewhat more reserved, but will from time to time contribute ideas when he or she has something to share. The third personality type is a bit more enigmatic. These are the reserved, quiet types who appear to be engaged, but remain as silent as the Sphinx.

We call this third personality type the Silent Thinkers.

When you observe a Silent Thinker, you can see the wheels turning in their heads, you may even notice them jotting down ideas, but they never open their mouths to contribute. The frustrating part is that Silent Thinkers often have very good ideas locked away inside. But for a variety of reasons, they rarely share out loud.

Why are they silent?

If we were to create a personality profile of the Silent Thinker, we would find they are typically individuals who are bright, sensitive, and somewhat introverted by nature. In many cases, they can be young, newly hired or promoted members of the organization.

Silent Thinkers tend to feel self-conscious about one or more of the following: their depth of knowledge; their level of understanding or experience; the value or worth of the ideas they conceive. And so Silent Thinkers shy away from situations where they might risk sounding silly, being proven wrong, or worse, getting judged negatively by others.

It is not uncommon for these sensitive group members to feel intimidated by the demonstrative prowess of the more confident, outgoing, experienced participants, especially when the boss or an authority figure is present.

Solving the riddle of the Sphinx

Silent Thinkers tend to feel more relaxed and comfortable contributing ideas in smaller groups. For this reason we recommend breaking up a larger group into a number of smaller teams of three to four members, creating a more intimate, collaborative environment that minimizes peer pressure.

Once Silent Thinkers feel more secure in sharing their ideas, you should quickly see an increase in your session's volume of new ideas.

It's also easier to get Silent Thinkers to contribute their ideas by using nonverbal writing activities and anonymous idea submission methods.

Tips for inspiring the Silent Thinker to greater contribution

Here are some simple things you can do both before and during your Smart-Storming sessions to help Silent Thinkers feel a greater sense of safety and confidence in sharing ideas:

Before your session: Give Silent Thinkers time to prepare

- Send participants the challenge, goals, and objectives a few days prior to the session.

- Request they read up and do their own research to better understand the subject, issues, and/or challenges. This can help build their knowledge and confidence.

- Request that each participant show up at the session with three initial ideas.

- Buddy up: Encourage Silent Thinkers to meet with one or two other participants prior to the session to kick around some ideas they may want to contribute.

- Invite Silent Thinkers to email their initial ideas before the session.

During your session: Minimize peer pressure

- Divide the group into smaller SmartStorming teams of three to four members. After one or two rounds of generating ideas, reshuffle participants into new team formations.

- Request that everyone write down three to five ideas on a piece of paper, then submit those ideas anonymously. Have a volunteer serve as the session Reporter to read the ideas out loud and write them down for the group to consider.

- Create a roundtable discussion where participants take turns sharing one idea.

- Have Silent Thinkers and junior-level participants present their ideas first; the more demonstrative, experienced, or senior-level members go later.

- Pair up junior-level and senior-level participants as a team.

- Invite Silent Thinkers to add to or help improve existing ideas presented.

Use idea-generation techniques that make it fun to share ideas

- Use silent, collaborative writing techniques such as Brainwriting or Group Graffiti to make it less intimidating for Silent Thinkers to share their ideas and collaboratively build upon the ideas of others.

- Play Bad2Good, a fun technique where everyone is asked to contribute the worst idea they can imagine. The group then tries to reverse those ideas to discover new possibilities within.

- Or use sticky notes, and have everyone write down three to five ideas (one per sticky note) and post them on a wall.

(You will find full instructions for each of the idea-generation techniques mentioned above in Chapter 20: Idea-Generation Techniques and Tools.)

What to remember

- Silent Thinkers often have good ideas locked away inside, but they rarely share out loud. They often shy away from situations where they might risk sounding silly, being proven wrong, or worse, being judged negatively by others.

- It's common for these sensitive group members to feel intimidated by the demonstrative prowess of more confident, outgoing, experienced participants.

- Engage the Silent Thinkers by minimizing peer pressure. Divide a large group into smaller SmartStorming teams of three to four members. After one or two rounds of generating ideas, reshuffle participants into new team formations.

- Use silent, collaborative writing techniques such as Brainwriting or Group Graffiti to help them feel more confident contributing ideas.

- Use fun, counterintuitive ideation techniques like Bad2Good, a technique where everyone is asked to contribute the worst idea they can imagine. The group then tries to reverse those ideas to discover new possibilities within.

- Ask everyone in the group to contribute ideas anonymously; then have the ideas read out loud and written down by the session Reporter.

CHAPTER 18

Managing Groups of Different Sizes

*"Coming together is a beginning. Keeping together is progress.
Working together is success."*

—Henry Ford

SmartStorming sessions occur in a variety of sizes and venues. Some are small, informal gatherings that last an hour or less, attended by a handful of participants. Other sessions are larger, organized meetings that can last half a day or longer, which may be attended by twenty or more participants. And at the upper end of the spectrum, there are multiday conferences with a hundred or more participants in attendance.

Recently we had the unique experience of piloting one of our largest Smart-Storming sessions to date: 140 senior-level marketing executives from a leading global corporation. Just a few days later, we piloted one of our smallest SmartStorming sessions: seven participants from a small, fast-growing public relations firm.

The two sessions could not have been more different. The first was held in a cavernous hotel ballroom, complete with support staff, a stage, and full a/v (microphones and an elaborate, multiscreen presentation display). The second session was held in a small conference room equipped with only the most basic necessities.

Both of these SmartStorming sessions were equally successful at generating a wide range of innovative new ideas. Both sessions were relatively easy to manage (once we had diligently thought through all of the details using the SmartStorming Pre-Session Planner checklist).

While the size of a group certainly does affect the complexity and logistical challenges of the session, rest assured that the proven Six-Step SmartStorming process, combined with the principles, skills, tools, and techniques covered in this book, will provide everything you need to effectively pilot productive idea-generation sessions for groups of any size.

Sizing up the size of your session

When preplanning a SmartStorming session, it is important to first get an accurate picture of the size and character of the group scheduled to attend. As the size of your group grows, so does the complexity of logistics such as scheduling, room size and location, quantities and arrangement of tables and chairs, supplies, equipment, assistance, etc.—all the things you need to consider when organizing and choreographing your session to ensure that it flows smoothly.

The challenges of managing large groups

Just as it is easier to conduct a quartet of musicians than it is to lead a full philharmonic orchestra, it is easier to lead a small SmartStorming session with eight participants than a large-scale session with eighty.

A brainstorming group is an assembly of individuals who come together to achieve a common goal. But while the group as a whole may share a sense of unified purpose, it is important to appreciate that each individual within the group is unique in his or her temperament, personality, beliefs, knowledge, experience, and style of relating to others. The larger the group, the greater the number of personalities (and, by definition, interpersonal dynamics) there are to manage.

Most groups you will lead will be good-natured and collaborate easily with one another. Other groups may be more serious in temperament and require a bit of coaxing to loosen up and spontaneously share ideas. And on a few rare occasions, you may find yourself managing a challenging group that gets easily embroiled in internal politics or Darwinian contests for dominance.

But regardless of the size and demeanor of your group, it will be your job as the SmartStorming Pilot to get everyone aligned toward a common goal, fully engaged, and contributing new ideas.

What is the ideal size for a brainstorming group?

We are often asked during our SmartStorming training programs whether smaller groups are more productive than larger groups. Or, are larger groups more productive because they contain more diversity (in knowledge, experience, and viewpoints) and provide greater opportunity for the cross-pollination of ideas? What is the ideal size for a brainstorming group?

While there is little specific research data on the subject, there does seem to be a consensus among brainstorming thought leaders that five to fifteen participants is a productive size range. Alex Osborn, the father of brainstorming, originally believed that the ideal number for a brainstorming group was between five and ten.[17] In later years, he revised his ideal group size number up to "about a dozen."[18]

In our own experience, we find groups of six to twelve participants to be an easy-to-manage and highly productive size.

Of course, the ultimate size of your group may be dictated by a number of factors, such as the size and scope of the challenge or project to be addressed, the number of stakeholders involved, and the range of knowledge, experience, or expertise required to successfully address the challenge.

The secret to managing groups of any size (S, M, L, or XL) is learning how to configure your session for ease of piloting and maximum productivity.

How to configure your sessions for easier piloting

Generally speaking, there are three distinct strategies you can employ to effectively manage a group during a SmartStorming session:

1. Have participants generate ideas together as a single group.

2. Divide larger groups into smaller SmartStorming teams.

3. Use a combination of the two approaches—have a group work together for part of a session, then divide the group into smaller teams for specific idea-generation activities.

When we facilitate SmartStorming sessions for our clients, we often use the third approach, a combination of both full group and team piloting strategies.

If the group size is relatively small (eight participants or fewer), we will have everyone generate ideas together as a single group throughout the session.

If the group size is larger (ten to twenty-five participants, or more), we'll employ a combination of both the group and team approaches in the session.

For a large group, we'll start the session with an all-inclusive group icebreaker activity. This allows participants to become acquainted with one another early in the process. When it's time to generate ideas, we'll first start off with an ideation activity that involves the entire group. Then afterward, we divide the large group into smaller teams of equal size for the ideation activities that follow.

In our years of experience, we've found that when it comes to leading large groups, it is far easier and more efficient to manage a small number of motivated, self-directed teams than a room full of individual personalities (and all of the interpersonal dynamics that go along with it). We believe this approach is the key to successfully managing large group ideation sessions.

Here are some of the other advantages to using this smaller team approach:

- There is less peer pressure in smaller teams than in larger groups. Team members feel less self-conscious about sharing ideas with fellow teammates.

- Small teams allow for a more equitable contribution of ideas; there is less opportunity for strong personalities to dominate.

- Team members develop a sense of camaraderie and mutual collaboration.

- Teams can quickly and easily self-select (harvest) their own best ideas.

- Teams can share (cross-pollinate) ideas, inspiring one another to higher levels of performance and productivity.

- Teams members can be easily reshuffled (after each ideation activity) to form new and different teams. This strategy of recombining participants into new team configurations helps keep everyone engaged, team dynamics fresh, and the session's productivity high.

Strategies for leading groups of different sizes

It takes a certain degree of confidence, experience, and solid leadership skills to manage a sizable group of participants for an entire session. This is another reason we recommend dividing larger groups into smaller, easier-to-manage SmartStorming teams. While there are no hard rules for how to configure and manage your sessions, we have found the following guidelines to work effectively:

Six or fewer participants—Begin the session with a group icebreaker; then have participants continue to generate ideas as a single group throughout the session.

Eight to twelve participants—Begin the session with a group icebreaker; then have participants continue to generate ideas as a single group for one or two ideation activities. Then, for variety, divide the group into smaller teams of equal size for the remaining ideation activity.

Twelve to twenty-five participants—Begin the session with a group icebreaker; then divide the group into smaller teams of four to five participants to generate ideas. Be sure to reshuffle participants to form new team configurations after each ideation activity. Keep a watchful eye for participants who prefer to stick together with the same colleagues. Try to discourage this behavior; in brainstorming, familiarity tends to breed predictable ideas.

Twenty-five to fifty participants—Divide the group into table teams of five to eight participants. Begin the session with an icebreaker activity that can be done simultaneously at each table. Afterward, team members can work together at the same table throughout each ideation activity, or you can reshuffle participants after each activity to form new table team configurations. Encourage participants to team up with new and different people after each round.

Fifty to one hundred or more participants—Divide the group into table teams of six to ten participants. Begin the session with an icebreaker activity that can be done simultaneously at each table. Team members should continue working together at the same table during each ideation activity.

Empowering your SmartStorming teams

When you divide a large group into smaller SmartStorming teams, it is important to make sure each team is well organized and self-sufficient, and has everything it needs to function autonomously during the idea-generation process.

As the master session Pilot, you can either assign participants to specific teams or empower the group to divide up and form their own. It is important to make sure that the number of participants on each team is as equal as possible. Don't allow lopsided team formations to occur.

Next, instruct your teams to select one member to serve as the team Pilot and another to serve as the team Reporter, responsible for writing down all the team's ideas.

Once your teams are set, take a moment to instruct the team Pilots that they are responsible for creating a safe, judgment-free environment where all ideas are welcome. The Pilot should also actively encourage all teammates to contribute as many ideas as possible in the time allotted.

The power of a little friendly competition

The legendary sportscaster Howard Cosell once said, "The ultimate victory in competition is derived from the inner satisfaction of knowing that you have done your best and that you have gotten the most out of what you had to give."

This same spirit will ring true for the teams generating ideas in your Smart-Storming session. In fact, the most satisfying and productive sessions you will experience are the ones where your SmartStormers push themselves and their creative problem-solving performance to new levels.

As we discussed earlier, look for opportunities to inject a little dynamic tension in the form of friendly competition into your ideation activities. The key to using competition effectively in SmartStorming is to keep the gamesmanship fun, lighthearted, and laser-focused on achieving your goals for the session.

What to remember

- SmartStorming sessions occur in a variety of sizes and venues.

- Get a clear picture of the number of participants attending your session. Keep in mind that as the size of your group increases, so does the level of complexity and number of logistics to manage.

- Plan ahead: Think through the most efficient ways to lead and manage the group, based on the number of anticipated participants. Decide whether it would it be more efficient to pilot your session with a single group or to divide the group into a number of smaller teams. It is usually easier to manage a smaller number of motivated, self-directed teams than a room full of individual personalities.

- Make teams self-sufficient. Be sure each team has an assigned team Pilot and Reporter.

- Team Pilots are responsible for creating a safe, judgment-free environment where all ideas are welcome. They are also responsible for actively encouraging teammates to contribute as many ideas as possible.

- Injecting a little lighthearted, friendly competition into your team's idea-generation activities can help push their creative problem-solving performance to new levels.

CHAPTER 19

SmartStorming Leadership: Frequently Asked Questions

In our live SmartStorming Brainstorm Leadership workshops, we find many of the same questions being asked from session to session. Here are some of the most common questions we hear.

Q: What is the ideal number of participants to invite to a session?

A: After many years of piloting SmartStorming sessions ourselves, we've found the ideal group size to be between six and twelve participants. The size of a group is often determined by how many stakeholders need or wish to participate, plus the type of expertise, knowledge, and experience necessary to successfully address the challenge at hand. For larger groups, we recommend dividing participants into smaller ideation teams of equal size. A few smaller teams are usually easier to manage than a single large group, and will typically generate a greater number and variety of ideas.

Q: How long should a session last?

A: As we mention earlier in Chapter 5, the length of a SmartStorming session is largely determined by the nature of the challenge you plan to address. If the challenge is relatively simple and straightforward, it can usually be handled in a session lasting just a few hours (or less). If you are tackling multiple issues (or aspects to a challenge), a session may require a full day, or multiple days.

The more challenges there are to address, the greater the number and variety of ideation techniques you will want to plan on using.

A simple formula you can use to ballpark the optimal length of a session is to add up the approximate amount of time each activity might take. For example:

Icebreaker activity = 10 to 15 minutes
Review brainstorming rules = 5 minutes
Introduce challenge, goals, and objectives = 10 minutes

Generate ideas = 15 to 60 minutes per ideation technique
Idea selection = 20 to 30 minutes
Next steps = 10 minutes
Breaks = 10 minutes (every 75 to 90 minutes)

Of course, these examples can be modified to accommodate the specific challenge(s) at hand, or the time constraints of your group.

Q: How do I know if I've identified the right challenge statement to address the challenge?

A: While there is no surefire way to test a challenge statement before a session (the proof will be in the pudding—or more precisely, the quality and quantity of ideas generated), there are things you can do to ensure that you've written an effective statement. First, don't simply settle for the first challenge statement you write. There's an old expression that says, "Writing is *re*writing." So keep at it until you feel your statement is clear, concise, and provocative, serving as a springboard for the imagination. Then, do a little research—share your statement with a few of your colleagues or group members and ask if they find the statement compelling; it's wise to double-check whether the challenge statement identifies the right problem or opportunity to address.

If you're having trouble crafting powerful challenge statements on your own, you might try collaborating with a colleague who is a particularly good wordsmith. After just a few minutes of going back and forth with your statement, you're certain to find it better than when you started.

Q: What is the best way to handle participants who dominate a session or constantly judge or criticize other people's ideas?

A: It is common to have some participants who are confident and vocal, and who might knowingly or unknowingly dominate a session. When you encounter such an individual, it is critical to actively manage the situation in order to prevent total disruption of your session. The most effective approach is to simply redirect the focus of the group by saying something like, "Thank you for your enthusiastic contribution, John/Jen. Now, let's hear ideas from some other people." The key is to keep it light and nonaccusatory; dominating participants are rarely deliberately trying to derail the session. They just have a lot to say! By continually redirecting in this manner, the dominator will get the message, and others will feel more comfortable sharing.

As for someone who judges or criticizes other's ideas, again, these people are usually not trying to be offensive. In fact, most actually believe they are performing a valuable service by helping the group stay focused and on track, and not wasting time on frivolous ideas.

The best way to handle these people, first and foremost, is by reviewing the Rules of the Game before the session begins (see Chapter 4). Ideally, the rules should be displayed on a poster in the room. Call particular attention to the first rule, "Suspend All Judgment," ask everyone to agree, and then announce a zero-tolerance policy for negativity in the session. A very effective method of enforcement when someone exhibits any type of negative behavior is to have the entire group immediately bombard the offender with crumpled paper balls. Again, keep it light; even make it a game. Encourage everyone in the room to participate in order to create a self-policing environment. While it may seem silly, this technique is a playful, good-natured way to remind a culprit of his or her transgression, and allow the group to enforce the "Suspend All Judgment" rule.

Q: How can I get a group back on track if it goes off on unproductive tangents?

A: Whenever a group meanders off on a tangent, simply ask a series of "refocusing" questions to shift their thinking back on a productive track. Good questions to ask include, "What is the most important thing to focus on here?" "In what ways does this area of discussion relate to our challenge?" "Are we on track for achieving our goal?" or, "How can we adapt this/that idea to solve our specific challenge?"

Q: How can I keep a group's enthusiasm and momentum high?

A: There are a number of things you can do to help keep a group's enthusiasm and productivity at peak levels throughout a session. First, be sure to use a mix of two to three (or more) different types of ideation techniques to engage your group's thinking in new and different ways. Second, pepper your session with a lot of different thought-provoking questions (see: 25 Piloting Questions for Any Challenge on page 259), and third, make jumps to new topics or lines of inquiry or exploration each time a group's ideation momentum begins to plateau. The key is to make a jump *before* the momentum drops too low for too long.

Q: Is it okay to inform the group about practical limitations before they start to generate ideas—like budget restrictions, technology limitations, etc.?

A: In general, we recommend against informing a group about too many specific limitations prior to generating ideas. Remember, during the idea-generation phase, you want to encourage and maximize divergent, anything goes thinking. This is what leads to truly innovative ideas. The same can be said for introducing your idea selection criteria (developed during the preplanning process) prior to idea generation. When people know ahead of time what will determine an idea's value, their thinking can be hindered.

That said, if you are leading a group of particularly creative or imaginative individuals—people who have no problem thinking out of the box—there is less danger in introducing preexisting limitations or selection criteria. Such a group will probably still be able to generate strong ideas, and might have a greater tendency to generate too many impractical ideas. But even with such a highly imaginative group, you might want to keep restrictions to yourself. Just be sure to actively pilot them, to ensure they stay focused on a strategy.

Q: How do I know which idea-generation techniques would be best for my type of challenge?

A: Each of the twenty ideation techniques included in this book will help a group achieve superior results when generating ideas. We encourage you to test-drive them all. As you become familiar with the way each one works and the results it produces, you will quickly develop a strong intuitive sense of the best ones to use for specific challenges. For example, a fast-paced, beat-the-clock technique like Idea Sprinting is good to use when you want a group to generate a lot of ideas in a short amount of time. A silent, collaborative group writing exercise like Brainwriting will help guarantee everyone contributes ideas; it will also help silence dominating personalities. A technique like SmartSWOT will help a group explore a wide range of different perspectives in regard to a challenge. And visual techniques like Mind Mapping and Vision Boards will help stimulate a group's spontaneous associative-thinking abilities. (See instructions in Chapter 20: Idea-Generation Techniques and Tools.)

Q: What's the best approach for determining a set of selection criteria to use for evaluating ideas?

A: First, you'll need to determine a clear vision for the end results you want your ideas to achieve; next, try to extrapolate five or six *must have* characteristics, traits, or attributes a winning idea would need to possess in order to successfully address the challenge. For example, the benchmarks for a winning concept might be "innovative," "affordable," "doable," or "reinforces our brand character." Remember, once you've identified your list of criteria, do your best to describe each one in the simplest, most concise way possible by distilling the essence of each criterion down to a single key word, usually an adjective or verb, followed by a concise, one-sentence descriptive definition.

Q: Are icebreakers really that important? I'd rather use that valuable time for generating ideas.

A: Icebreaker activities are well worth the investment of a few minutes of time at the beginning of a session. An enjoyable activity helps participants relax, get to know one another, free up their attention from outside matters, and quickly transform a room of individuals into an aligned team, focused on achieving a common goal.

Part Four
SmartStorming Pilot's Toolkit

CHAPTER 20

Idea-Generation Techniques and Tools

Welcome to the SmartStorming Pilot's Toolkit. Here you will find a valuable collection of proven idea-generation techniques and tools designed to help you and your group more effectively think outside the box and tackle challenges in new and more innovative ways.

The featured techniques and tools will help free a group from old, habitual ways of thinking and make it easier for them to view issues and challenges from fresh perspectives, make new connections, and generate a greater depth and breadth of new ideas.

Each of the techniques works differently in the way it engages a group's curiosity, imagination, and thought process. We encourage you to become familiar with all of the techniques; simply read the easy-to-follow instructions and test-drive each one. As you become familiar with the results they produce, you will develop an intuitive sense for which are the best to use for specific challenges, and how to mix and match different techniques in a session. (As a reminder, we recommend that you select two to three different techniques to use in each SmartStorming session you pilot.)

In the pages ahead, you will find a list of twenty idea-generation techniques, a reference chart with recommendations for when to use different techniques, and step-by-step instructions for how to lead each of them. We have included a number of proven, well-known techniques, as well as a sampling of our own original or modified techniques.

Many of the techniques also feature Solo SmartStorming instructions (which follow immediately after group/team instructions) for those times when you are working on a challenge by yourself and wish to liberate more of your own individual creative genius.

This collection of techniques and tools is intended to serve as an easy-to-access reference, ready whenever you have to find the right tool for the job.

20 proven idea-generation techniques

1-4-All—Individual and collaborative idea generation (Group)

Bad2Good—Counterintuitive idea generation (Group/Team/Solo)

Brainwriting—Silent, collaborative writing activity (Group/Team)

Channeling Genius—Collaborative idea generation via identities (Group/Team)

Escaping the Box—Challenging conventions (Group/Team/Solo)

Frankensteining—Forced-association idea generation (Group/Team/Solo)

Group Graffiti—Collaborative wall-writing activity (Group)

Idea Mashup—Forced-association idea generation (Group/Team)

Idea Speed Dating—Rapid collaborative idea generation (Group)

Idea Sprinting—High-velocity idea generation (Group/Team/Solo)

In Their Shoes—Empathy-based idea generation (Group/Team/Solo)

Mind Mapping—Visual associative thinking (Group/Team/Solo)

Pre-Storming—Pre-session idea generation (Group/Team)

Pump Up the Value—Adaptive idea generation (Group/Team/Solo)

Reimagine It!—Analogy/metaphor idea generation (Group/Team/Solo)

SCAMPER—Adaptive idea generation (Group/Team/Solo)

SmartSWOT—Exploring multiple viewpoints (Group/Team/Solo)

Think Much, Much Bigger—Idea-expansion process (Group/Team/Solo)

Vision Boards—Visual inspiration and idea generation (Group/Team/Solo)

What If...?—Challenging conventions/status quo (Group/Team/Solo)

Guide for determining when to use different techniques

Goal/Objective	Appropriate Technique(s)
To help a group think up new, bigger, and better ideas	Channeling Genius What If...? Think Much, Much Bigger
To help a group think outside its comfort zone	Bad2Good Escaping the Box
To help energize a group and fuel its idea-generation momentum	Group Graffiti Idea Speed Dating Idea Sprinting
To help liberate a group from old, habitual thinking patterns	Channeling Genius Frankensteining Idea Mashup Mind Mapping Reimagine It! SCAMPER What If...?
To help a group explore new and different perspectives about a challenge	In Their Shoes Mind Mapping SmartSWOT
To help a group find new ways to improve or innovate a product, process, or service	Pump Up the Value SCAMPER What If...?
To help make sure everyone in the group is contributing ideas	1-4-All Brainwriting Group Graffiti Pre-Storming
To help silence dominating or attention-seeking personalities	Brainwriting Group Graffiti

1-4-All
Individual and collaborative idea generation

At a glance

This simple, yet powerful triple-strength creative problem-solving approach helps compound and amplify the problem-solving genius of individuals, small teams, and an entire group, all in one activity. There are three parts to the technique that allow participants to contribute their own unique ideas, as well as collaborate with other group members to explore a wide range of new ideas.

In Part 1, group members work independently, generating ideas to address the challenge. In Part 2, participants are grouped into small teams of four to share and build upon one another's ideas and generate new ideas together. In Part 3, teams share their best ideas; then all participants join forces as a single collaborative group to build upon and improve the best ideas presented.

Number of participants 8–24

Duration 45–60 minutes

How to pilot

1. Introduce the challenge to be addressed.

2. **Part 1: Individual idea generation**
   Instruct participants to work independently (solo) to write down as many ideas as possible.

3. When finished, ask participants to select two to three of their best or most interesting ideas.

4. **Part 2: Team idea generation**
   Next, divide up your group into four-person teams. Ask team members to share their best ideas (generated in first round) with one another; then work collaboratively to build upon and/or improve promising ideas or generate new ones.

5. When finished, ask each team to select a short list of its best or most innovative ideas.

6. **Part 3: Group idea generation**
   Begin the third round by asking teams to take turns sharing their short list of best ideas with the entire group. Have a volunteer serve as the Reporter to write down all of the ideas on a large flipchart pad or whiteboard.

7. When the best ideas from all the teams have been written down, challenge the group as a whole to collaborate on ways to build upon, improve, or evolve any of the ideas in the Idea Bank.

Piloting tips

- Encourage participants to think boldly outside the box, pushing the boundaries of what is expected.

- Encourage participants to also think visually; challenge them to sketch or doodle ideas.

- If your group size is less than eight participants, you can create smaller teams, with two or three members per team.

Bad2Good
Counterintuitive idea generation

At a glance

Bad2Good is a provocative technique based on the premise that often, bad-sounding, counterintuitive ideas can actually contain the seeds of an innovative, game-changing idea if effectively turned around. Counterintuitive thinking techniques have been around for a long time and are widely used by innovators and inventors.

If you wonder how seemingly bad ideas can really lead to good ideas, consider this example. Suppose you were brainstorming ideas for how to keep football players more comfortable, cooler, and drier during a game. What could be worse than suggesting, "Let's have football players wear women's lingerie?" But that is essentially the bad idea that helped launch an innovative, billion-dollar sports apparel brand called Under Armour. Under Armour founder Kevin Plank envisioned using a special fabric (used in women's lingerie) to create a base-layer T-shirt that would be more comfortable than cotton, and more effectively wick moisture away from the skin—an ideal fabric for helping to keep athletes cooler and drier.

See how good a bad idea can be? This highly entertaining, 180-degree thinking technique helps free a group's imagination from the confines of conventional thinking. Expect a lot of laughter as participants generate dozens of fresh, new ideas.

Number of participants 4–25

Duration 30 minutes

How to pilot

1. Introduce the challenge to be addressed.

2. **Part 1: Imagine a lot of really bad ideas**
   Instruct the group to imagine as many absolutely dreadful ideas as they can to address the challenge. Invite your group to have fun—the wilder, more outrageous, and more preposterous the ideas, the better. Anything goes! Here are some fun, provocative questions you can ask to get the ball rolling:

   "What are the most obvious bad ideas that come to mind?"

   "What are the most outlandish, ridiculous, or preposterous ideas we can imagine?"

   "What truly awful ideas would get us fired, or arrested for insanity?"

   "What crazy ideas might just solve the problem/challenge instantly?"

   "How would a mad scientist or a five-year-old solve this type of challenge?"

3. **Part 2: Select the most intriguing of the bad ideas**

   Once a significant number of really bad ideas have been generated, ask your group to quickly narrow them down to a manageable short list of their favorite (most awful) ideas.

4. **Part 3: Turnaround—Identify the seeds of good ideas**

   Now it's time to challenge your group to see how well they can turn around or transform those bad ideas into good or even great ideas. The goal is to identify the seeds of good ideas within the bad ones. You can guide your group through this counterintuitive thinking process with the following prompts:

   > "Is there something interesting, provocative, or potentially beneficial in this bad idea that could transform it into a good idea?"

   > "If we turned this idea around and did the complete opposite, could we come up with something really good?"

   > "What are the most obvious ways this bad idea can be transformed into a good, useful idea?"

   > "In what ways can this bad idea be adapted, modified, reimagined, or reengineered to create a good idea?"

   > "How could we accomplish the same thing this bad idea does, but in a positive way?"

5. At each step in the process, have a volunteer Reporter write down the group's ideas.

Piloting tips

- This exercise should be an enjoyable activity. Encourage your group to let go of any sense of seriousness or inhibitions (being juvenile, inappropriate, or outrageous is perfectly acceptable).

- When it's time for your group to turn around its bad ideas, encourage them to collaboratively share insights and build upon one another's ideas. For fun, introduce a little friendly competition to see who (or which team) can come up with the best idea turnaround in the room.

- If a group runs into any difficulty transforming a bad idea into a good one, re-ask the questions in Part 3. Also, encourage your group to explore different ways a bad idea can be adapted, modified, reversed, or reimagined to transform it into a great idea.

- This versatile technique can also be used as a fun icebreaker exercise.

Bad2Good: Solo SmartStorming instructions

1. **Part 1: Imagine a lot of really bad ideas**
   Focus on the issue, challenge, or opportunity to be addressed.

   Next, deliberately imagine as many absolutely dreadful ideas as you can to address the challenge. Have fun—the wilder, more outrageous, and more preposterous the ideas, the better. Anything goes! Here are some fun, provocative questions you can ask yourself to get the ball rolling:

   "What are the most obvious bad ideas that come to mind?"

   "What are the most outlandish, ridiculous, or preposterous ideas you can imagine?"

   "What truly awful ideas would get you fired, or arrested for insanity?"

   "What crazy ideas might just solve the problem/challenge instantly?"

   "How would a mad scientist or a five-year-old solve this challenge?"

2. **Part 2: Select the most intriguing of the bad ideas**
   Once you've generated a number of really bad ideas, narrow them down to a short list of your favorite (most awful) ideas.

3. **Part 3: Turnaround—Identify the seeds of good ideas**
   Now it's time to challenge yourself to see how well you can turn around or transform those bad ideas into good or great ideas. The goal is to identify the seeds of good or great ideas within the bad ones.

   Try answering the following questions:

   Is there something interesting, provocative, or potentially beneficial in this bad idea that could transform it into a good idea?

   If I turned this idea around and did the complete opposite, could I come up with something really good?

   In what ways can this bad idea be adapted, modified, reimagined, or reengineered to create a good idea?

   Is there another version or variation on this bad idea that would make it a good one?

   How could I accomplish the same thing this bad idea does, but in a positive way?

Brainwriting
Silent, collaborative writing activity

At a glance
Brainwriting is a well-known, enjoyable, silent, collaborative writing technique that begins with individual problem solving and then grows exponentially to involve every member of the group. Participants begin by writing down an idea to address the challenge. Ideas are passed from person to person, and built upon until the process comes full circle and everyone has contributed to each of the original ideas.

This simple technique is an excellent "contribution equalizer." Because it is performed nonverbally, Brainwriting creates a safe, nonjudgmental environment for those quiet or self-conscious Silent Thinkers in your group, making it much more comfortable for them to contribute ideas. It also effectively silences intimidating, opinionated, or dominating personalities, in effect, leveling the playing field so that all participants have an equal opportunity to share.

Number of participants 5–8. For larger groups, divide participants into smaller teams of equal size.

Duration 20–30 minutes

How to pilot
To begin, divide your group into teams of five to eight in a circle formation. Provide each participant one sheet of writing paper and a pen. Instruct participants to number their ideas and write them as legibly as possible.

1. Introduce the challenge to be addressed.

2. Instruct participants to write down one single idea to solve the challenge at the top of their sheets of paper, and number it #1.

3. Next, each participant passes his or her sheet to the person immediately next to them, on their right or left side (make sure everyone goes in the same direction). Each person then silently reads the idea written on the paper they have just received and either builds on it, further develops it, or adds a totally new idea below the original. Sheets are then passed to the next person in line, and the process is repeated.

   (Note: Encourage participants to be as quick and spontaneous as possible in reading the ideas on their sheet and writing down ideas, spending no more than one minute per turn.)

4. The group continues passing sheets and building on one another's ideas until each person gets back his or her original sheet. Brainwriting ends when everyone has their original idea sheet back in their possession.

5. Harvesting the best ideas: Ask participants to review all the ideas on their sheet and select the two or three they think most successfully address the challenge. Once everyone has selected their favorite ideas, go around the room and ask each participant to share the ideas they have selected with the group. Have a volunteer serve as the Reporter to write down all of the ideas on a large flipchart pad or whiteboard.

Piloting tips

- Limit group sizes to five to eight participants. If a group circle size gets too large, the collaborative idea-generation process can become laborious and time-consuming.

- Encourage participants to generate ideas as spontaneously as possible to keep the flow (of sheets of paper) moving at a swift pace. A good target goal is approximately one idea per minute.

- To avoid directional confusion, be sure to establish the (clockwise or counterclockwise) direction in which participants will pass their sheets. Announce the direction before beginning the activity.

- As the Brainwriting activity progresses, it is normal for the pace of the action to slow, since participants have more ideas to read, consider, and add to. Monitor the progress of each team and give verbal prompts (if needed) to keep the activity moving efficiently.

Channeling Genius
Collaborative idea generation via identities

At a glance

In this imaginative role-playing technique, the group selects a groundbreaking visionary, innovator, inventor, artist, or performer (living or legend) such as Steve Jobs, Albert Einstein, Walt Disney, Oprah Winfrey, or Mother Teresa; or a fictional character such as Sherlock Holmes, MacGyver, or the Terminator to serve as its problem-solving inspiration.

The objective is to develop a range of new ideas to address a challenge in the same style or manner (creative thought process) as the chosen innovator/visionary might have approached it.

For example, "In what ways could Steve Jobs or Mother Teresa have solved our customer service issue?" Steve Jobs might have looked for ways to dramatically redesign the entire customer service process until it provided a simpler and more elegant customer experience. Mother Teresa, on the other hand, might have approached the challenge by inspiring a greater sense of empathy and compassion among the customer service staff.

Number of participants 4–20. Divide a group larger than 8 into smaller teams of equal size.

Duration 45–60 minutes

How to pilot

Setting the stage for your activity:

- Provide a copy of the list of innovative leaders with descriptions of their special talents (on pages 194–195) to each participant.

- Next, instruct the group/teams to select one renowned person from the list. If working in teams, ask each team to select a different personality to assure diversity in creative problem-solving approaches.

- Allow the group/teams a few minutes to get into character by discussing the unique personality traits, problem-solving strengths, talents, and abilities of the individual they selected.

As the Pilot, you can help facilitate this process by asking questions such as:

"Who is/was this person? What is/was he or she known for?"

"When you think of this person, what are some of the defining traits or characteristics that make/made them unique?"

"What aspects of their personality or talent make/made them outstanding in their field?"

"What are some of the defining characteristics or benefits of what he/she invented, discovered, innovated, or achieved?"

"How do you imagine this person approached problem solving?"

Piloting the activity:

1. Introduce the challenge to be addressed.

2. Instruct your group/teams to generate as many innovative ideas as possible by channeling their efforts through the unique problem-solving genius, personality, and talents of its selected individual (i.e., discover ways to solve the problem in the same style or manner he/she might have solved it).

3. When the time is up, instruct your group/teams to select a short list of the most interesting or effective ideas to address the challenge.

4. Repeat the process by instructing the group/teams to select a new personality to serve as their problem-solving inspiration. Remember to allow a few minutes for the group/teams to get into character by discussing the unique personality traits and characteristics of that person.

5. When the time is up in round two, instruct your group/teams to select a short list of the most interesting or effective ideas to address the challenge.

6. Harvesting the best ideas: When idea generation is complete, ask the group/each team to share which individuals they chose, and then what ideas they developed. Have a volunteer serve as the Reporter to write down all of those ideas on a large flipchart pad or whiteboard.

Piloting tips

Before beginning the idea-generation process:

- Make sure participants clearly understand the concept of channeling (or mimicking) the creative problem-solving style of the person they selected *before* generating ideas.

- This is an imagination-driven activity, so encourage participants to have fun channeling the creative problem-solving genius of their innovative leader.

- In addition to the names below, you/your group can also create your own list of creative problem-solving personalities, including any superhero, movie character, business leader, athlete, innovator, politician, historical figure, etc.

Examples of innovative leaders and their special talents and characteristics

Albert Einstein "The Theorist"
Insightful, scholarly, playful, creative, imaginative, and a big-picture thinker. He solved challenges by envisioning new connections—blending science with imagination to reveal new ways of looking at the universe.

Alexander the Great "The Strategic Conqueror"
Analytical, strategic, tactical, resourceful, adaptive, powerful, and single-mindedly focused on winning. He solved challenges by shrewdly analyzing a situation and the competition, then strategizing innovative tactics to achieve his goal.

Donald Trump "The Brand Empire-Builder"
Ambitious, self-assured, shameless self-promoter, visionary, empire-builder, resilient, learns from mistakes, and highly adaptive. He solves challenges by developing and promoting his brand, which caters to the aspirations, hopes, and dreams of others (for quality and status).

MacGyver "The Super-Resourceful"
Smart, cunning, inventive, adaptable, resourceful, with a strong talent for improvisation. He solved challenges by repurposing and transforming ordinary objects and things into extraordinarily effective devices that saved the day.

Madonna/Lady Gaga "The Trendsetter"
Bold, audacious, provocative, shrewd, charismatic, seductive, opportunistic, engaging, controversial, entrepreneur, zeitgeist spirit of her time and culture. She solves challenges by identifying the latest trends and leveraging them to her advantage.

Mark Zuckerberg "The Social Networker"
Brilliant, confident, controversial, opportunistic, visionary, adaptive, risk-taker, sees future realities others cannot imagine. He solves challenges by leveraging technology to create beneficial connections between people, things, and events.

Martin Luther King "The Peacemaker"
Courageous, visionary, inspiring leader, had big dreams, believed in equality and fairness, protector, movement organizer, eloquent speaker. He solved challenges by expressing a compelling vision for a better future for everyone.

Mother Teresa "The Empathizer"
Empathic, compassionate, helper, healer, admired, involved, trustworthy, symbol of hope and healing, a miracle worker. She solved challenges by seeing the goodness in human nature and taking empathy-based action to comfort others.

Oprah Winfrey "The Queen of Media"
Influential, charismatic, caring, confident, curious, savvy advocate for learning and self-empowerment, media empire-builder. She solves challenges by identifying issues of concern to her audience and creating forums to discuss the issues, educate, and self-empower others.

Sherlock Holmes "The Detective Super Sleuth"
Highly perceptive, discerning, deductive reasoning, dogmatic, systematic, an eye for details, connects the dots others miss, presents conclusions with flair. He solved challenges by observing the smallest of details and discerning new connections that solved mysteries.

Steve Jobs "The Visionary"
Entrepreneurial, innovator, perfectionist, showman, thought differently, demanded simplicity and outstanding design and functionality; accepted no limitations or barriers. He solved challenges by questioning conventional thinking (status quo) and boldly envisioning new possibilities.

Terminator "The Unstoppable"
Determined, relentless, highly adaptive, resourceful, and unyielding in pursuit of his goal. He solved challenges by ruthlessly and single-mindedly overcoming all obstacles that stood in the way of achieving his goal or objectives.

Thomas Edison "The Inventor"
Intuitive, prolific tinkerer, methodical problem solver, opportunist, adaptive, relentless, resourceful, practical, insightful, makes new connections. He solved challenges by identifying "what could be," and then methodically experimenting and tweaking his inventions until they became new realities.

Walt Disney "The Imagineer"
Prolific storyteller, enchanter, imaginer of new worlds, marketer, icon-maker, character developer, empire-builder, and skillful orchestrator of creative talent. He solved challenges by captivating audiences with imaginative storytelling and endearing characters.

Escaping the Box
Challenging conventions/status-quo thinking

At a glance

An assumption is a preconceived idea or belief about *the way things are* or *the way they should be;* it can also be a belief about *what is* or *is not* possible. It is an unexamined belief that we perceive to be true, but for which we have little to no evidence or proof.

The more assumptions and beliefs an individual, group, or organization has about an issue or challenge, the more limited their options can appear. That is why limiting preconceptions are such a huge impediment to innovative thinking.

Unexamined assumptions can impede the flow of a group's curiosity, wonder, and sense of discovery by creating a false sense of limitations. When people say, "We need to think outside the box," what they really mean to say is, "We need to think outside of our self-limiting assumptions."

For example, a radical-sounding idea was presented to a group of executives at a large supermarket chain: to allow local farmers to set up a weekly farmer's market in the parking lots of a number of the chain's locations. The idea was controversial because several of the executives *assumed* the farmer's markets would compete head-to-head with their stores—siphoning away both shoppers and the company's profits.

Was it true? Perhaps not.

In reality, the farmer's markets could actually boost the supermarkets' reputation in the communities and attract new customers who would shop in the supermarkets for items not available at the farmer's markets. (In fact, several years ago Barnes & Noble took a similar, radical business approach by not only allowing, but encouraging customers to sit in their stores and read books and magazines, without purchasing—and they revolutionized the bookselling industry in the process.)

See how preconceived notions can prevent us from considering a potentially game-changing idea? This provocative questioning technique can help dramatically free up a group's creative problem-solving process, allowing it to explore a wider range of new possibilities.

Number of participants 4–20

Duration 45–60 minutes

How to pilot

Escaping the Box is a simple, yet powerful three-part process: Part 1 helps a group identify hidden assumptions and limiting beliefs members may have about a challenge. In Part 2, the group identifies those specific beliefs that can impede its ability to succeed. In Part 3, the group challenges (disproves) the validity of those beliefs and generates new ideas (new possibilities).

1. Introduce the challenge to be addressed.

2. **Part 1: Identifying limiting beliefs**
   Ask the group to free-associate a list of any and all assumptions or preexisting notions or beliefs they may have about the issue, challenge, or situation (or its ability to successfully address the challenge). It's worth mentioning that no presumption is too small or inconsequential to be written down.

3. **Part 2: Selecting the most limiting notions or beliefs**
   Once your group is finished identifying a list of notions or beliefs, instruct them to narrow down the items to a short list of those that feel absolutely true (difficult to dispute), or those that they believe would most limit their ability to succeed. This selection process should be done as swiftly as possible. Keep an eye out to make sure your group does not get bogged down in prolonged conversations or debates.

4. **Part 3: Challenge Assumptions (a.k.a. "The Drill-Down")**
   In this final part, instruct your group to challenge each assumption on their short list head-on by asking and answering the following three questions, one at a time, in sequence:

   1. "Is this belief true?"

   2. "Is it absolutely true, all the time, without exception, always? Can we imagine a circumstance in which it might not be true?"

   3. "If it's NOT absolutely true, all the time, what are the possibilities?"

   By walking through this diagnostic process, your group should discover that a surprisingly large number of their original assumptions and limiting beliefs were proven false—a liberating experience, indeed! As one assumption after another dissolves under objective analysis, instruct your group to generate new ideas. Ask, "What becomes possible once the old limitations are gone?"

5. At each step in the process, have a volunteer Reporter write down the group's ideas.

Piloting tips

- Before you begin your session, assess the size of your group to determine whether it is better to pilot this activity with the group as a whole or to divide it into smaller teams of four to six.

- If working in teams, each team can generate its own list of assumptions, then challenge those assumptions to see what new ideas become possible.

More about the three "drill-down" questions

"Is this belief true?"

When piloting your group through the three questions, make sure the participants are with you each step of the way. For example, when asking the first question, *Is this belief true?* listen to hear whether the group is generally aligned in their answer or needs time to reach a consensus (it does not have to be unanimous).

"Is it absolutely true, all the time, without exception, always?"

This second question always stimulates a good, healthy discussion. Allow a few minutes for the discussion. If the group gets too deeply embroiled in a debate, point out that very few, if any things in life are *absolutely true, all the time, without exception, always.* The goal is to help the group see a new glimmer of freedom or new pathways of opportunity where none may have existed before.

"If it's NOT absolutely true, all the time, what are the possibilities?"

This final question should stimulate a shift in viewpoint within the group/teams from a sense of limitations to an expanded sense of new possibilities.

An assumption by any other name

- It's helpful to recognize that limiting beliefs can show up in a number of different guises. Ever hear people say things like, "It's common knowledge that...," "The prevailing wisdom says...," "Our presumption is...," "Experts say...," or "We can't do/say that; this is just the way things are."?

- As we mentioned earlier, groups will find that a surprisingly large number of the assumptions challenged will be proven *not* to be true. But occasionally, a group may get stuck on an assumption (a fixed belief) they find difficult to disprove. When this occurs, shift tactics and ask your group:

  "Does this assumption or belief help or impede our efforts to succeed?"

  "Imagine if this assumption weren't true; what would be possible?"

  "In what ways can we move beyond the limitations of this belief?"

Escaping the Box: Solo SmartStorming instructions

1. Focus on the issue, challenge, or opportunity to be addressed.

2. **Part 1: Identify limiting beliefs**
   Write down a spontaneous list of any and all assumptions or preexisting notions or beliefs you may have about the issue, challenge, opportunity, or your ability to successfully address the challenge. Consider no presumption too small or inconsequential.

3. **Part 2: Select the most limiting notions or beliefs**
   Once you have finished identifying a list of assumptions, narrow it down to the ones that you feel are absolutely true (difficult to dispute) or most strongly limit your ability to succeed.

   Note: This selection process should be done as swiftly as possible, using intuition as your guide.

4. **Step 3: Challenge assumptions (a.k.a. "The Drill-Down")**
   In this final part, you challenge each belief on your short list by asking the following three questions, one at a time, in sequence:

   1. "Is this belief true?"

   2. "Is it absolutely true, all the time, without exception, always? Can you imagine a circumstance in which it might not be true?"

   3. "If it's NOT absolutely true, all the time, what are the possibilities?"

   By walking through this diagnostic process, you should discover that a surprisingly large number of your original assumptions and limiting beliefs are proven false. As one assumption after another dissolves under objective analysis, generate new ideas for what becomes possible when the old limitations are gone.

Frankensteining
Forced-association idea building

At a glance

Frankensteining challenges participants to discover ways to combine two (or more) seemingly unrelated ideas to create a distinctly new and unique product, service, process, or thing.

This combinatory-play approach of merging different ideas, ingredients, features, functions, attributes, or characteristics to create something altogether new is a hallmark of the innovation process. For example, someone combined a telephone and a photocopier to create the fax machine. The company Mars Brands combined two popular food items (a pretzel nugget and cheddar cheese) to create the popular snack Combos; automotive companies around the world are designing hybrid gas/electric cars that get better fuel economy with lower emissions. And Apple combined the features of a cell phone, digital music player, web browser, GPS system, calendar, camera, and video recorder to create the miraculous, all-in-one iPhone.

This Frankensteining technique encourages participants to switch off their logic-based thinking and enjoy the process of creatively tinkering and experimenting like a mad scientist at play to discover new, unexpected possibilities.

Number of participants 6–12

Duration 30–60 minutes

What you will need

- Sticky notes or small writing pads for each participant
- Pens, crayons, or color markers

How to pilot

1. Introduce the challenge to be addressed.

2. Generate a lot of ideas—Ask participants to generate as wide a range of different ideas as possible. You may use *any* SmartStorming idea-generation technique you wish for this first step. Instruct participants to write down or draw each idea on its own separate sticky note or sheet of paper (i.e., one idea per sticky note or sheet of paper).

   (Note: You can skip Step 2 by asking participants to show up to the session with three to five ideas, or by using preexisting ideas generated in an earlier activity.)

3. When the group has finished generating concepts, ask participants to select the most interesting, creative, or innovative ideas; then post those ideas on the wall.

4. Next, ask your group to quickly cluster ideas on the wall according to similarities in subject matter, theme, category, type, style, etc.; combine ideas that are similar, and eliminate any duplicate concepts.

These ideas will serve as the inspiration/stimuli/ingredients for the next step: combinatory play.

5. Now it's time to Frankenstein! Ask your group to look over all the ideas on the wall and search for imaginative ways to blend, combine, commingle, marry, merge, mix, or synthesize two (or more) ideas—until new and uniquely different ideas emerge.

This process should be enjoyable, so encourage participants to playfully experiment, collaborate, and build upon one another's ideas with abandon. Anything goes! There is no idea or new combination of ideas that is too wild or outrageous.

Piloting tips

- Before you begin this activity, assess the size of your group to determine whether it would be more productive to pilot this activity with the group as a whole, or to divide the group into smaller teams.

- Remember to tell participants to write down or draw each idea on its own separate sticky note or sheet of paper (i.e., one idea per sticky note).

- Encourage participants to think visually by sketching or doodling ideas.

- As a reminder, this activity should feel like a fun, exhilarating experience. The goal is to conjure up the most interesting, imaginative, or innovative combination of ideas possible. The more audacious the ideas, the better! As the saying goes, "You never know how far you can go until you've gone too far." It's better to push ideas to the outermost edge of plausibility than play it too safe.

Frankensteining: Solo SmartStorming instructions

1. Focus on the issue, challenge, or opportunity to be addressed.

2. Generate a lot of ideas—as wide a range of new and different ideas as possible. Write down or draw each idea on its own separate sticky note or sheet of paper (i.e., one idea per sticky note).

   (Note: You can skip Step 2 by using preexisting ideas generated in an earlier activity.)

3. When you are finished generating concepts, select the most interesting, creative, or innovative ideas; then post those selected ideas on a wall or on a desktop.

4. Next, quickly cluster ideas according to any similarities in subject matter, theme, category, type, style, etc.; ideas that are similar may be combined, and any duplication should be eliminated. These ideas will serve as the inspiration/stimuli/ingredients for combinatory play.

5. Now it's time to Frankenstein! Look over all the ideas and search for imaginative ways to boldly blend, combine, commingle, marry, merge, mix, or synthesize two (or more) ideas—until new and uniquely different ideas emerge.

6. Have fun playing and experimenting like a mad scientist. Anything goes! There is no idea or new combination of ideas that is too wild or outrageous.

Group Graffiti
Collaborative wall-writing activity

At a glance
Group Graffiti is an energizing, collaborative idea-building activity that gets participants up out of their seats and thinking on their feet. As its name implies, Group Graffiti is an interactive writing and drawing activity in which participants walk back and forth along a blank "concept wall" and fill it by writing down new ideas. Participants are encouraged to spontaneously build upon one another's ideas until the entire graffiti wall is filled. This process stimulates the cross-pollination of ideas in a fun, interactive physical activity.

Number of participants Any size group

Duration 20–30 minutes

What you will need
- A long, smooth wall (eight to fifteen feet long) or a series of shorter walls in close proximity to one another (a hallway wall outside your session room could also work well)
- Several large sheets of stick-on flipchart paper or a long roll of brown paper
- Markers for each participant

How to pilot
Setting the stage for your activity:

First, prepare the wall space you plan to use for your Group Graffiti activity *prior* to beginning your session. Tape several (six to twelve) large sheets of stick-on flipchart paper next to one another (or a long sheet from a roll of brown paper) on a smooth wall. Write down the problem/challenge statement on the top of the first sheet.

Piloting the activity:
1. Introduce the challenge to be addressed.

2. Next, ask the group to walk back and forth along the blank graffiti wall and spontaneously write down or draw any ideas they wish to contribute. Encourage participants to actively build on and develop each other's ideas—or create entirely new ideas inspired by concepts their colleagues have already written. The goal is to cover the full length of the wall with as many new and different ideas as possible within the time limit.

3. Harvesting the best ideas: Once the group has finished, ask participants to step back, evaluate all of the ideas written on the wall, then identify (with an

asterisk or check mark) those ideas that could best address the challenge.

Next, ask participants to read all selected ideas out loud. Have a volunteer serve as the session Reporter to write down those ideas on a large flipchart pad or whiteboard.

Piloting tips

- When setting up your wall, make sure there is more than enough unobstructed space to comfortably accommodate the number of participants in your activity. If your group is large (eighteen or more), you may want to consider using two separate walls near each other. Also, consider using the hallway outside your session room, or another large public space.

- It's a good idea to test the paper with a marker to make sure it won't bleed through and leave marks on the wall underneath. If it does, double up the sheets of paper.

- Keep everyone participating. As Group Graffiti progresses, keep a watchful eye on the number of participants actively writing down ideas on the wall versus those standing back reading the wall or socializing with others.

- If a number of participants have stopped contributing ideas, a gentle nudge can get them back into action. A good tactic is to challenge everyone in the group to add at least two or three more ideas to the wall before the time expires.

- Group Graffiti can also be used for crowd-sourcing ideas. It's easy; just post large sheets of paper (or a long, rolled-out sheet of brown paper), along with the challenge statement, in a public hallway or space so passersby can stop and contribute ideas.

Idea Mashup
Forced-association idea generation

At a glance

This popular idea-generation approach takes advantage of the mind's amazing ability to link two (or more) disparate items—such as words, images, objects, subjects, and ideas—and use the new associations to develop fresh, unexpected solutions.

Forced associations help override a group's linear thought processes; using random external triggers forces participants to make new connections between the challenge and the trigger item. These trigger items challenge participants to stretch their imaginations and think outside their familiar comfort zones.

For example, let's say your group's challenge is to develop new approaches for marketing a brand of dog food, and the random trigger item chosen is an MRI medical imaging device. The group would explore associations between the two disparate items (dog food and an MRI device) to address the challenge, such as:

- An MRI sees into the body to reveal what's inside. What if we designed a distinctive new see-through dog food package?

- MRIs are used in health screenings. What if we sponsored a free mobile canine health-screening clinic that traveled from city to city?

- An MRI is a scanning device. What if we offered a special "smart card" that could be scanned for special product discounts and gifts?

- An MRI generates images. What if we held a photo contest? The winning dog image could appear on our products and promotions.

As you can see, this technique is a powerful way to expand a group's problem-solving perspective beyond the expected.

Number of participants 4–25

Duration 45–60 minutes

How to pilot

Setting the stage for your activity:

To prepare, ask each participant (in a round-robin manner) to randomly name any word, object, or thing (e.g., airplane, ocean, farm, circus, perfume, Hollywood, book, video game). Have a volunteer serve as the session Reporter to write down the ideas on a large flipchart pad or whiteboard. The goal here is to build a master list of random stimuli that teams can then use to trigger new associations and connections.

Piloting the activity:

1. Introduce the challenge to be addressed.

2. Begin the activity by randomly selecting one of the words, objects, or things on the master list; then instruct the group to begin making associations between the random item selected and the issue/challenge to be addressed. Encourage participants to have fun and stretch their imagination to identify novel or unexpected connections.

3. You can help stimulate the group's thinking by asking:

    "How is this issue/challenge like __(selected item)__?"

    "What traits, characteristics, or properties do they share in common?"

    "How can the traits, characteristics, or properties of __(selected item)__ be applied to address this issue/challenge?"

4. Repeat the activity: Select another item randomly from the master list and repeat the forced-association exercise using the new item as the trigger.

5. Continue this process for several more rounds until the group has generated a wide range of novel ways to address the challenge.

Piloting tips

*   Encourage participants to think boldly outside the box, pushing the boundaries of what is expected. No idea or association is too wild or outrageous.

*   Encourage participants to also think visually by drawing ideas.

*   Other ways to generate random items for this activity:

    Pass out index cards to each participant. Ask everyone to write down one random word, object, or thing per card. Collect the cards, shuffle the deck, then pick a card to begin the activity. Pick a new card every few minutes to stimulate new associations and connections.

    Open a dictionary to any page and randomly pick out a word, or use a random word-generator app, software, or website.

    Ask participants to each write down one random word on a sheet of paper. Next, have them fold the paper and place their paper in a hat, box, or bag. Randomly select an item to begin the activity.

Idea Speed Dating
Rapid collaborative idea building

At a glance

This fun, collaborative idea-building activity was inspired by the social networking concept of speed dating. Participants first work individually to generate some initial ideas for how to solve an issue or challenge. Next, participants meet one-on-one with other SmartStormers in a series of brief, round-robin, idea-building sessions that last only ten to fifteen minutes each.

During each mini session, idea partners share their ideas and exchange insights for how to improve, develop, or build upon one another's ideas. The tight time limit keeps the collaborative idea-generation activity energized, focused, and highly productive.

Number of participants 6–18

Duration 60–90 minutes

What you will need

- A large, open (uncluttered) space or room
- Chairs to accommodate the number of participants

Idea Speed Dating rule

- Instruct your group to keep all comments about one another's ideas unconditionally positive and 100 percent free of any judgments or negativity. The goal of each round is not to critique the merits of ideas, but rather to help idea partners identify the strongest, most innovative ideas, and then collaborate on ways to improve, evolve, or build upon them.

How to pilot

Setting the stage for your activity:

- The ideal venue for this activity is a large, open (uncluttered) room, set up with sets of two chairs facing one another either in a large circle formation or in rows. Be sure to leave space between the sets of chairs for a little privacy.

- Divide participants into two groups. Members of group one (we'll call them Residents) will remain in their seats throughout the entire activity. Members of group two (we'll call them Visitors) will rotate to new partners after each round.

Piloting the activity:

1. Introduce the challenge to be addressed.

2. The activity begins with independent idea generation: Participants are first instructed to work independently to generate as many new ideas as possible.

3. Next, ask participants to select their two best ideas.

4. Begin idea speed dating: Ask all members of group two (Visitors) to select an idea speed-dating partner (from among the seated Resident members) to collaborate with during the first round of ideation. Once everyone has paired off, instruct idea partners to take turns sharing their ideas, and to discuss ways to improve, develop, or build on one another's ideas. (Time limit: 10–15 minutes per round)

5. Round-robin changing of idea partners: When time is up, instruct members of the Visitors group to switch idea partners by getting up and moving to the person sitting at the next set of chairs. Once again, instruct idea partners to take turns sharing their best ideas and discussing ways to improve, develop, or build on one another's ideas.

6. Repeat this round-robin changing of idea partners every ten to fifteen minutes until each participant has had the chance to work with a number of different idea partners.

7. To harvest the best ideas: Have each participant select the two to three most innovative ideas on his or her list.

8. Finally, ask participants to take turns sharing their selected ideas with the group as a whole. Have a volunteer serve as the session Reporter to write down those ideas on a large flipchart pad or whiteboard.

Piloting tips

- Speed and spontaneity are key ingredients in this activity. To use time efficiently, instruct participants to take only a few minutes each to share ideas; use the balance of the time remaining to help improve and build upon each other's ideas, or create entirely new concepts. Provide time alerts when five minutes remain in the round.

- Keep a watchful eye on participants to ensure they don't get sidetracked socializing or in off-topic conversations.

Idea Sprinting
High-velocity idea generation

At a glance

Idea Sprinting, as the name implies, is a fast-paced, beat the clock idea-generation technique. It's specifically designed to help a group generate a large quantity of new ideas quickly over a short period of time. For example, "Let's shoot for twenty-five new ideas in the next five minutes!" The group is challenged to meet (or exceed) the number of ideas requested within the time frame defined.

This high-velocity activity gets participants' attention focused, adrenaline pumping, and creative juices flowing; there is no time for inhibition or self-consciousness. Idea Sprinting can help your group generate dozens, if not hundreds, of new ideas. It's a surefire way to get your SmartStorming session off to a roaring fast start.

Number of participants 4–25

Duration 5–10 minutes. This activity can be repeated multiple times.

How to pilot

1. The Pilot begins by presenting his or her group with an ambitious goal for the number of new ideas to achieve within a short time frame. For example:

   "Let's shoot for fifteen or more new ideas in the next three minutes!"

   "Let's shoot for twenty-five or more new ideas in the next five minutes!"

   "Let's shoot for thirty-five or more new ideas in the next ten minutes!"

   Try and make the activity sound like a fun game or contest—introduce the ambitious target goal with a sense of playful enthusiasm.

2. Set a countdown timer to the number of minutes you've decided on.

3. Next, introduce the challenge as a provocative question.

4. When everyone is ready to begin the Idea Sprint, announce loudly, "Time begins…NOW!" Start the timer immediately.

5. To help fuel the group's idea-generation momentum, ask a rapid-fire set of provocative questions throughout the contest (see the list of questions on next page).

6. Have a volunteer serve as the session Reporter to write down those ideas on a large flipchart pad or whiteboard.

Piloting questions for Idea Sprinting

Here are some thought-provoking questions you can ask your group to help keep the idea-generation activity moving quickly:

"What's the most obvious idea we can think of?"

"What's the opposite of that?"

"What are similar/different ways to…?"

"What are some really bad ideas?"

"How do we turn them into good ideas?"

"What else haven't we thought of yet?"

"What are two or three other ways or options to…?"

"What if…?"

"What is the most outrageous thing we can think of?"

"What would solve this problem quickly or easily?"

"What would Apple, Google, or Nike do?"

"If we knew we couldn't fail, what would we do?"

"How would a five-year-old solve this challenge?"

"If we had all the money and resources in the world, what would we do?"

"What idea/solution would change everything?"

Piloting tips

- To keep a group's outflow of ideas high, ask lots of provocative questions. When the flow of ideas begins to ebb, immediately switch to a new line of questioning to spark fresh thinking. You can use the Pilot's cheat sheet of 25 Piloting Questions for Any Challenge (on page 259).

- Idea Sprinting is a focused, high-energy activity, so it's important to keep the session momentum high.

- Idea Sprinting is a great activity to get your group off to a fast start. It can be used to boost your group's energy and enthusiasm after lunch or during the afternoon doldrums, or it can be used as an icebreaker at the start of a session.

- For large groups, divide the group into smaller teams of equal size. Ask each team to designate a team Reporter to capture the team's ideas. When the Idea Sprint is completed, each team can take turns sharing their best ideas.

Idea Sprinting: Solo SmartStorming instructions

1. Focus on the issue, challenge, or opportunity to be addressed.

2. Challenge yourself to come up with an ambitious number of new ideas to achieve within a tight time frame. For example:

   Ten (or more) ideas in the next five minutes!

   Fifteen (or more) new ideas in the next ten minutes!

   The goal of this exercise is to go for *quantity over quality*. Generate ideas as quickly and spontaneously as possible without thinking too long about an idea. Remember to postpone all judgment. Go for wild and edgy ideas.

   Use sticky notes for this exercise. Write (or draw) one idea per note.

3. Set a timer to the number of minutes you've decided on.

4. When you are ready to generate ideas, say out loud: "Time begins...NOW!" Start the timer immediately.

5. When you are done, select your most promising ideas. Set them aside for now. Take a short break to clear your mind, then repeat the Idea Sprinting process as many times as you wish.

In Their Shoes

Empathy-based idea generation

At a glance

Empathy is the ability to compassionately appreciate the emotional state (feelings, thoughts, needs, desires, etc.) another person is experiencing within the frame of reference of that other person's reality.

This empathy-based idea-generation technique is designed to help a group develop deeper understanding and insight into the *emotional drivers* that influence or motivate a person, group, or target audience.

Whether the challenge is to find effective new ways to engage teenagers via social media, improve the quality of a customer's shopping experience, or motivate aging Baby Boomers with a medical condition to see their doctors, have your group imagine (as detailed as possible) what a typical day (or a specific situation or condition) in the life of that person, group, or audience would feel like. They will gain valuable new insights that can be used to develop meaningful and effective solutions, as well as identify new opportunities.

Number of participants 4–12

Duration 30–60 minutes

How to pilot

1. Introduce the challenge to be addressed.

2. **Part 1: Understanding the person, group, or audience**
   Ask the group to imagine and discuss, in as much detail as possible, what a typical day (or a specific situation or condition) in the life of the person or group would look and feel like. What would it be like to walk a day in their shoes? To feel like they feel? To experience what they experience? Some good discussion starters are:

   Who are they?

   What specific issue, problem, challenge, or situation do they face?

   What thoughts and emotions are they experiencing?

   What physical or emotional needs/wants are not being met?

   What is/are the best way(s) to reach them?

   What would it look and feel like to be in their shoes?

   Have the group keep a list of any interesting or important insights that surface during their discussions.

3. **Part 2: Exploring ways to fulfill wants and needs**

   Next, instruct your group to use all of the insights they gained in Part 1 to generate ideas. The goal is to identify new and innovative ways to 1) satisfy the person's or group's unmet needs or wants; 2) solve their problem/issue; 3) improve their situation/condition; or 4) achieve a specific goal. Some good questions to prompt the ideation process:

   What specific unmet need(s) can we help satisfy?

   In what ways can we satisfy them?

   In what ways can we help them achieve/acquire what they want?

   What specific issue, situation, or condition can we help improve, change, or resolve?

   In what ways can we do it?

   What are some meaningful things we can do or say?

   If there were no limitations, what would we do or say?

4. Have a volunteer serve as the session Reporter to write down those ideas on a large flipchart pad or whiteboard.

Piloting tips

- Prior to the start of the ideation process, it is helpful to discuss with your participants the distinction between needs and wants.

  Needs: their emotional drivers, the must-haves to feel safe or whole

  Wants: something wished for or desired

- Encourage participants to really feel into each question rather than thinking about it on a purely intellectual or analytical level. Thinking and feeling are two completely different ways of relating.

- Ask participants to do some field work prior to the session—observing the person/persons in their environment or situation. For example, if the target audience is teenagers, then ask your group to spend some time observing and speaking with teenagers in the real world. Learn where they like to hang out, how they relate to one another, where they shop. Listen to their favorite music, watch their television shows, movies, videos, etc., and explore their favorite social media sites. The goal is to get a true sense of what it feels like to be, act, and think like a teenager.

In Their Shoes: Solo SmartStorming instructions

1. Focus on the issue, challenge, or opportunity to be addressed.

2. **Part 1: Understanding the person, group, or audience**
   Imagine in as much detail as possible what a typical day (or a specific situation or condition) in the life of the person, group, or target audience would look and feel like. Write a list of any insights that come to mind about what it would be like to walk a day in their shoes...to feel like they feel...to experience what they experience.

   Who are they?

   What are they like?

   What specific issue, problem, challenge, or situation do they face?

   What thoughts/feelings/emotions are they experiencing?

   What needs/wants are not being met?

   Who are they interacting with and where?

   What is/are the best way(s) to reach them?

3. **Part 2: Exploring ways to fulfill wants and needs**
   Next, look over all of your insights and imagine new and innovative ways to 1) satisfy the person's or group's unmet needs/wants; 2) solve their problem/issue; 3) improve their situation/condition; or 4) achieve a specific goal.

   In what ways can their specific unmet need(s) be satisfied?

   What specific issue, situation, or condition can you/we help improve, change, or resolve? In what ways can you/we do it?

   What are some meaningful things you/we can do or say?

   What would make them truly happy or satisfied?

   What would rock their world?

Mind Mapping
Visual associative-thinking activity

At a glance
Mind Mapping is a popular visual ideation technique that closely mimics the way the human brain naturally absorbs, processes, and retrieves mental stimuli to make new connections. While the technique has been around for centuries in various forms, it was fully developed by Tony Buzan, author of *The Mind Map Book*. The technique helps individuals and groups diagrammatically represent ideas and see related concepts arranged around a core concept.

Mind Mapping begins with a single key word or symbol (representing the topic or issue) written in the center of a sheet of paper. Participants then spontaneously write down any associations (ideas/themes) triggered by the key word or symbol. Lines are drawn to connect these new associations with the central topic. Next, building on each of the new associations, participants branch out into subassociations. This process is repeated a number of times until the Mind Map is filled with a diverse range of associations, all connecting back to the central topic. On paper, these ideas (radiating out in all directions) resemble the branches of a tree, a root system, or even a spider's web.

Mind Mapping is a powerful tool for fully exploring a topic in a visual manner. It helps identify, connect, and organize a broad range of information. The technique can be used for a wide range of challenges, such as solving complex problems, identifying and developing new business opportunities, setting goals, etc.

Mind Maps can be created by an individual, a team, or even a large group.

Number of participants Any size group.

Duration 20–45 minutes

What you will need
- A flipchart-size writing pad or large poster-size sheets of paper for each team
- A separate work area or wall space area for each team
- Adhesive tape
- Pens and crayons or markers for each participant

Setting up for Team Mind Mapping
Divide your group into small teams of three to four members. Each team will need their own large flipchart pad or whiteboard, or wall space with a large sheet of flipchart paper taped to it, as well as pens and crayons or markers.

How to pilot

1. Introduce the challenge to be addressed.

2. Instruct teams to write down a key word or draw a symbol to represent the main topic in the center of the paper. For example, let's say the topic is to identify ideas, themes, or activities for "things people enjoy." To begin, teams could write down "Enjoyment" as the key word in the center of the sheet of paper.

3. Next, instruct teams to draw a series of six to ten short lines that radiate out from the central word/image like the branches of a tree in all directions. Teams can use a variety of colored crayons/markers to differentiate each new branch.

4. Ask teams to free-associate ideas triggered by the key word/symbol. Ideas should be written down (in single key word form) above the lines/branches drawn; additional lines may be added to match the number of ideas generated.

5. When this first level of idea generation is finished, ask teams to look over their ideas, and begin a second level of free associations based on the first. Ask teams to draw smaller sub-branches that sprout outward from each original idea, to accommodate the new associations.

6. Teams should continue free-associating new ideas, building and adding third- and even fourth-level branches until their Mind Map is filled.

7. When completed, instruct each team to carefully look over and assess their collective Mind Map. Using intuition and discernment as a guide, ask teams to identify the most interesting or valuable ideas, themes, or insights to emerge.

   - What immediate solutions or areas of opportunity does the Mind Map reveal?

   - What previously unseen concepts, themes, trends, or areas of importance emerge?

   - What new insights, directions, or opportunities reveal themselves, warranting further exploration or development?

8. Harvesting ideas: Ask each team to share its most interesting insights. Have a volunteer serve as the session Reporter to write down those ideas on a large flipchart pad or whiteboard.

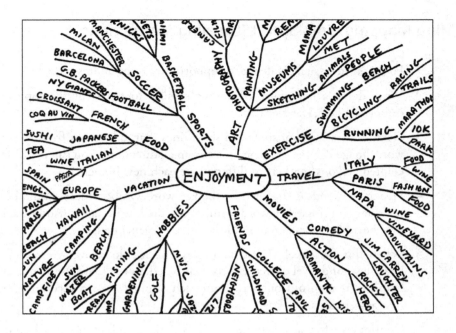

Piloting tips

- Use large, oversized sheets of flipchart paper for Mind Mapping.

- Keep all key words/symbols simple and concise (one to two words) and be sure they clearly communicate the essence of the issue/topic to be addressed. For example, if the challenge is to identify ways to increase ice cream sales in Alaska, a good key word to use would be *Alaska* or *Ice cream,* or perhaps, even better, draw the image of someone wearing a parka eating an ice cream cone.

- Size matters: Instruct teams to write down the key word/symbol in a modest size in the center of the paper in order to leave plenty of room for ideas to radiate out in all directions.

- A picture is worth a thousand words. Encourage your SmartStormers to draw pictures, symbols, or icons to communicate the essence of an idea, rather than relying solely on words.

- Encourage collaborative idea-building and sharing of insights.

Mind Mapping: Solo SmartStorming instructions

1. Focus on the issue, challenge, or opportunity to be addressed.

2. Write down a key word or graphic symbol to represent the topic in the center of a large sheet of paper.

3. Next, draw a series of six to ten short lines that radiate out from the central word/image like the branches of a tree in all directions. You can use different-colored crayons/markers to differentiate each new branch.

4. Free-associate ideas triggered by the key word/symbol. Ideas should be written down (in single key word form) above the line branches. Additional lines may be added to match the number of ideas generated.

5. When this first level of associations is finished, look over your ideas, and begin a second level of free associations based on the first. Draw smaller sub-branches that sprout outward from each original idea to accommodate the new associations.

6. Continue to free-associate new ideas, building and adding third- and even fourth-level branches until your page is completely filled. (See illustration on previous page.)

7. When you are finished, carefully look over and assess your Mind Map. Using intuition and discernment as your guide, identify the most interesting or valuable ideas, themes, or insights to emerge.

   - What immediate solutions or areas of opportunity does the Mind Map reveal?

   - What previously unseen concepts, themes, trends, or areas of importance emerge?

   - What new insights, directions, or opportunities reveal themselves, warranting further exploration or development?

Pre-Storming
Pre-session idea generation

At a glance

One of the simplest and most effective ways to amass a large number of new ideas quickly is to instruct participants to show up to the SmartStorming session with three initial ideas ready to share. Think of these ideas as the ticket for admission into the session; no ideas, no entry!

Asking participants to pre-storm ideas prior to the session accomplishes two positive things: First, it motivates participants to familiarize themselves with the challenge and goal; and second, it allows insights and ideas time to percolate in the unconscious mind for several days—often resulting in new, unexpected connections.

What's impressive about Pre-Storming is that if you have ten SmartStormers scheduled to attend your session and each brings three ideas—that's thirty new ideas in the bank *before* your session even begins!

This foolproof process may seem so obvious that it's barely worth mentioning as a technique. However, you might be surprised by how few brainstorm facilitators actually take advantage of Pre-Storming.

Number of participants Any size group

Duration 20–30 minutes

How to pilot

1. Send your participants a meeting invitation several days before the scheduled session; include an attachment with the following information and request:

   - A brief statement of the issue or challenge to be addressed, plus the specific goals and objectives for the session.

   - All relevant background or support information necessary to understand the issue, problem, or challenge.

   - A formal request for each participant to read over the information provided, and to bring three (or more) initial ideas to share at the beginning of the session to help spark discussions.

2. Send a follow-up reminder a couple of days prior to the scheduled session.

3. Pre-Storming makes an ideal icebreaker activity. Simply go around the room and ask each participant to quickly share his or her ideas. As participants share their ideas, identify the most interesting or provocative ones. Use them as the points of departure for a new round of group idea generation.

4. Have a volunteer serve as the session Reporter to write down those ideas on a large flipchart pad or whiteboard.

Piloting tips

- Be sure to provide all the necessary background information participants will need to fully understand the challenge.

- Encourage participants to think boldly outside the box. These initial ideas should be imaginative and push the boundaries of what is expected or possible. Wild and edgy ideas are welcome!

- Also encourage participants to think visually by sketching ideas, bringing in pictures, or creating montage inspiration or mood boards.

Pump Up the Value
Adaptive idea generation

At a glance

In today's innovation-driven, global economy, consumers have become more discerning and more demanding. They expect more and better value in the products and services they buy.

Value can be defined as the perceived worth, merit, or importance of a product, service, or process based on price/cost. In other words, does it meet or exceed expectations for what it should be or do? Is it worth the price?

This innovative technique helps participants imagine new ways to pump up the value proposition in its products, services, or processes—i.e., make it better, simpler, faster, cheaper, easier to use, more reliable, more satisfying, more beautifully designed, or even more emotionally endearing.

To help your group more effectively pump up the value, we have provided a versatile reference tool called the SmartStorming Value Compass. This compass points to a variety of different directions (ways and/or areas) in which your group can drive innovation by adding greater value.

Number of participants 4–20

Duration 30–45 minutes

What you will need

- A photocopy of the SmartStorming Value Compass (on page 249) for each participant or team.

How to pilot

1. Introduce the challenge to be addressed.

2. Instruct the group to select a direction (an attribute or feature) on the Value Compass.

3. The goal is to generate as many new ideas as possible for ways to dramatically improve, innovate, or reimagine that specific attribute or feature in regard to the challenge. (Set a five-minute time limit for each direction selected.)

   For example, if the direction selected is "Simplicity," ask the group, "In what ways can we dramatically simplify some aspect or feature of this product/service/process?"

4. When the time is up, ask the group to quickly note their most promising or interesting ideas with a check mark or asterisk.

5. Next, instruct the group to select another direction on the Value Compass and repeat the idea-generation and selection steps. Again, allow five minutes for conceptualizing ideas, and just a few minutes to quickly note the most promising ideas.

6. Have the group explore as many different Value Compass directions as possible in the time you've allotted for the activity.

7. When finished exploring directions on the Value Compass, instruct the group to review the promising ideas they noted after each round, and select the best ones. Ask the group/teams to read their best ideas out loud. Have a volunteer serve as the Reporter to write down all of the ideas on a large flipchart pad or whiteboard.

Value Compass

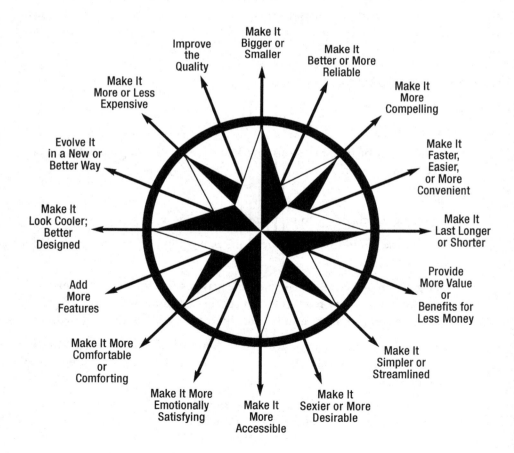

Piloting tips

- Before you begin your activity, assess the size of your group to determine whether it is better to pilot them as a single group or to divide the group into smaller teams of equal size.

- Make a photocopy of the SmartStorming Value Compass (on page 249) for each participant or team.

- The Value Compass provides a wide range of different directions to explore. To keep your activity moving efficiently, remember to set a firm five-minute deadline for each direction. (Note: If one or two directions stimulate an especially rich vein of new ideas, you can extend the time limit.)

- Encourage participants to build upon one another's ideas.

- Get visual. Provide participants with a pad of sticky notes and a pen. Ask them to sketch or draw any ideas they have in response to each direction. When the activity is completed, sketches can be arranged on a larger board according to each direction explored.

Pump Up the Value: Solo SmartStorming instructions

Note: You will need a copy of the Value Compass for this activity (on page 249).

1. Focus on the issue, challenge, or opportunity to be addressed.

2. Select a direction (an attribute or feature) on the Value Compass.

3. Your challenge is to generate as many new ideas as possible for ways to dramatically improve, innovate, or reimagine that specific attribute or feature in regard to the challenge. Set a five-minute time limit for each direction you select.

   For example, if the direction you have selected is "Simplicity," ask yourself, "In what ways can this product/service/process be dramatically simplified?"

4. Next, select another direction on the Value Compass and repeat the idea-generation process. Again, allow five minutes for conceptualizing ideas.

5. Explore as many different Value Compass directions as possible in the time you've allotted yourself for this activity.

6. When you have finished exploring directions on the Value Compass, select the best or most promising ideas you've generated in each category (compass direction).

Reimagine It!
Analogy/metaphor idea generation

At a glance

One of the best ways to gain a fresh perspective on an issue, challenge, or opportunity is to use your creativity to reimagine it in the context of an analogy, metaphor, or fictional characterization. By using creative visualization, imagery, storytelling, or fiction, a group can grasp the nature of a challenge in new, visceral ways. This enjoyable technique invites a group to reframe its challenge as either:

1) **An analogy**—a similarity between two things that share common features, properties, or characteristics; for example, *the similarity between a human heart and a mechanical pump.*

2) **A metaphor**—something representational or symbolic of something else; for example, *the battle between Coke and Pepsi for market share as a form of marketing warfare.*

3) **An anthropomorphized character**—animal, object, subject, issue, or situation to which human attributes, traits, or characteristics are ascribed; in other words, bringing a problem or challenge to life as if it were a central character in a Disney movie. For example, characterizing a hurricane as a colossal, one-eyed, swirling rain monster named "Slamming Sammy," an elemental creature that draws its destructive strength from warm ocean waters.

Number of participants 4–12

Duration 30–45 minutes

How to pilot

1. Introduce the challenge to be addressed.

2. Instruct your group to creatively reinterpret the issue, challenge, or opportunity as a colorful analogy, metaphor, or character. Tell them to imagine they are part of a Disney storytelling team with the task of reinterpreting the challenge in a symbolic or metaphorical way, like a story for the big screen.

3. Encourage them to let go of all logical thinking and to have fun engaging the power of their imaginations. Also encourage creative play, such as drawing, storytelling, storyboarding, and making clay model characters (optional).

4. Next, when your group has reimagined the challenge as an analogy, metaphor, or character, ask them to investigate all the different aspects of the story or character to identify any new insights into the challenge.

You can jump-start your group's creative problem-solving efforts by asking the following questions:

"What other types of situations or things does this challenge remind us of?"

"What kinds of metaphors or analogies come to mind?"

"If this situation were a fictional person or character, who would it be?"

"If this situation were an animal or creature, what would it be?"

"If this situation were an object or thing, what would it be?"

"What kind of character would Disney turn this situation into?"

Follow-up questions:

"What would the character's name be?"

"What type of personality would the character have?"

"What is its motivation or reason for being?"

"What nourishes or strengthens the problem? What aggravates it?"

"What forces, substances, or situations does the character fear?"

"What are some solutions for dealing with this character?"

Piloting tips

- This is an imagination-driven activity. You can enhance the process by having arts and crafts supplies on hand to stimulate your group's creativity—boxes of crayons, colored markers, colored paper, modeling clay, glue sticks, pipe cleaners, rolls of brown paper; also toys or props like small dolls, cars, stick-on eyes, noses, mouths, etc.

- Encourage your group to visualize the analogy, metaphor, or character/creature they developed as a drawing, storyboard, or three-dimensional object.

- Ask participants to make a short presentation to share the idea behind their analogy, metaphor, or character. Why did they choose or create it? What story does it tell? What insights did they learn by exploring it? What solutions to the challenge or pathways of opportunities did they discover?

- Pre-storm the challenge before the session—send the goal, objectives, and challenge a few days in advance, and ask everyone to show up with one (or more) ideas about how the challenge can be reinterpreted as an analogy, metaphor, or character/creature.

- To help participants better understand the distinctions between analogy, metaphor, and anthropomorphism, provide each participant a copy of the descriptions on the next page.

More about analogy, metaphor, and anthropomorphosis

Examples of analogy

An analogy draws a direct parallel between two objects, things, concepts, processes, or relationships. It's a way to understand a new idea in terms of ideas that we know from the past. For example:

- Just as the Earth revolves around the sun, an electron revolves around the nucleus.
- What a general is to his/her army, a CEO is to his/her company.
- Fish is to water as bird is to air.
- What a note is to a composer, a word is to a writer.
- What a sail is to a ship, an engine is to a car.
- Our lungs are like bellows that draw air in and out.

Examples of metaphor

A metaphor is a figure of speech that uses a tangible story, image, or thing to represent or express a more intangible (ethereal) thing, quality, or concept. For example:

- There's a new Darwinism in business: Innovate or perish.
- Poor decision-making has landed him/her in a sea of trouble.
- America is a melting pot of different cultures.
- The marketing campaign is running out of steam.
- She/he is a rock star in our sales department.

Examples of anthropomorphism

Anthropomorphosis is the process of ascribing human attributes, traits, or characteristics to an animal, object, subject, issue, situation, or concept. For example:

- Love/attraction can be anthropomorphized into the myth of Cupid, a winged cherub shooting lovers with his arrows.
- A big, diversified company (involved in many industries) can be anthropomorphized into a giant octopus with many tentacles.
- Indecisive management can be anthropomorphized into Doctor Doolittle's "Push-Me/Pull-You" two-headed llama.
- The characteristics of a cereal can be anthropomorphized into three cartoon characters named "Snap," "Crackle," and "Pop."
- A long-lasting battery can be anthropomorphized into a lovable toy rabbit beating a drum (the Eveready Bunny) that keeps going...and going...and going.

Reimagine It!: Solo SmartStorming instructions

1. Focus on the issue, challenge, or opportunity to be addressed.

2. Explore different ways to reinterpret the challenge as a colorful analogy, metaphor, or character. Imagine you are a part of a Disney storytelling/animation team with the task of reinterpreting the challenge in a symbolic or metaphorical way for the big screen. Let go of all logical thinking. Have fun engaging the power of your imagination, and play with creative activities such as drawing or storytelling.

3. Once you have reimagined the challenge as an analogy, metaphor, character, or creature, investigate all the different aspects of the story or character to identify new insights. This process itself can lead to new ways to address the challenge.

4. Thought-provoking questions to ask yourself:

   "What other types of situations or things does this challenge remind you of?"

   "What kinds of metaphors or analogies come to mind?"

   "If this situation were a fictional person or character, who would it be?"

   "If this situation were an animal or creature, what would it be?"

   "If this situation were an object or thing, what would it be?"

   "What kind of character would Disney turn this situation into?"

   Follow-up questions:

   "What would the character's name be?"

   "What type of personality would the character have?"

   "What is its motivation or reason for being?"

   "What nourishes or strengthens the problem? What aggravates it?"

   "What forces, substances, or situations does the character fear?"

   "What are some solutions for dealing with this character?"

For more information about analogy, metaphor, and anthropomorphosis, see previous page.

SCAMPER
Adaptive-thinking idea generation

At a glance

SCAMPER is a well-known idea-generation technique based on the theory that every new invention or innovation is, in some way, shape, form, or function, an adaptation of something that already exists or has existed.

The word "SCAMPER" is an acronym that serves as an innovator's checklist. Each letter of the acronym suggests a different way a group can tinker with the characteristics of a product, service, or process to stimulate totally new ideas:

S = Substitute something
C = Combine it with something else
A = Adapt something (another idea, part, process, etc.)
M = Modify, magnify, or minimize
P = Put to other uses
E = Eliminate (or simplify) something
R = Rearrange (or reverse)

For example, if a product development team in an athletic footwear company wanted to design the next generation of its best-selling running shoe, you could ask the team:

"What aspect of our current running shoe can be *substituted* (ingredient, material, part, pattern, process, etc.)?"

"What can be *combined* (alloyed, attached, integrated, merged, packaged together, etc.)?"

"What can be *adapted* (copied, duplicated, emulated, incorporated, imitated, knocked off, etc.)?"

"What can be *modified, magnified, or minimized* (altered, enlarged, embellished, expanded, reduced, redesigned, reorganized, shrunk, etc.)?"

"What can be *put to other uses* (new functionality, purpose, activities, markets, etc.)?"

"What can be *eliminated* (omitted, reduced, removed, simplified, subtracted, streamlined, etc.)?"

"What can be *rearranged* (reoriented, reorganized, repositioned, reversed, transposed, etc.)?"

Alex Osborn originally developed a list of "idea-spurring questions" that are the basis of the technique. They were later arranged and further developed by author Bob Eberle to form the acronym "SCAMPER."

Number of participants 4–20

Duration 45–60 minutes

How to pilot

1. Introduce the challenge to be addressed.

2. Take your group through each of the seven SCAMPER questions below, one at a time. Be sure to fill in the subject or issue of your specific challenge at the end of each sentence (i.e., to innovate our product, to increase sales, to streamline our billing process).

3. Pause for five to ten minutes after each question to allow your group to generate ideas.

    What can be *substituted* (ingredient, material, part, pattern, personnel, process, etc.)?

    What can be *combined* (alloyed, attached, blended, integrated, merged, packaged together, etc.)?

    What can be *adapted* (copied, cloned, duplicated, emulated, incorporated, imitated, knocked off, matched, etc.)?

    What can be *modified, magnified, or minimized* (altered, enlarged, embellished, expanded, reduced, redesigned, reorganized, shrunk, etc.)?

    What can be *put to other uses* (new function, purpose, design, applications, processes, markets, etc.)?

    What can be *eliminated* (excluded, omitted, removed, simplified, subtracted, streamlined, etc.)?

    What can be *rearranged* (reoriented, reorganized, repositioned, reversed, transposed, etc.)?

4. Harvesting the best ideas: Once the ideation process is completed, instruct the group to select a short list of ideas (from each of the seven SCAMPER categories) it believes best address the challenge. Have a volunteer serve as the Reporter to write down all the best ideas on a large flipchart pad or whiteboard.

(For a list of additional SCAMPER questions you can ask your group, please see 50 Great SCAMPER Questions on pages 232–233.)

Piloting tips

- **Piloting teams:** If your group is large, divide it into a number of smaller teams of four to six. Teams should be of equal size. Instruct each team to select one member to serve as the Reporter to write down the team's ideas.

- Your role as the session's Pilot is to lead your teams through each of the seven questioning steps in the SCAMPER process.

- To keep the activity moving efficiently, set a five- to ten-minute time limit for each of the seven steps. If one or two of the steps in the process stimulates an especially rich vein of new ideas, you are free to extend those segments for a longer period of time.

- **Make SCAMPER fun:** Encourage your group to be spontaneous and have fun with the activity. Challenge them to think outside the box…wild or radical ideas are welcomed, because even the worst-sounding ideas can contain the seed of a great idea within.

- **Try Visual SCAMPER:** For a change of pace, try this technique as a visual problem-solving activity. Simply provide each participant a small pad of sticky notes and a pen. Ask them to sketch or draw any ideas that they have in response to each question. It's helpful to remind your group that artistic talent is not required for this activity. Stick figures and doodles work fine as long as they can communicate the essence of their idea. When the activity is finished, sketches can be arranged on a larger board according to each of the SCAMPER categories.

SCAMPER: Solo SmartStorming instructions

1. Focus on the issue, challenge, or opportunity to be addressed.

2. Ask yourself each of the seven SCAMPER questions below, one at a time. Be sure to fill in the subject/goal of your specific challenge at the end of each sentence (e.g., to increase sales, to streamline our billing process). For each question, take five to ten minutes to generate ideas.

   "What can be *substituted* (ingredient, material, part, pattern, personnel, process, etc.)?"

   "What can be *combined* (alloyed, attached, blended, integrated, merged, packaged together, etc.)?"

   "What can be *adapted* (copied, cloned, duplicated, emulated, incorporated, imitated, knocked off, matched, etc.)?"

   "What can be *modified, magnified, or minimized* (altered, enlarged, embellished, expanded, reduced, redesigned, reorganized, shrunk, etc.)?"

   "What can be *put to other uses* (new function, purpose, design, applications, processes, markets, etc.)?"

   "What can be *eliminated* (excluded, omitted, removed, simplified, subtracted, streamlined, etc.)?"

   "What can be *rearranged* (reoriented, reorganized, repositioned, reversed, transposed, etc.)?"

3. When you are finished, go back through each of the seven SCAMPER categories and select those ideas you believe best address the challenge.

(For a list of additional SCAMPER questions you can ask yourself, please see 50 Great SCAMPER Questions on next pages.)

50 great SCAMPER questions

Here are over fifty thought-provoking questions to help stimulate new creative problem-solving ideas and insights:

Substitute

What other types of ingredients or materials can be substituted?

What other people, places, or things can be substituted?

What other methods, processes, or procedures can be substituted?

What other parts, components, or technology can be substituted?

What other power/energy source can be substituted?

What else can be replaced/interchanged?

What are the most obvious things that can be substituted?

What colors, textures, details, or finishes can be substituted?

Combine

What ingredients, materials, or parts can be combined?

What two or more ideas can be combined?

What else could be added, merged, or blended?

What steps, functions, or processes can be combined?

What features can be combined?

What functions can be integrated/combined?

How can we combine uses with something else?

How can we combine our efforts and resources with others to succeed?

Adapt

What else is like/similar to this?

What can be copied or imitated?

How can _____ be adjusted/changed to fit another purpose?

What has worked before?

Who is/what is a highly successful role model to emulate?

What product, service, or process is worthy of copying/emulating?

What are five other uses or purposes we can imagine for this?

How can _____ be adapted to provide greater/additional value?

Modify/Magnify/Minimize

In what ways can it be bigger, stronger, longer lasting, or more durable?

In what ways can it be smaller, lighter, shorter, or more compact?

In what ways can it be embellished, exaggerated, or more attention grabbing?

How can it be faster or take less time?

How can it be friendlier and easier to use?

In what ways can color, form, function, or design be improved?

What new/additional features can be added?

What can add extra value?

Put to Other Uses

In what ways can _____ be used other than its original intended use?

Who else might be able/interested to use _____ ?

What other markets/niches can _____ be used in?

What else can _____ be used for other than its original purpose?

What are five different ways _____ can be used?

What other unmet needs can _____ fulfill?

What new ways can _____ be used, marketed, or sold?

In what ways would a bunch of five-year-olds use/play with _____ ?

Eliminate

What can be taken away, removed, or streamlined?

What parts or pieces aren't really necessary?

What rules, steps, or procedures aren't really necessary?

What can be subtracted, deleted, or omitted?

What would not be missed if eliminated?

What is unnecessary or redundant?

What aspect of our product or service provides little value?

What can be minimized, condensed, or compacted?

Rearrange

What parts or features can be rearranged?

What components can be interchanged?

How can _____ be laid out in a different pattern/configuration?

What can be reversed?

What can be reorganized or transposed?

What can be redesigned or reengineered?

What can be reformulated?

What would be unexpected/provocative?

SmartSWOT
Exploring multiple viewpoints

At a glance

The SWOT Analysis is a well-known strategic-planning technique that helps groups and organizations identify the **Strengths** and **Weaknesses**, as well as the **Opportunities** and **Threats,** they face in relation to an issue, situation, or challenge. The insights gained from this analysis can help them more effectively leverage their strengths, minimize weaknesses or blind spots, mitigate threats, and identify and capitalize on new opportunities.

SmartStorming's SmartSWOT adds several additional viewpoints to the traditional SWOT analysis methodology, to help your group gain a well-rounded set of valuable insights for creative problem solving.

The seven SmartSWOT perspectives

Strengths—The traits or characteristics of the organization, team, product, service, or process that provide a distinct advantage (e.g., a good reputation, proprietary know-how, a strong brand name, exclusive resources or technology).

Weaknesses—The traits or characteristics of the organization, team, product, service, or process that can be perceived as a disadvantage (e.g., a poor or unreliable reputation, a weak brand name, high cost structure, the lack of access to resources or technology).

Opportunities—The external factors, influences, situations, or conditions that can offer new or favorable circumstances for profit, growth, or improvement (e.g., emerging new markets, unfulfilled customer needs, deregulation of the market, emerging technologies).

Threats—The external factors, influences, changes, or challenges that can potentially undermine or thwart the organization's ability to profit, grow, or thrive (e.g., new or increased competition, a shift in customer taste or preference, new restrictive regulations or barriers to trade).

Facts/Information—An objective accounting of the hard facts, data, or information that can affect or influence the issue, situation, or challenge.

Perceptions—The subjective perceptions, beliefs, opinions, and biases that can affect or influence the issue, situation, or challenge.

What Else/All Else—All other miscellaneous facts, perceptions, issues, influences, or considerations that arise that do not fit neatly into one of the other categories.

Number of participants 4–25

Duration 45–60 minutes

How to pilot

Setting the stage for your activity:

- Explain each of the seven SmartSWOT perspectives to your group and how they pertain to the topic or challenge to be addressed.

- The goal of this activity is to have the group (as a whole) explore each of the seven facets of the topic or challenge, one at a time, from the same frame of reference. If someone offers a perspective that would fall under a different SmartSWOT category than the group is currently exploring, ask the group member to hold his or her insight until it's time to explore that specific perspective.

- All comments, insights, and opinions should be welcomed as a valid viewpoint to consider. There is no need for arguments or debates. It's perfectly okay if contradictory facts or opinions appear in different categories.

- Have the session Reporter write down all the insights.

(Note: For a helpful list of SmartSWOT questions you can ask any group, please see 35 Great SmartSWOT Questions on pages 239–240.)

Piloting the SmartSWOT activity

1. Introduce the challenge to be addressed.

2. Begin with the category: **Facts**
   The goal of this first category is to identify the *objective* information, facts, or data surrounding the issue, situation, challenge, or opportunity to determine what information is known to be true, what information may be questionable, and what information may still be needed. Try and keep subjective (personal) beliefs, opinions, or biases out of this discerning process—you are looking for just the facts.

   Have the Reporter write the word "Facts" at the top of a large sheet of flipchart paper; then record all of the group's insights and comments. Make sure the Reporter numbers each item on the list.

3. Next, move on to the second category: **Perceptions**
   The goal of this next category is to identify the *subjective* (personal) feelings, beliefs, perceptions, hunches, and opinions surrounding the challenge or problem. This is an opportunity for the group to freely share its likes, dislikes, uncertainties, and intuitive impressions about the issue, situation, challenge,

or opportunity, or the organization's ability to succeed; also include any notable perceptions from others outside the situation or organization. (Note: It's important to keep this portion of the activity 100 percent free of any judgments or criticism. All subjective perceptions, opinions, and feelings are welcome as viewpoints to consider.)

Have the Reporter write the word "Perceptions" at the top of a new sheet of flipchart paper; then record all insights and comments.

4. Then move on to the third category: **Strengths**
   The goal of this category is to identify those traits or characteristics of the organization, team, product, service, or process that provide a distinct advantage (e.g., a good reputation, proprietary know-how, a strong brand name, exclusive access to resources or technology).

   Have the Reporter write the word "Strengths" at the top of a new sheet of flipchart paper, and record all insights and comments.

5. Next, move on to the fourth category: **Weaknesses**
   The goal of this category is to identify those traits or characteristics of the organization, team, product, service, or process that can be perceived as a disadvantage (e.g., a poor or unreliable reputation, a weak brand name, high cost structure, the lack of access to resources or technology).

   Have the Reporter write the word "Weaknesses" at the top of a new sheet of flipchart paper; then record all insights and comments.

6. Next, move on to the fifth category: **Opportunities**
   The goal of this category is to identify those external factors, influences, or things that can offer new or favorable circumstances for profit, growth, or improvement (e.g., emerging markets, unfulfilled customer needs, market deregulation, emerging technologies).

   Have the Reporter write the word "Opportunities" at the top of a new sheet of flipchart paper; then record all insights and comments.

7. Next, move on to the sixth category: **Threats**
   The goal of this category is to identify those external factors, influences, changes, or challenges that can undermine or threaten the organization's ability to profit, grow, or thrive, or undermine its ability to solve or address the challenge at hand (e.g., new or increased competition, a shift in customer taste or preference, new restrictive regulations, or barriers to trade).

   Have the Reporter write the word "Threats" at the top of a new sheet of flipchart paper and record all insights and comments.

8. Finally, move on to the seventh and final category: **What Else/All Else**

   The goal of this category is to identify any other miscellaneous insights, facts, perceptions, issues, influences, or considerations that do not fit neatly into one of the previous categories and that could be relevant to the challenge at hand.

   Have the Reporter write "What Else/All Else" at the top of a new sheet of flipchart paper; then record any insights and comments.

9. Harvesting ideas: Post all seven completed category sheets on a wall next to each other. Review each category, one by one, with the group to identify the most relevant insights or ideas within each category.

   Next, summarize the findings with your group, then ask them to SmartStorm what new insights or opportunities have emerged in relation to solving or addressing the challenge. Have the session Reporter record the group's insights.

Piloting tips

- As a reminder, the goal of this activity is to have the group (as a whole) explore each of the seven facets of the topic/challenge one at a time, from the same frame of reference. Try to keep your group aligned and focused on one topic at a time; avoid conversations that jump back and forth between different categories.

- Be sure to establish a judgment-free zone where all points of view are welcome. Encourage participants to share their ideas and opinions freely; establish the rule that states, "There is no such thing as a bad, wrong, or erroneous idea or opinion."

- Watch to make sure everyone has the opportunity to contribute. If one or two participants are dominating the conversation, thank them for their insights, then say, "Let's hear some new perspectives from other group members."

SmartSWOT: Solo SmartStorming instructions

1. Focus on the issue, challenge, or opportunity to be addressed.

2. Begin with the category: **Facts**
   Write the word "Facts" at the top of a sheet of paper. Make a list of the objective information, facts, or data surrounding the issue, situation, challenge, or opportunity to determine what information is known to be true, what information may be questionable, and what information may still be needed.

3. Next, move on to the second category: **Perceptions**
   Write the word "Perceptions" at the top of a sheet of paper. Make a list of all feelings, beliefs, hunches, and opinions surrounding the challenge or problem. Identify likes, dislikes, uncertainties, and gut feelings about the issue, situation, challenge, opportunity, or your/your organization's ability to succeed.

4. Then move on to the third category: **Strengths**
   Write the word "Strengths" at the top of a sheet of paper. Make a list of all the traits or characteristics you, your team, your organization, your product, service, or process provides that offer a distinct advantage (e.g., a good reputation, proprietary know-how, a strong brand name, exclusive access to resources or technology).

5. Next, move on to the fourth category: **Weaknesses**
   Write the word "Weaknesses" at the top of a sheet of paper. Make a list of all of those traits or characteristics you, your team, your organization, your product, service, or process perceived as a disadvantage (e.g., a poor or unreliable reputation, a weak brand name, high cost structure, the lack of access to resources or technology).

6. Next, move on to the fifth category: **Opportunities**
   Write the word "Opportunities" at the top of a sheet of paper. Make a list of all the external factors, influences, or things that can offer new or favorable circumstances for profit, growth, or improvement (e.g., emerging markets, unfulfilled customer needs, market deregulation, emerging technologies).

7. Next, move on to the sixth category: **Threats**
   Write the word "Threats" at the top of a sheet of paper. Make a list of all the external factors, influences, changes, or challenges that can undermine or threaten you, your team, or your organization's ability to profit, grow, or thrive, or undermine the ability to solve or address the challenge at hand (e.g., new or increased competition, a shift in customer taste or preference, new restrictive regulations, or barriers to trade).

8. Finally, move on to the seventh and last category: **What Else/All Else**
   Write "What Else/All Else" at the top of a sheet of paper. Make a list of any other miscellaneous insights, facts, perceptions, issues, influences, or considerations that arise that do not fit neatly into one of the previous categories and could be relevant to the challenge at hand (e.g., "What else haven't I/we thought of yet?" "Are there any blind spots I/we might have missed?" "What areas or issues might I/we have stepped over or ignored?").

9. When finished, place all seven completed category sheets on a wall, next to each other. Look over all of your insights to see if you can identify the most relevant ideas/insights within each category that can help solve or address the challenge.

35 great SmartSWOT questions

Here are thought-provoking questions to help stimulate new creative problem-solving ideas and insights:

For exploring **Facts**

What are the facts surrounding this challenge, problem, or opportunity?

What information, facts, or data is/are important to consider?

What information, facts, or data do we need?

What information, facts, or data don't we know or understand?

What unanswered questions need to be addressed?

For exploring **Perceptions**

How does the group feel about this issue, challenge, or opportunity?

What is the group sensing in particular?

What do you feel are the most important things for us to consider?

What does the group's intuition or gut feeling tell us?

What might people outside this situation think or feel about this?

For exploring **Strengths**

What are our greatest strengths and assets?

What do we do better than anyone else?

What unique advantages do we have or offer?

What sets us uniquely apart from all others?

What unique resources, know-how, and capabilities can we draw upon?

For exploring **Weaknesses**

What are our weaknesses as an organization or team?

What do we need to improve? Where do we need to make these improvements?

Where are we vulnerable or at risk?

What assets, resources, know-how, or experience do we lack or need?

How do our weaknesses interfere with our ability to succeed?

For exploring **Opportunities**

What are the most apparent opportunities we can see or imagine?

What emerging trends play to our strengths?

What product or service area(s) have others overlooked?

What kinds of internal resources can we leverage in new ways?

What challenges can be turned into opportunities?

For exploring **Threats**

What kinds of threats or obstacles do we face?

What kinds of competitive threats do we face?

What kinds of internal threats do we face?

What kinds of external threats do we face?

In what area are we most vulnerable?

For exploring **What Else/All Else**

What else haven't we thought of yet?

Are there any blind spots we might have missed?

What's been left unsaid or understated?

What unaddressed areas or issues might we have stepped over or ignored?

If there's one important area or issue that's been left out, what is it?

Think Much, Much Bigger

Idea-expansion process

At a glance

Contrary to popular belief, most organizations do *not* suffer from a lack of new ideas. But in today's innovation-driven world, a good idea just isn't good enough!

This idea-building technique is an effective way to take the most promising ideas previously generated in a SmartStorming session and push or expand them to an exponentially bigger/larger realm for significantly greater potential. In other words, Think Much, Much Bigger helps you take good ideas and transform them into game-changing concepts.

Number of participants 4–12

Duration 45–60 minutes

How to pilot

Setting the stage for your activity:

- To prepare, identify a short list of promising ideas (previously developed) that you believe have the potential to become bigger and better ideas. These ideas will serve as the catalysts for this idea-expansion activity.

- Note: This idea-generation activity is a three-part process.

Piloting your activity:

1. Introduce the challenge to be addressed.

2. Next, select an existing idea for the group to consider. Be sure to describe the concept (and context) behind the idea so everyone understands it clearly.

3. **Idea expansion level 1:** Begin the idea-expansion process by asking your group, "In what new and different ways can we make this concept a BIGGER and better idea (in concept, scope, magnitude, importance, effectiveness, or in added value, benefits, features, etc.)?"

   Encourage your group to think outside the box and encourage wild, even audacious ideas.

4. When finished, ask the group to quickly select what it considers the single biggest or best idea developed.

5. **Idea expansion level 2:** Next, instruct your group to take that selected idea and imagine, "In what new and different ways can we make this concept a MUCH BIGGER and better idea (in concept, scope, magnitude, importance, effectiveness, or in added value, benefits, features, etc.)?"

6. When finished, ask the group to once again quickly select what it considers the single biggest or best idea developed in this step.

7. **Idea expansion level 3:** For one last time, see how far your group can push the edge of the envelope to see what's possible. Instruct your group to take the idea selected and boldly imagine, "In what new and different ways can we make this concept a MUCH, MUCH BIGGER and better idea (in concept, scope, magnitude, importance, effectiveness, or in added value, benefits, features, etc.)?"

Note: By this point, the group may be laughing or groaning, but tell them to press on—often the best ideas come when a group thinks it has exhausted all possible ideas.

8. When finished, select a short list of the biggest, best, and most innovative ideas. For fun, compare those ideas to the original idea that served as the catalyst for the process. We are confident the new concepts will indeed be much, much bigger and better ideas.

9. **Optional step:** You and your group can repeat this three-part idea-expansion process with each of the remaining ideas on your original list. Be sure to briefly discuss each idea first to make sure everyone understands the concept clearly.

Piloting tips

- Parallel process ideas: If you divide your group into small teams of equal size, you can have teams work on different ideas (from the original short list) simultaneously. Simply ask each team to select an idea from the original list, then take itself through each of the three parts of the idea-expansion process.

- Encourage participants to generate ideas as spontaneously and quickly as possible at each step in the process. Note: It's normal for the pace of the action to slow down as participants are forced to think more and more expansively in each successive step. It's wise to continuously monitor the progress of the group and issue verbal prompts to keep the activity moving efficiently.

- If group members get stuck and can't imagine new ways to make ideas bigger, you can help stimulate new avenues of thinking by asking:

  "If we had no limitations, what could we do/say?"

  "If we knew we couldn't fail, what could/would we do?"

  "What is the most audacious thing we could do, say, or imagine?"

  "What are other ways we can add greater value or additional benefits?"

Think Much, Much Bigger: Solo SmartStorming instructions

Setting the stage for your activity

Identify a short list of the most promising ideas generated during an earlier session. These ideas will serve as the catalysts and stimuli for this idea-expansion activity. Note: This solo idea-expansion activity is a three-part process.

To begin

1. Focus on the issue, challenge, or opportunity to be addressed.

2. **Idea expansion level 1:** Pick an idea, then imagine, "In what ways could this concept be made into a BIGGER and better idea (in concept, scope, magnitude, importance, effectiveness, or in added value, benefits, features, etc.)?" Generate as many bigger and better ideas as possible.

3. When finished, select what you consider the single best idea.

4. **Idea expansion level 2:** Next, take that selected idea and imagine, "In what ways could this concept be made into a MUCH BIGGER and better idea (in concept, scope, magnitude, importance, effectiveness, or in added value, benefits, features, etc.)?"

5. When finished, select what you consider the single best idea from that round.

6. **Idea expansion level 3:** One last time, take the idea you selected and imagine, "In what ways could this concept be made into a MUCH, MUCH BIGGER and better idea (in concept, scope, magnitude, importance, effectiveness, or in added value, benefits, features, etc.)?" Really push the envelope during this last round.

7. When finished, select a short list of your biggest, best, and most innovative ideas.

Tip

- If you get stuck at any point and can't imagine new ways to make ideas bigger, you can discover new avenues of thinking by asking yourself:

  "If there were no limitations, what would/could be possible?"

  "If I knew I couldn't fail, what could be done or achieved?"

  "What is the most audacious thing that can be done or imagined?"

  "What if...?"

Vision Boards
Visual inspiration and idea generation

At a glance

It has often been said that a picture is worth a thousand words. Images possess the power to inspire a wealth of fresh, new ideas. Also known as mood boards or inspiration boards, these visual collages are often used by creative professionals like fashion, product, and interior designers and architects to explore new ways of approaching a project and visualizing future realities. Why? Because images can quickly provoke strong, emotional responses that inspire new insights, often much more effectively than words alone.

When tackling a project or challenge, or exploring new opportunities, vision boards can very quickly help a group develop a clear understanding of what they find appealing, what is possible, what works, and what doesn't. Vision boards can act as inspirational stimuli for stocking the creative pond before generating ideas.

Plus, they're fun! Searching online for interesting, inspirational images, or even combing through magazines, catalogs, and books allows your imagination to run wild.

Number of participants Any size group

Duration 45–90 minutes

What you will need

- Poster/illustration board for each participant (if working in teams, one large-size board for each team).
- Pictures/photos—A large variety of different images, either downloaded from online sources (such as Flickr, Pinterest and Google Image Search), various types of magazines (such as lifestyle, fashion, nature, business, or sports), catalogs, photographs, reference materials, etc. You can also ask participants to bring in their own images.
- Scissors and glue sticks for each participant.
- Drawing paper and color markers or crayons.
- Tabletop work surfaces for everyone to spread out and work.

How to pilot

Setting the stage for your activity:

- To begin, provide each participant with a sheet of poster board, a pair of scissors, and a glue stick.
- Also provide participants with a variety of images, as well as some magazines, catalogs, or other visual materials they can use and share.

Piloting the activity:

1. Introduce the challenge to be addressed.

2. Next, instruct participants to create their own vision boards by cutting and pasting together (in a collage fashion) any images they feel represent their feelings, insights, and ideas about the topic or challenge.

   Participants should include any images they like, even if they don't seem directly related to the topic—as long as they inspire an insight or idea.

   For example, if you are generating ideas for ways to save on operating expenses in your company, an image of an arctic landscape might suggest that the air-conditioning in the office is kept at too low a temperature. Raising the thermostat could help reduce expenses.

3. When participants have finished creating their vision boards, ask them to take turns briefly discussing their boards—the meaning behind the images they chose, plus any ideas or insights that their board inspired.

4. After everyone has shared, encourage the group as a whole to discuss and build on any interesting insights or ideas.

5. Have a volunteer serve as the session Reporter to write down the ideas and insights presented.

Piloting tips

- Encourage participants to have fun! Being too serious or analytical in thinking can turn vision boards into a tedious task. The more imaginative and playful participants can be, the more interesting and valuable their vision board(s) will be.

- Participants can also draw their own pictures and add them to their collage. Be sure to have some drawing paper and color markers or crayons on hand.

Vision Boards for Pre-Storming

- Vision boards are also an ideal activity to use for pre-storming. Here's how it works: A few days prior to the session, ask participants to create a vision board based on the challenge. Tell them that their vision board is the price of entry into the session.

  Begin the session with participants taking turns presenting their vision boards to the group. Afterward, encourage the group to discuss what insights, ideas, or themes resonated as important to addressing the challenge at hand. Have a volunteer serve as the session Reporter to write down all ideas of interest.

What If...?
Challenging conventions/status quo

At a glance

Real, game-changing innovation is driven by bold, visionary ideas—ideas with the power to break through the barriers of conventional thinking and redefine what's possible.

This thought-provoking, three-part technique is designed to help your group challenge the status quo by encouraging it to think as far outside the box as possible—to shoot for the most ambitious, forward-thinking, and disruptive *What if...?* ideas imaginable. Afterward, the most intriguing ideas are reevaluated to determine how they can be adapted or modified to become practical, real-world solutions.

Here are some examples of bold *What if...?* thinking that have become realities:

What if...we built a new kind of reusable spaceship that can make space tourism an affordable reality? (Virgin Galactic's vision for space tourism)

What if...all of our customers' digital content were stored in the "cloud" rather than on their electronic devices? (Amazon.com's vision for Cloud storage)

What if...we designed smart products that could be operated with a single function button? (Apple's vision for the iPhone and iPad)

What if...our search engine could anticipate what a user was searching for the moment his/her fingers started typing? (Google's vision for "Google Instant")

Number of participants 6–18

Duration 45–60 minutes

How to pilot Note: This technique is a three-part idea-building process.

1. Introduce the challenge to be addressed.

2. **Part 1: Generate *What If...?* ideas**
   Ask participants to think as far outside the box as possible. You're looking for the boldest, most far-fetched, radical, or even audacious ideas they can imagine to address the challenge at hand. You can help stimulate your group's imagination by asking the following prompts that begin with the words *What if...?*:

   "What if there were no limitations whatsoever on what we could do, say, or create? What would be possible?"

   "What if we had all the time, money, and resources in the world? What would be possible?"

   "What if we could change anything we wanted? What becomes possible?"

"What if we could channel the creative genius of Einstein, Disney, or Steve Jobs? What innovative ideas or solutions could we imagine?"

"What if we time-traveled one hundred years into the future; how would we address this challenge?"

3. **Part 2: Select the most provocative ideas**
   Ask your group to look over all of its visionary ideas, then narrow them down to a short list of the most provocative or forward-thinking ideas.

4. **Part 3: Transform the provocative into the possible**
   Next, instruct your group to take each of the ideas on its short list and figure out ways to adapt, modify, or transform them into real-world applications or solutions.

   You can help prompt your group's problem-solving thinking by asking:

   "In what ways can these audacious ideas be adapted, modified, reimagined, or reengineered into a good real-world solution?"

   "Is there a seed or hint of a useful, practical solution hiding within this outrageous concept? How can we retain that seed and turn it into a practical solution?"

   "What are the most obvious ways to translate this radical idea into a real-world solution?"

   "How can we harness the power of this idea and package it in a more accessible/practical way?"

   "Is there another version or variation on this wild idea that would make it a good practical one?"

5. At each step in the process, have a volunteer Reporter write down the group's ideas.

Piloting tips

- This exercise should be a fun, exciting experience. It's designed to help shift a group out of linear, day-to-day thinking and propel it into a fertile realm of the imagination. So encourage your group to really let go of inhibitions or limitations.

- Encourage participants to collaboratively build upon one another's ideas.

- If a group runs into difficulty transforming a wild idea into a more practical one, re-ask the questions in Part 3 of these instructions. Also, encourage them to explore different ways a wild idea can be reimagined into a great solution.

What If...? Solo SmartStorming instructions

1. **Part 1: Generating *What If...?* ideas**
   Focus on the issue, challenge, or opportunity to be addressed. Deliberately think as far outside the box as possible. Try to think of the wildest, boldest, most far-fetched, radical, or audacious ideas you can imagine to address the challenge at hand. Spark your imagination by asking yourself the following prompts that begin with the words *What if...?*

   "What if there were no limitations whatsoever on what could be done or created? What would be possible?"

   "What if there were all the time, money, and resources in the world? What would be possible?"

   "What if anything could be changed or manipulated any way you wanted? What becomes possible?"

   "What if I could channel the creative genius of Einstein, Disney, or Steve Jobs? What innovative ideas/solutions could I imagine?"

   "What if I time-traveled one hundred years into the future; how would I address this challenge?"

2. **Part 2: Select the most provocative ideas**
   Look over all of your ideas, then narrow them down to a short list of the most provocative or forward-thinking ideas that can address the challenge.

3. **Part 3: Transform the provocative into the possible**
   Next, take each of the ideas on your short list and work out ways to adapt, modify, or transform them into possible real-world applications or solutions. You can stimulate your creative problem-solving process by asking:

   "In what ways can this audacious idea be adapted, modified, reimagined, or reengineered into a good real-world solution?"

   "Is there a seed or hint of a useful, practical solution hiding within this outrageous concept? How can I retain that seed and turn it into a practical solution?"

   "What are the most obvious ways to translate this radical idea into a real-world solution?"

   "How can I harness the power of this idea and package it in a more accessible/practical way?"

   "Is there another version or variation on this wild idea that would make it a good practical one?"

SmartStorming Value Compass

Value can be defined as the perceived worth, merit, or importance of a product, service, or process compared to its cost. In other words, does it meet or exceed expectations for what it should be or do? Or even more simply, is it worth the price?

This innovative tool can help you imagine new ways to pump up the value proposition of a product, service, or process to make it better, simpler, faster, cheaper, easier to use, more reliable, more satisfying, more beautifully designed, or even more emotionally endearing.

The SmartStorming Value Compass provides reference points to a variety of different ways in which you can drive innovation by adding greater value. To begin, just pick a direction and start imagining ways to add greater value based on that prompt.

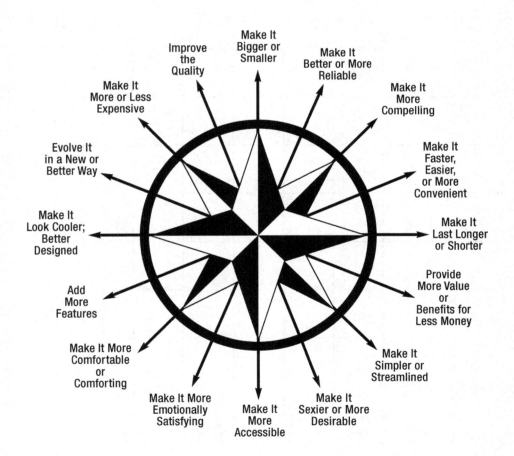

SmartStorming Idea Selection Diagnostic Matrix

This diagnostic tool can help you/your groups identify the most promising ideas with minimal personal subjectivity or bias. To use the matrix, simply post your selection criteria (as key words) across the top. Then write your most promising ideas down the left-hand side (in an abbreviated form). The ideas are then judged against each of the criteria. Those ideas that meet all (or most) of the criteria are solid winners; those ideas that fail to meet three or more of the criteria should be discarded. (For full instructions, please see pages 107–109.)

Selection Criteria:

Ideas:

CHAPTER 21

Guides, Planners, and Worksheets

In this Toolkit chapter, you will find all the support materials you will need to more easily and effectively plan and lead productive SmartStorming sessions.

The pages ahead contain a wealth of useful SmartStorming tools—planners, guides, lists, and even cheat sheets—to help you masterfully design and lead your sessions. While many of these resources appear elsewhere in the book in the chapters that fully describe their use, this chapter is intended to serve as an easy-to-access resource, ready whenever you need to find the right tool for the job.

Guides

- **Rules of the Game**—List of essential rules to tell a group before generating ideas.

- **Rules for Selecting Ideas**—List of rules to tell a group before evaluating and selecting ideas.

- **25 Great Icebreaker Activities**—Instruction guide for twenty-five activities that will help create group alignment and collaboration, and get your session off to a fast start.

- **25 Piloting Questions for Any Challenge**—A handy cheat sheet that provides a range of provocative questions designed to stimulate a group's thinking.

Planning worksheets

- **SmartStorming Pre-Session Planner**—helps you develop a comprehensive blueprint for a successful session.

- **Solo SmartStorming Pre-Session Planner**—helps you develop a comprehensive blueprint for your own individual Solo SmartStorming session.

- **Determining Your Challenge, Goals, and Objectives Worksheet**—helps you gain greater clarity about a challenge, determine your goal(s) and objectives, and develop a compelling challenge statement.

- **SmartStorming Participant Selection Planner**—helps you to determine the best participants (knowledge/experience) to invite to your session.

- **Idea Selection Criteria Worksheet**—helps you determine the objective selection criteria you'll need for evaluating ideas.

- **SmartStorming Next Steps: 5-As Action Planner**—helps you identify the action steps that will need to happen (after your session) to bring your ideas to life.

- **SmartStorming Six-Step Session Flowchart**—a useful reference tool that provides a clear, easy-to-understand bird's-eye view of the sequential steps in the SmartStorming process.

- **Piloting Your First Session Checklist**—a comprehensive checklist designed to help you effectively plan, prepare, and lead your first SmartStorming session.

Rules of the Game

Suspend all judgment
Criticism and judgment will inhibit participants from sharing ideas; ideas will be evaluated later on, during the selection process.

There is no such thing as a bad idea
Hey, you never know. Even the worst-sounding idea can contain the seed of a great idea within it.

Maintain an ego-free zone
In a collaborative group problem-solving effort, the originator of any idea is irrelevant.

Go for quantity, not quality
For every 100 ideas generated, only a few will be truly original ideas with potential.

Embrace wild, audacious ideas
You never know how far you can go until you've gone too far. It's better to push concepts to the edge than be too conservative.

Build upon one another's ideas
A group working collaboratively can generate bigger and better ideas than individuals working alone.

One conversation at a time
Side conversations create distractions and split the session's focus.

Nothing is impossible
Yesterday's impossible ideas (flying, personal computers, 3-D movies, etc.) are today's realities. Think forward.

No texting or emailing during the session
Multitasking is a myth; texting distracts participants from the goal of generating ideas.

The boss speaks last
When an authority figure participates in a brainstorm, his or her comments and opinions often sway or inhibit a group's exploration of ideas. Ask respectfully that the boss hold comments until all others have shared.

(A poster-size version of the Rules of the Game can also be downloaded in digital format at http://SmartStormingBook.com/Toolkit.htm.)

Rules for Selecting Ideas

Just as there are rules of the game for the idea-generation stage of a SmartStorming session, there are a few rules that help foster group alignment in the evaluation and selection process. We recommend sharing these rules with your group or committee before evaluating ideas.

Keep discussions convergent

The goal of the selection process is to narrow down the number of ideas to a short list that best addresses the challenge.

Respect differences of opinion

All points of view are valuable to hear and consider. If differences of opinion arise, focus upon those points the group does agree on.

Radical ideas should not be dismissed

Even the wildest, most audacious idea can contain the seeds of an innovative, game-changing idea.

Select ideas first, improve ideas later

Don't stop the selection process to fix ideas. Select them now; then schedule a meeting to improve ideas at a later time.

Combine ideas where possible

Eliminate redundancy; look for ways to combine ideas that share similar themes, approaches, traits, or attributes.

The boss votes last

When an authority figure participates in the selection process, his or her opinions can often sway a group's evaluation of ideas. Ask the boss to hold comments until all others have discussed the merits of each idea.

25 Great Icebreaker Activities

An icebreaker is an essential part of the SmartStorming process because it helps quickly free up participants' attention from outside concerns, lower interpersonal barriers, and foster an atmosphere of spontaneous collaboration.

Here are twenty-five proven icebreaker activities that will help get creative juices flowing and your session off to a fast start.

1. Pre-Storming

A few days prior to your session, instruct participants to pre-storm two to three initial ideas for how to solve the challenge at hand. At the start of your session, begin your icebreaker activity by asking everyone to take turns sharing their initial ideas. Once participants have shared ideas, challenge the group to see if they can find creative ways to improve or evolve the most promising ones, or combine two (or more) ideas to create something altogether new.

2. Roses Are Red

Ask participants to compose a simple four-line rhyming poem that incorporates some aspect of the challenge and a solution. For example:
Roses are red,
Lilies are white,
Higher prices haven't helped us,
But a new website might!
Next, ask each participant to stand and recite his or her poem to the group.

3. Think Like a Famous Problem-Solver

Divide your group into small innovation teams. Ask each team to select a famous visionary, innovator, or creative problem-solver (living or legend), such as Steve Jobs, Donald Trump, Oprah Winfrey, Walt Disney, Albert Einstein, Mother Teresa, or Picasso. Next, instruct the teams to generate ideas for how to solve the challenge in the same style and manner its iconic leader might have. For example, "In what ways would Donald Trump solve our sales issue?"

4. What If…?

Ask everyone to silently write down three of the wildest, most ambitious, or audacious *What if…?* ideas they can imagine to solve the challenge. In this fun, anything goes icebreaker activity, the more imaginative the concepts, the better! Afterward, have participants take turns sharing their *What if…?* ideas with the group.

Option: Invite everyone to search for ways some of the wild ideas can be adapted or modified to become practical, real-world solutions.

5. Future Perfect

Ask your group to imagine what the ideal solution to the challenge would look and feel like, in its most perfect form. Then have the group work backward, through deductive reasoning and leaps of imagination, to identify the steps necessary to achieve their vision.

6. Idea Sprinting

Idea Sprinting is a fun, fast-paced, beat-the-clock activity for generating ideas. To begin, give your group a challenge or problem to solve. Next, challenge your group to generate a target number of ideas within a tight time frame. For example, "Let's shoot for twenty (or more) new ideas in five minutes." This process is very effective for getting the creative juices flowing and generating an abundance of new ideas very quickly.

7. Guess My Secret Talent

Ask everybody to write down a special talent or ability they possess that nobody in the room knows about. Participants then pass their papers to the Pilot, who reads them aloud. Everybody tries to guess which talent belongs to whom.

8. Cartoon Caption Contest

Find an interesting cartoon and eliminate the caption. Present it to your group and have them each write a new caption. The cleverest new caption wins. (You can find excellent *New Yorker*-style cartoons at www.cartoonbank.com.)

9. Animal Personality

Ask each participant to answer the question, "What animal best represents your personality and why?"

10. Superpowers

Ask, "If you could have just one superpower, what would it be and why?" Examples: the ability to fly, the ability to travel through time, the power of invisibility, the ability to read minds, etc.

11. Dream Vacation

If you could go on a two-week, all-expenses-paid dream vacation anywhere in the world, where would you go, and why? What would you do there?

12. Quick Million

Ask participants to imagine the fastest way to make a million dollars without playing the lottery...or resorting to a life of crime.

13. Things in Common

Partner people up and give them two minutes to discover three things they have in common. Then have each pair share their discovery with the entire group.

14. Dinner with the Famous

If you could have dinner with any three famous celebrities or historical figures (past or present), who would you invite, and why?

15. One Truth and a Lie

Participants take turns stating one truth and one lie about themselves. The group must decide which statement is true and which is false.

16. Worst Job

Each participant describes his or her worst or first job.

17. My Own Reality Show

If you were to star in your own reality TV series, what would it be called? Why?

18. SmartStorm the Absurd

Have the group quickly and energetically SmartStorm ideas for an absurd challenge. Examples:
How can the beef industry convince vegetarians to buy its products?
How can the ice cream industry sell more of its products in Alaska?
How can the hot tub industry increase sales in the Caribbean?

19. Celebrity Spouse

If you could marry any celebrity, who would it be, and why?

20. Collaborative Storytelling

Begin by having your group form a circle. Select one person to begin telling a story. It can be about any subject in any genre—fiction, nonfiction, or fairy tale. They simply begin a story. After a few sentences, they look at the person to their right and hand off the storyline. The next person must take the story in any direction he or she wishes. The storytelling continues around the circle until the person who started the story is reached. He or she gets to create the ending.

21. Desert Island Wish List

Ask your group, "If you were stranded on a desert island, what three things would you want to have in your possession? How do you plan to use those items on the island?"

22. The Story of Your Name

Each participant tells either what their name means or where it comes from, and if they think that it accurately represents them as a person. If not, and they could rename themselves, what name would they choose, and why?

23. Lucky Lottery Tickets

Give each group member a real, scratch-off lottery ticket. Have each person take turns describing what he or she would do if they won the jackpot prize. When everyone has shared, have the group simultaneously scratch off their tickets to see if anyone won! The winner may be excused from the meeting to celebrate.

24. Time Traveler

If you could go back (or forward) in time, what year or period would you go to, and why?

25. Yes, and...

This well-known and popular improvisation technique is an excellent ice-breaker, and sets the stage for positive collaboration during the session. Begin a simple story for the group; for example, "Once upon a time there was a man who lived in a blue house. And right next door lived a woman in a green house." Then pass the story on to the person to your left, who must start off by saying, "Yes, and..." and then continue the story. The idea here is that they must accept your storyline ("yes") and add to it ("and"). Saying "no" or "but" is not allowed. When everyone has contributed to the story, either begin a new one or just continue with the same story.

Note: You can invite your group to create their own list of fun icebreaker activities.

25 Piloting Questions for Any Challenge

Here are twenty-five effective questions you can ask in regard to any challenge to stimulate your group's imagination and problem-solving ability:

What is the simplest, most obvious solution to this challenge?

What are three other ways to solve/address this challenge?

If all limitations were taken away, what would we do or say?

If we knew we couldn't fail, what would we do, try, or pursue?

Let's quickly free-associate all the things that __(subject)__ reminds us of.

What else is similar to/different from this/that?

What is the most audacious thing we can do, say, or imagine?

What would Apple, Google, or Nike do in this situation?

What haven't we thought of yet?

What's the most important thing to focus on here?

What are some radically new or different ways to approach this challenge?

What idea(s) can we push further?

What possibilities have we missed or not considered yet?

What if we…?

What can we simplify, combine, reverse, modify, or eliminate?

If we dug down deeper, what would we discover?

How would a five-year-old solve this challenge?

What opportunities haven't we seen or taken advantage of yet?

Where is there an unmet need we can fulfill?

How would they solve this challenge fifty years in the future?

What are some of the worst ideas we can think of? (Wait for bad ideas to be offered, then ask...) How can we reverse them to find the seeds of a good idea?

How can we take this wild idea and make it more practical/applicable?

What do our customers really want, need, or desire?

What would an insanely great idea or solution look like?

In what ways can we turn this challenge into a golden opportunity?

These 25 Piloting Questions for Any Challenge can also downloaded in digital format at http://SmartStormingBook.com/Toolkit.htm.

SmartStorming Pre-Session Planner

The SmartStorming Pre-Session Planner helps you develop a comprehensive blueprint for leading a successful SmartStorming session. It will help you clarify your challenge, goal, and objectives; identify the best participants to invite; determine the best ideation techniques and selection criteria to use; and discern the best action steps to take once your session has ended.

Be sure to set aside some quality time to carefully think through and fill in each of the planning sections below.

1. **Goal/Objective:** What specific outcome, end result, or deliverable do you wish to achieve from this session?

2. **Challenge Statement:** What is the simplest, most concise and compelling way to present this challenge? (Formulate a thought-provoking question, e.g., "In what ways can we...?")

3. **Participants:** Who are the best people (based on talent/knowledge/experience) to help you succeed? Create a problem-solving dream team. Be sure to invite diversity.

4. **Background Information:** What essential information, data, or context does your group need to know? What sources of inspiration would be helpful?

5. **Icebreaker:** What activity would quickly foster a spirit of collaboration and focus the group's attention? (See 25 Great Icebreaker Activities on page 255.)

6. **Ideation Techniques:** What idea-generation techniques would best inspire your group's problem-solving thinking in new, innovative ways? (Select two or three different techniques for your session. See Ideation Techniques in Chapter 20.)

7. **Selection Criteria:** What specific objective criteria will you use as a yardstick for measuring the merits of a winning idea? (See Idea Selection Criteria Worksheet on page 264.)

8. **Next Steps:** What specific action steps need to occur immediately after this session? Who are the best people to assign responsibilities to?

Solo SmartStorming Pre-Session Planner

This version of the Pre-Session Planner will help you develop a comprehensive blueprint for your own Solo SmartStorming session. It will help you clarify your goals/objectives; identify the support you need; determine the best ideation techniques and selection criteria to use; and establish what action steps need to occur after you've selected your best ideas.

1. Situation: The specific issue, challenge, or opportunity to be addressed is:

2. Goal/Objective: The specific outcome or deliverable I wish to achieve is:

3. Support: The people whose specific talent, knowledge, and experience I can call upon (or access via social media) to help me succeed are:

4. Background Information: The essential information, data, or context I need to know/understand is:

5. Stocking the Pond: Some rich sources of inspiration for this project are:

6. Ideation Techniques: The idea-generation techniques I plan to use to best inspire my problem-solving thinking in new, innovative ways are (select two or three different Solo SmartStorming techniques from Chapter 20):

7. Selection Criteria: The five specific objective criteria I will use as a yardstick for measuring the merits of ideas are (see Idea Selection Criteria Worksheet on page 264):

8. Next Steps: The specific action steps that will need to occur after I have selected my winning ideas are:

Determining Your Challenge, Goals, and Objectives Worksheet

This worksheet can help you gain greater clarity about a challenge; determine your goal(s) and objectives; develop a compelling challenge statement; and determine the target number (and types) of ideas you wish your group to achieve.

1. What is the specific issue, challenge, or opportunity to be addressed?

2. What is/are the most likely, specific underlying cause(s) of this issue, challenge, or opportunity (its point of origin)?

3. What would need to change in order for this issue, challenge, or opportunity to be permanently solved/addressed?

4. What are the specific goal(s) and objective(s) of your SmartStorming session?

5. What is the most concise and compelling way to state this issue, challenge, or opportunity (Challenge Statement)?

6. What deliverables (the target number and type[s] of ideas) do you want your group to generate in your session?

SmartStorming Participant Selection Planner

Who you invite to your SmartStorming session can have a dramatic impact on its ultimate success. When you deliberately include a diverse group from different backgrounds, genders, age groups, talents, skills, knowledge, and expertise, you increase your group's ability to deliver innovative solutions.

This participant selection planner will help you to decide the best people to invite to your session and, just as importantly, *not* to invite.

1. Situation: The specific issue, challenge, or opportunity to be addressed is:

2. Skills: The people with the best skills/talents to help solve this challenge are:

3. Knowledge: The people with the best knowledge/understanding to help solve this challenge are:

4. Experience: The people with the best experience/expertise to help solve this challenge are:

5. Creativity: The people who can help inspire fresh, new thinking are:

6. Diversity: The people who can help bring fresh, new perspectives are:

7. Outside perspectives: The people outside the team, company, and organization who can bring new skills, knowledge, expertise, or perspective are:

8. Who not to invite: The people who should *not* be invited to this session (Attention Seekers, Dominating Personalities, Idea Assassins, etc.) are:

Idea Selection Criteria Worksheet

Your selection criteria serve as the objective benchmarks (reference points) to help identify those specific characteristics, attributes, or benefits a winning idea must possess in order to successfully address the challenge at hand.

To determine the most appropriate criteria, visualize as clearly as possible the perfect solution or end result you wish to achieve.

For example, if you wanted to develop a set of criteria for selecting ideas for a new product to bring to market, you could extrapolate the *must have* characteristics, attributes, or benefits a winning idea would need to possess in order to create a highly successful product introduction, such as:

- **Innovative**—new, uniquely different, and better than other products
- **Defining**—what we want our company/organization to be known for
- **Desirable**—speaks directly to, or satisfies an unmet customer need or want
- **Value-adding**—provides more benefits/features than the competition
- **Differentiating**—looks and feels different from the competition

(For more examples of selection criteria, please see pages 101–102.)

Keep your criteria list short, simple, and to the point

We recommend you limit the number of selection criteria you develop to a manageable short list of five to six attributes. Too many criteria can bog down the selection process.

Once you have determined your list of criteria, do your best to communicate each one in the simplest, most concise way possible. A good format to follow is to distill the essence of each criterion down to one single key word, usually an adjective or verb, followed by a concise, one-sentence descriptive definition (as in the examples above).

Use the following three-step process to help identify the best set of selection criteria for your SmartStorming session:

1. **Visualize the end result first**
   The perfect solution (or end result/end product) to this challenge, problem, or opportunity would look like:

   _____

   _____

2. Identify the DNA of winning ideas

To create this successful outcome, a winning idea must possess the following characteristics, attributes, or benefits (e.g., simple, effective, easy to use, memorable, different, affordable, flavorful, adds value):

_____

_____

3. Narrow down your selection

From the list of characteristics, traits, or attributes above, select the five or six most important. Remember to format each of your criteria using the following formula:

(Key word) + (Simple, concise description of meaning) = Criterion

For example:

Innovative—new, uniquely different, and better than other products

Key word	Simple, concise description
1. _____	_____
2. _____	_____
3. _____	_____
4. _____	_____
5. _____	_____
6. _____	_____

SmartStorming Next Steps: 5-As Action Planner

The 5-As Idea Implementation Process is an effective, top-line approach for ensuring that your ideas move forward in a positive and productive way, increasing the odds that they survive the journey from concept to new reality. This planner will help you clarify the five steps in the process: Act, Assess, Assign, Agree, and Activate.

Step 1: Act—Foster an action-oriented attitude. (What can you do to ensure that your team is enthusiastic and motivated to take action? How can you more effectively inspire them?)

Step 2: Assess—Size up the big picture; then break it down into action steps. (What is the scope of the project in terms of time, complexity, and resources? What skills/capabilities are necessary? What adjustments need to be made to existing responsibilities and schedules to ensure the team has the time and attention necessary?)

(What subprojects make up the overall project? Identify major milestones, then individual tasks, for each subproject.)

Step 3: Assign—Establish specific roles, responsibilities, and deliverables. (Who is the very best person to assign to each task, based on their talents, skills, and individual traits?)

Step 4: Agree—Create team alignment and personal accountability. (What is the best way to establish agreement about specific timelines and deliverables *before* participants leave the room?)

Step 5: Activate—Pull the trigger; make it happen! (What needs to happen to get the project started today?)

SmartStorming Six-Step Session Flowchart

1 Pre-Session
In step 1, you create your blueprint for leading the session; send out invitations, including all necessary background information the group may need.

Fill Out SmartStorming Pre-Session Planner

2 Icebreaker
In step 2, you help participants get to know one another and create group alignment with an enjoyable icebreaker activity.

10-Minute Group Icebreaker Activity

3 The Challenge
In step 3, you introduce the session's goals and objectives, and announce the challenge statement—make it a provocative call to action!

Introduce Goals and Challenge Statement

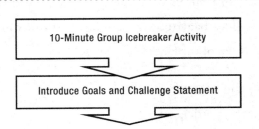

4 Idea Generation
In step 4, you inspire and guide the group through a series of 2-3 different idea generation activities.

Be sure to harvest the group's best ideas after each ideation activity and have the session Reporter write them down on the Idea Bank.

Idea Generation Activity #1

Harvest Ideas

Idea Generation Activity #2

Harvest Ideas

Idea Generation Activity #3

Harvest Ideas

I D E A   B A N K

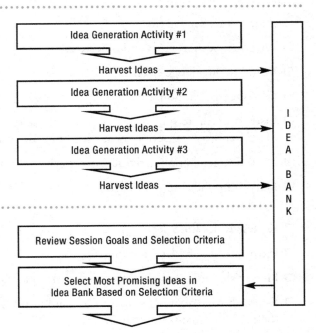

5 Evaluation and Selection
In step 5, you begin by reviewing the selection criteria with the group before evaluating ideas.

The selection criteria establish the benchmarks by which the group (or a selection committee) can more objectively evaluate the strengths and weaknesses of ideas.

Review Session Goals and Selection Criteria

Select Most Promising Ideas in Idea Bank Based on Selection Criteria

6 Next Steps
In step 6, you announce the action steps necessary to move winning ideas forward to the next stage of their development. Be sure to specify deadlines and assign roles and responsibilities.

Review Next Steps with Group; Assign Deadlines, Roles, and Responsibilities

End Session, Thank Group

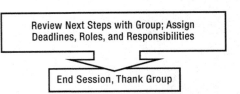

Piloting Your First Session Checklist

Before the session

❏ Define the specific issue, challenge, or opportunity to be addressed.

❏ Fill out SmartStorming Pre-Session Planner.

❏ Set up for your session (supplies, flipchart, whiteboard, etc.).

❏ Set up Idea Bank (one sheet of flipchart paper for each ideation activity).

❏ Post Rules of the Game.

During the session

❏ Welcome participants.

❏ Review Rules of the Game.

❏ Pilot icebreaker activity.

❏ Introduce session goals and objectives.

❏ Introduce challenge statement.

❏ Pilot idea-generation activity #1.

❏ Instruct group to quickly select (harvest) the few best/most promising ideas. Have Reporter transcribe those ideas into Idea Bank.

❏ Pilot idea-generation activities (two to three if possible).

❏ Harvest best ideas and have Reporter transcribe to Idea Bank after each activity.

❏ Review Rules for Selecting Ideas.

❏ Introduce set of selection criteria.

❏ Pilot evaluation and selection process (from ideas in Idea Bank).

❏ Establish next steps, deadlines, roles, and responsibilities (before participants leave the room).

❏ Thank participants for their contributions.

Part Five
Solo SmartStorming

CHAPTER 22

Solo SmartStorming—
Liberating Your Own Creative Genius

"My ideas usually come not at my desk writing but in the midst of living."
—Anaïs Nin, Author

The primary focus of this book is how to lead super-productive group idea-generation sessions. But the SmartStorming methodology is so versatile, it can easily be adapted by individuals aspiring to unleash more of their own innate creative problem-solving genius.

And so we have included this chapter, which will help you run your own personal Solo SmartStorming sessions. Many of the principles are similar to those discussed in previous chapters, but have been modified here to make them practical for your own personal application. Everything in this chapter is designed to enhance your idea-generation performance.

The difference between group and Solo SmartStorming

There are many who believe that individual idea generation is actually a more productive process than group brainstorming. In fact, several studies appear to support this. However, our own experience, and that of many of our colleagues and clients, shows that group idea generation offers tremendous advantages (i.e., the richness in diversity and the collaborative sharing of viewpoints, knowledge, backgrounds, and experience). And other studies have concluded that when conducted properly, by skilled facilitators, group brainstorming is highly effective.

But group brainstorming may not always be an option. At one time or another, we all find ourselves in situations where we need to generate creative solutions with no one else there to lend a hand. Fortunately, there is no reason an individual, working alone, cannot experience an "Aha!" flash of insight with the power to transform markets, lives, or even the world as we know it. In fact, it happens every day!

Overview: The Solo SmartStorming process

Solo SmartStorming is designed to take your intuitive approach to problem solving and channel it through a more structured and productive process, just as Smart-Storming does for groups. The best part about Solo SmartStorming is that you don't have to change the way you think or the manner in which you like to work. Just follow each of the steps in the Solo SmartStorming process, and let your creativity flow.

By following each of the steps in this solo process, you will find your own exploration of new ideas more organized, enjoyable, and productive than in the past.

The five Solo SmartStorming steps

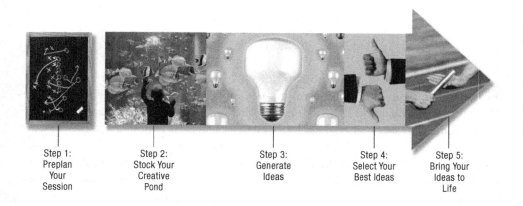

Step 1:
Preplan
Your
Session

Step 2:
Stock Your
Creative
Pond

Step 3:
Generate
Ideas

Step 4:
Select Your
Best Ideas

Step 5:
Bring Your
Ideas to
Life

Step 1: Preplanning—Visualizing the end before you begin

The process begins with preplanning. It covers several of the same elements considered by SmartStorming Pilots when planning their group sessions, but with a few important differences. Once you have created your game plan, you will have a strong foundation for staying focused and productive while generating ideas on your own.

The planner prompts you to clarify your goals and objectives for your ideation session; identify the information, expertise, and resources you will need to succeed; select the best ideation techniques to help inspire your creativity; and determine a set of selection criteria to use for objectively evaluating the ideas you will have generated.

The final part in the preplanning process will help you map out the initial action steps you will have to take in order to transform your ideas from concept to reality, largely by enlisting the support of others.

Set aside some quiet quality time to fill out your pre-planner—the more thoughtful preparation you put into your planning process, the smoother and more enjoyable the process of exploring ideas will be.

Solo SmartStorming Pre-Session Planner

Situation: The specific issue, challenge, or opportunity to be addressed is:

Goal/Objective: The specific outcome, end result, or deliverable I wish to achieve is:

Support: The people whose specific talent, knowledge, and experience I can call upon (or access via social media) to help me succeed are:

Background Information: The essential information, data, or context I need to know or understand is:

Stocking the Pond: Some rich sources of inspiration for this project are:

Ideation Techniques: The idea-generation techniques I plan to use to help best inspire my problem-solving thinking in new, innovative ways are (select two or three different Solo SmartStorming techniques from Chapter 20):

Selection Criteria: The five specific objective criteria I will use as a yardstick for measuring the merits of ideas are (see Idea Selection Criteria Worksheet on page 264):

Next Steps: The specific action steps that will need to occur after I have selected my winning ideas are:

Step 2: Stock your creative pond

The most productive creative thinkers are those who actively seek out new sources of inspiration. So before you go fishing for ideas, it is important to first stock up on all the important background information, support materials, and fresh, inspirational stimuli you can find.

Finding new sources of inspiration (words, stories, pictures, movies, concepts, etc.) is essential for triggering new associations and connections. The more stimuli you have percolating around in your head, the more new connections and combinations you can imagine, and the easier it is to net a wide range of fresh, new ideas. (See Chapter 8 for more information about stocking your creative pond.)

Tap into the inspiration of your social networks

If you are generating ideas on your own but desire new input, information, feedback, or a fresh perspective, why not tap into the collective wisdom of your personal or professional social networks?

In today's networked world, collaborative partners are only a text, tweet, email, wall post, video chat, or phone call away.

There are many ways you can utilize your social network to function as your own personal virtual think tank:

1. Use your network as a sounding board for your ideas.

2. Solicit suggestions for improving, strengthening, or building on ideas.

3. Gain access to greater knowledge, understanding, or expertise.

4. Ask others to contribute ideas of their own.

5. Ask others where they find new sources of inspiration.

Step 3: Generate ideas!

In Step Three, you unleash the creative power of your conscious and *un*conscious mind to generate new ideas. This is the fun part of the Solo SmartStorming process—the part where you get to roll up your sleeves and allow the creative, spontaneous flow of ideas to emerge.

Before you begin, it's always a good idea to remind yourself that the same Rules of the Game that apply to groups in a SmartStorming session also apply to you as a solo idea generator. By embracing these simple rules, you will experience a lighter, less self-judgmental mindset while generating ideas. Here are a few good rules to keep in the forefront of your mind:

Suspend all judgment

Go for quantity, not quality

There is no such thing as a bad idea

Go for wild, audacious ideas

Push your ideas to the edge

Build on your ideas

Nothing is impossible

Approach the process of generating ideas as "play with purpose"

Two approaches to generating ideas

There are two distinct approaches you can use to generate new ideas.

The first way is to *deliberately* focus all of your mental faculties (your curiosity, knowledge, memory, intuition, and imagination) on tackling your challenge head-on. The purpose of this approach is to deliberately stimulate new associations and connections that can produce new concepts.

This is the approach we employ each time we use an ideation tool or technique. The goal of this on-demand approach is to generate as many different ideas as possible within a defined period of time.

Conversely, the other approach is to relax your concentrated efforts and allow your unconscious mind to take over, wander, and improvise in making its own spontaneous associations and connections (intuitive combinatory play). You do this by deliberately taking a break from your concentrated problem-solving efforts. Go out for a walk, do some gardening, cook a meal, listen to music, play a game, solve a Sudoku puzzle, or engage in any other enjoyable activity that helps you relax. Have you ever had a great idea or the solution to a problem come to you in the shower? If so, you have experienced intuitive combinatory play.

Many creative professionals make it a practice to alternate between the two processes, first intensifying their attention on a challenge, then releasing attention to allow their unconscious mind to make new connections. They will repeat this process a number of times until a moment of insight arrives.

Give this process of alternating between intensifying and then releasing your attention a try. Discover for yourself how effortless and productive conceptual problem solving can become.

Solo SmartStorming ideation techniques

Many of the ideation tools and techniques introduced in earlier chapters are well suited for individual use, and will help stimulate your thinking in new and different ways—even while you are sleeping, taking a shower, walking your dog, or sitting on the beach. (See Chapter 20: Idea-Generation Techniques and Tools for more information and instructions. Solo instructions follow immediately after group instructions for each technique.) These techniques are the same proven, powerful ones used by groups, but modified with simple, easy-to-follow instructions that will help you generate a greater number and range of fresh, new ideas than ever before.

Here are brief descriptions of the solo ideation techniques you can use in your creative problem-solving exploration:

Bad2Good—This engaging, counterintuitive ideation technique is based on the theory that within every bad idea may lie the seed of a great idea. By reversing your conventional thinking 180 degrees, inhibitions fall away, and new, unexpected possibilities emerge. The technique is fun and easy to do. You deliberately come up with the worst ideas you can imagine to solve your challenge. Next, you simply turn each idea around to find that seed of a great idea hidden within.

Escaping the Box—When people say they need to think outside the box, what they really mean is that they need to think outside of their current limiting assumptions and beliefs. This powerful technique will help you identify and successfully challenge the status quo, move beyond any perceived limitation or barriers, and by doing so, empower you to imagine bold new possibilities.

Frankensteining—Frankensteining is an engaging idea-generation technique that challenges you to discover ways to combine two (or more) seemingly unrelated ideas to create a distinctly new and unique product, service, process, or thing. This combinatory-play approach of merging different ideas, ingredients, features, functions, attributes, or characteristics to create something altogether new is a hallmark of the innovation process. For example, someone combined a telephone and a photocopier to create the fax machine.

Idea Sprinting—Idea Sprinting is a fast-paced, beat-the-clock technique in which you challenge yourself to conceive of as many ideas as possible within a tight time deadline (say, fifteen new ideas in five minutes). This process is very effective for overcoming self-consciousness, getting the creative juices flowing, and generating an abundance of new ideas quickly.

In Their Shoes—This empathy-based idea-generation technique is designed to help you develop greater awareness, empathy, and emotional connection with a specific target audience or customer. By imagining, in as vivid detail as possible, what a typical day in the life of the end user would look like—or a specific condition, situation, or unmet need they might experience—you will be better able to generate new insights that can be used to develop meaningful and effective solutions.

Mind Mapping—Mind Mapping is a well-known idea-generation technique that mimics the brain's natural process of making spontaneous associations. The technique starts with a key word, image, or issue written in the center of a piece of paper. Related ideas and insights triggered by the key word, and subsequent associations, radiate outwardly in all directions. Individual ideas are interconnected by lines. Mind Mapping is a powerful way to visually conceive, connect, extrapolate, combine, and organize information about a topic or subject.

Pump Up the Value—Customers and clients today demand more value in the products and services they buy. Increased competition makes value-added innovation the primary differentiator between brands. This technique challenges you to identify ways to make a product or service better, simpler, faster, cheaper, easier to use, more reliable, friendlier, and more endearing. This technique provides you with a Value Compass to help you explore a myriad of different ways in which you can develop ideas that add/provide greater value.

Reimagine It!—A good way to gain a fresh perspective on an issue or challenge is to explore it through the context of an analogy, metaphor, or fictional characterization. By using creative visualization, imagery, storytelling, or fictional characterizations, you can grasp the nature of the challenge in new visceral ways.

SCAMPER—SCAMPER is a popular technique based on the philosophy that everything new is really an adaptation of something else that already exists. Each letter of the SCAMPER acronym represents a different way in which you can play with, modify, adapt, or change the characteristics of a product, challenge, issue, process, or service you want to innovate.

- **S** = Substitute
- **C** = Combine
- **A** = Adapt
- **M** = Magnify
- **P** = Put to Other Uses
- **E** = Eliminate (or Simplify)
- **R** = Rearrange (or Reverse)

SmartSWOT—The SWOT analysis is one of the most widely used strategic planning methods used by individuals, teams, and organizations. It can help you identify, highlight, and evaluate the **S**trengths, **W**eaknesses, **O**pportunities, and **T**hreats involved in pursuing a specific project, launching a new venture, or achieving a desired goal. This enhanced version of the technique adds several new dimensions for you to explore in order to gain greater insight and identify new strategies and tactics for achieving success.

Think Much, Much Bigger—This idea-building technique is an effective way to take the most promising ideas you've previously generated, then push or expand them to an exponentially bigger/larger realm for significantly greater potential. In other words, Think Much, Much Bigger helps you take good ideas and transform them into much, much bigger game-changing concepts.

What If...?—Real game-changing innovation is driven by bold, visionary new ideas, with the power to break through the barriers of conventional thinking and redefine what is possible. This thought-provoking technique is designed to help you think as far outside the box as you can—to shoot for the most ambitious, forward-thinking, and disruptive *What if...?* ideas imaginable. Then later, you will reevaluate your most intriguing ideas to determine how they can be adapted or modified to become practical, real-world opportunities or solutions.

Have fun with your power mind tools

We encourage you to test-drive each of the different techniques to see which ones help you produce the best results possible. You will find easy-to-follow solo instructions for each of these idea-generation techniques in Chapter 20. (Solo instructions follow immediately after group instructions for each technique.)

Capturing your ideas

Your ideas can be written down (as spontaneously as possible) on a pad of paper as an ongoing list, captured with keystrokes on a laptop or desktop computer, or jotted down on sticky notes (one idea per sticky note). Each of these approaches for capturing ideas is effective. You should select the method that you feel most comfortable using.

We strongly recommend you test-drive the sticky notes approach. Writing down each idea individually on its own sticky note allows you the option of moving around your ideas and clustering them later, according to similar themes, approaches, or attributes. This is very helpful in narrowing down your ideas during the evaluation and selection process.

Step 4: Select your most promising ideas

In the end, your Solo SmartStorming activity could easily generate dozens, if not a hundred or more new ideas. In Step Four, you will apply a simple and efficient method for evaluating and selecting your best ideas (the strongest, most innovative problem-solving concepts). To do so, you will use a combination of your intuition (sixth sense, gut feelings, etc.) and your objective selection criteria.

Getting Started

To begin your selection process, place all your ideas on a wall, on a large desk, or even down on the floor in front of you so you can view them all at once.

Next, spend a few minutes looking over your concepts and refamiliarize yourself with the big idea behind each. Once you are ready, follow this simple three-step process to identify and select the best of your ideas:

1. Organize your ideas

First, begin to organize your ideas by grouping them in clusters according to similarities in subject matter, category, approach, style, theme, etc.

Next, look for ways to combine ideas that appear similar. Be sure to eliminate any duplication to reduce the number of ideas to evaluate. Also weed out any weak ideas that immediately feel underdeveloped, are too complicated, or don't fully address the issue, challenge, or opportunity.

2. Rank your ideas

After you have narrowed down the number of concepts, rate each remaining idea based on how effective you believe it would be in solving your challenge. We recommend using a simple rating scale from zero to three possible stars (*Average idea, **Interesting idea, or ***Innovative idea).

Those ideas that fail to measure up should not be given any stars and immediately discarded. Be a discerning critic; your mission is to narrow down the field to only those few strongest, most innovative concepts.

Here is a description of each of the three rating categories:

*Average idea (Rating: 1 star)
These ideas may seem interesting at first, but on closer inspection they do **not** fully address the challenge. They may feel too vague, overly complicated, or unworkable. These ideas should be discarded.

**Interesting idea (Rating: 2 stars)
These ideas seem to have real potential. They can be fledgling ideas that contain the seeds of a good (or great) idea within. These ideas should be put aside for further development.

***Innovative idea (Rating: 3 stars)
These ideas really sizzle! They represent solutions that possess the potential to successfully address the challenge; or they may indicate a new path of opportunity. These ideas should be selected to move forward.

Using your predetermined selection criteria as a yardstick

When you have finished rating your concepts, immediately eliminate all of the ideas that ranked below two stars. This will narrow down the number of ideas to a short list of your strongest contenders.

The final step in your evaluation and selection process is to see how well your strongest ideas measure up against your predetermined objective selection criteria. This is the best way to objectively evaluate ideas strictly on the merits of their originality and potential effectiveness at addressing your issue/challenge/opportunity.

Note: To judge the merits of your final contenders, you will need to refer to the list of objective selection criteria you identified in your preplanning process.

Here's how it works:

Take each of your remaining ideas, one at a time, and evaluate how closely they meet all five of the selection criteria you've determined. (You can use the SmartStorming Idea Selection Diagnostic Matrix for this step. (See pages 107–109 for details.)

If an idea meets all five of the criteria—it is a strong, undisputed winner.

If an idea falls short in satisfying one (or two) of your selection criteria—it can be either set aside to be improved in those deficient areas or simply discarded.

If an idea falls short in three (or more) selection criteria areas—it should be discarded.

The beauty of using this diagnostic approach is that it reveals exactly where concepts measure up to the predetermined selection criteria and where they may fall short. This helps eliminate any doubt or second-guessing; plus, it also identifies the exact areas where promising ideas can be improved.

Ideas that pass this litmus test are guaranteed winners.

For more detailed information about the evaluation and selection process, please refer to Chapter 9.

Step 5: Next steps—Bringing your ideas to life

The final step in the Solo SmartStorming process is to enlist the time, effort, and resources of others to help transform your concepts into new realities. As we do in group SmartStorming, we will use the 5-As Idea Implementation Process.

Step 1: Act—Prepare yourself for taking action.
Do a quick self-assessment to ensure that you are ready to take action, have a positive, can-do attitude, and are prepared to identify and enlist the help and support of others.

Step 2: Assess—Size up the big picture; then break it down into action steps.
As quickly as possible, assess how big, time-consuming, and complex the project of bringing your ideas to life will be. Break large projects down into smaller, more manageable steps. And then assign yourself a deadline for completing each step.

Step 3: Assign—Identify specific roles, responsibilities, and deliverables.
Once you have assessed the task, it's time to decide what will be required in terms of skills, talents, and capabilities (and the specific people who possess them) to see it through to completion. Try to create an A-Team that can overcome any challenge!

Step 4: Agree—Create team alignment and personal accountability.
Once you have identified your support system, contact each person and secure their help. Clearly identify specific roles and responsibilities, and gain agreement on exactly what will be delivered and when.

Step 5: Activate—Pull the trigger; make it happen!
It's time to press the start button. If you have taken the time to go through each step, you and those supporting you should be in agreement.

For more detailed information on the SmartStorming 5-As Idea Implementation Process, please refer to Chapter 10.

What to remember

- In today's fast-changing, chaotic business environment, there is a good chance that the next big breakthrough product or service idea will be dreamed up by an individual working solo rather than a team huddled in a room.

- The Solo SmartStorming Pre-Session Planner will help you get organized, clarify your goal and objectives for the challenge or opportunity at hand, and identify the information, resources, and tools/techniques you will need to succeed. Once you have created your game plan, you will have a strong foundation for staying focused and productive while generating ideas on your own.

- Before you go fishing around for ideas, it is important to first stock your inner creative pond with all the background information, support materials, and fresh, inspirational stimuli you can find. The more mental stimuli you have floating around in your mental ecosystem, the more new connections and combinations you can imagine.

- If you're generating ideas on your own but desire new input, information, feedback, or a fresh perspective, tap into the collective wisdom of your personal or professional social networks. In today's networked world, collaborative partners are only a text, tweet, email, wall post, video chat, or phone call away.

- The task of selecting your strongest, most innovative ideas can be accomplished efficiently by: 1) using your intuition (sixth sense, gut feelings) to narrow down to a short list of the most promising ideas; and 2) evaluating how well each concept measures up against your predetermined selection criteria.

- Use the 5-As Idea Implementation Process to effectively move your ideas forward. Enlist the time, effort, and resources of others to help transform your concepts into new realities.

Part Six
Open Innovation and
Virtual SmartStorming

CHAPTER 23

Open Innovation and Virtual SmartStorming

"When you give everyone a voice and give people power,
the system usually ends up in a really good place."

—Mark Zuckerberg, co-creator of Facebook

Not so long ago, the very notion of a group of people collaborating effectively, in real time, from different physical locations was unheard of. In order to share thoughts and ideas, debate, and collaborate—at least without a significant time delay—meant sitting across the table from one another.

But while the face-to-face brainstorm is far from dead (it is still the most widely utilized process for group idea generation), technological advancements have made remote brainstorming a reality.

Perhaps even more important to realize, however, is that this ability for teams to collaborate in real time from different locations has become a necessity. The globalization of many organizations and openness to telecommuting, results in teams that are scattered across many geographic locations. The cost in terms of dollars and time, as well as the inconvenience of travel, makes it increasingly impractical to schedule face-to-face meetings. There are often corporate mandates in place to leverage technology investments for optimal efficiency. And of course, there is the desirability of crowd-sourcing—effectively leveraging talent and contributions across an entire organization and even outside its corporate walls.

But perhaps the most compelling reason virtual collaboration is necessary today is that our world of continuous change and reinvention demands it.

Pros and cons of virtual, collaborative idea generation

There are many advantages to virtual brainstorming and remote collaboration.

- Fewer scheduling challenges are encountered, since participants do not have to show up someplace, other than where they are.

- It significantly increases the potential pool of participants, since anyone, anywhere, can join in (as long as they have access to the technology required). In short, it provides the ultimate opportunity to invite diversity.

- Depending on techniques and technology used, virtual brainstorming can allow individuals to participate on their own time schedule, 24/7.

- Collaborating remotely minimizes the possibility of face-to-face, interpersonal challenges—ego struggles, negativity, dominating personalities, shy, nonparticipating silent thinkers, etc.

- In skilled hands, virtual brainstorming can lead to some new, innovative, technology-based techniques for generating ideas—some of which might be less applicable in a live setting.

Of course, there can be real challenges when conducting a virtual meeting.

- There is less opportunity for in-the-moment, cross-pollination of ideas and spontaneous idea-building among participants.

- The experience is less emotional. While this has some obvious advantages, the natural energy and enthusiasm that emerge in a face-to-face session are a powerful catalyst for inspiration, sharing, and debate.

- When some team members are together in the room and others are participating online or over the telephone, there is an imbalance in the energy and participation.

- Technology and bandwidth limitations can result in sound and/or video delays or even the complete drop-out of participants. Such issues throw off the timing and the flow of conversations and interactions. Participants are forced to constantly adjust and accommodate, reducing or eliminating spontaneity.

- Depending on the medium/technology utilized, some participants may find it more challenging to effectively express and explain their ideas to fellow participants.

- There is a much greater likelihood that participants will multitask and divide their attention among the brainstorm and other activities such as surfing the Web, texting, emailing, playing Angry Birds, etc.

Clearly we have entered the era of virtual, collaborative idea generation. And while there are certainly differences between live, face-to-face brainstorming and virtual brainstorming, there are also many similarities. Many of the very same factors that contribute to a face-to-face brainstorm's success—the processes, principles, tools, and techniques utilized in SmartStorming—can help ensure a more successful virtual SmartStorm as well.

If you haven't already, it is inevitable that you will be called upon to participate in and very likely organize and lead a virtual SmartStorm. Our goal here is to provide some insights about how to make the best use of your newly developed SmartStorming piloting skills in a virtual environment.

Virtual brainstorming technologies

Virtual brainstorming and remote collaboration can take many forms, from a few colleagues tossing around ideas via a telephone conference call all the way to large-scale, organization-wide, open innovation initiatives. Here is a quick look at some of the available technology platforms and their various advantages and disadvantages.

Telephone (conference calls/bridge lines)

Pros
- Easy and accessible.
- Familiar means of communication for everyone.
- Thanks to cell phones, people can participate from any location.

Cons
- Audio only—no way to share visual ideas/information.
- Confusing—no easy way to identify who is speaking in calls with a large number of participants.
- Gridlock/delays if multiple people want to share simultaneously.

Email (setting up an email chain)

Pros
- No time or location requirements—people can participate when convenient for them.
- Allows for sharing of written ideas as well as visual.

Cons
- Minimal opportunity for associative spontaneity, in-the-moment inspiration.
- Difficult to implement without a predefined, agreed-upon structure.

Video chatting (Skype, ooVoo, Google Hangouts, etc.)

Pros
- Allows both verbal and visual communication.
- Participants are able to actually see each other.

Cons
- Technology can sometimes be problematic (audio/video delays, inadequate bandwidth, poor audio/video quality, dropped video/call, etc.).
- Some limitation in terms of how many people can reasonably participate before it gets confusing.

Web conferencing (variety of platforms, with and without video)

Pros
- When there is video capability, probably the closest to a live, face-to-face brainstorm.
- Most popular technologies allow a range of ways to share ideas—audio, video, whiteboard, file uploads, polling, surveys, etc.

Cons
- Technology can be challenging for some people.
- Incompatible computer platforms or operating systems can lead to complications/issues.

Wikis (variety of platforms)

Pros
- Not dependent on real-time meeting—allows users to contribute any time of day, on their own schedule.
- In some ways, a simple, inexpensive, but far less flexible alternative to sophisticated, open innovation management systems (see below).

Cons
- No real-time interactivity or spontaneity.
- Can be complicated/intimidating for some users.
- Types of information you can share can be limited.

Open innovation management tools

Over the past several years, large organizations have woken up to the realization that there is an enormous amount of untapped brainpower and creativity out there. And today, the technological capability to access that resource exists. The result has been the introduction of a number of powerful, multifeatured, open innovation management tools. (At this time, it is difficult to identify a common term used to describe these products. But in general, while the various offerings differ somewhat in specific features and capabilities, they are all designed to facilitate soliciting, sharing, evaluating, and harvesting ideas on a large, potentially enterprise scale.)

These powerful technology tools represent virtual brainstorming and remote collaboration at their largest and most sophisticated level. Think of them as the modern-day equivalent of the company suggestion box—on steroids—because they make it possible for users to do much more than simply submit their ideas. Typically online-based, these systems provide a variety of tools for harnessing the collective brainpower of employees, business partners, customers—pretty much anybody and everybody the organization and project owner wish to include.

Open innovation management tools have been used successfully by major corporations to develop new product ideas, marketing campaigns, internal business improvements, etc. As of this writing, key players in the category include companies like Brightidea, Spigit, and Jive, each of which offers a somewhat different focus and suite of tools. But in general, they all provide the following capabilities:

- Sharing a challenge, opportunity, or question with a virtually unlimited number of users.
- Distributing related background information and content (files, images, videos, etc.).
- Collecting ideas from users.
- Organizing/categorizing ideas.
- Facilitating collaborative discussion about ideas.
- Voting on or rating ideas.
- In some cases, moving ideas forward into a project management phase.

An in-depth discussion of open innovation management tools is beyond the scope of the book. However, a discussion of virtual SmartStorming would be incomplete without touching on them. Clearly such systems open up very exciting possibilities in group idea generation and development. Here are some of their pros and cons:

Pros
- Allow for organization-wide collaboration—even beyond the organization, if so desired.
- Contributions can be made anytime, at the convenience of the participant.
- Designed to accommodate every step of the idea-generation and development process.
- Depending on the technology, a wide range of content can be shared.

- Some platforms have real-time interaction capability.
- Some combine idea generation with project management, helping to bridge the gap between ideation and implementation.

Cons
- Expensive, relative to other virtual collaboration platforms.
- Require a trained administrator.
- Depending on the specific platform, may not allow for real-time, spontaneous sharing of ideas.
- Can be technologically challenging/intimidating for some users.
- Often because the technology does so much of the work, it is assumed that less is required of the project owner.

SmartStorming in the virtual world

SmartStorming was originally conceived as a solution to the most common challenges encountered in traditional group brainstorming sessions, as typically practiced. It was intended to be a live, face-to-face methodology. That said, while remote collaboration in its various forms offers some very interesting and even exciting possibilities in this world of idea generation, it still faces many of the same challenges as live, in-the-room brainstorms.

The good news is that many of the same principles you have learned to apply to traditional, face-to-face brainstorms can also be utilized to increase the effectiveness of remote sessions. Here are a few insights that will make your virtual SmartStorms as effective as your live ones.

SmartStorming roles

One of the most common shortcomings of remote collaboration initiatives is that, because there is a central technology presumably holding everything together, people assume there is no need for active piloting (facilitating) of the process. But nothing could be further from the truth.

Since in virtual SmartStorming participants will be on their own, many will require even greater guidance and inspiration from the Pilot. Perhaps more important is the understanding that a Pilot is necessary at all. In many virtual brainstorming/idea-generation projects, someone is assigned to act as an administrator. But often this individual is focused primarily on managing the technical requirements of the process. These administrators are rarely, if ever, trained brainstorming facilitators applying their skills to maximize the output of the participants. A skillful SmartStorming Pilot (like you!), on the other hand, actively engages, inspires, nurtures, and guides his or her group in the ideation process—whether live or remote.

All too often, when an organization or team initiates an online-based brainstorming project, once the challenge is presented, there is an initial flood of ideas. But very quickly, the quantity and quality of contributions drop; that initial flow of ideas slows down to a trickle. Participants lose interest and the virtual brainstorming initiative fizzles out. (Note: As we discussed earlier, the same thing can and does happen in a traditional brainstorm—unless a skilled facilitator proactively pilots the group to maintain energy and enthusiasm.) Project administrators and stakeholders are generally clueless about how to reignite and maintain interest and participation during a virtual brainstorm that can go on for days, weeks, or even months. A trained SmartStorming Pilot, however, can apply proven skills to keep the process vital and productive.

If you are planning a virtual brainstorm, consider the piloting skills you have learned in this book (or in a SmartStorming workshop, if you have participated in one), and consider how they can be applied in a virtual setting—and then use them. Just as you would in a live SmartStorming session, keep your situational awareness on high. Course correct as necessary. Keep your team on track and productive, and you will achieve superior results.

Throughout the rest of this chapter, you will find specific suggestions for some of the SmartStorming principles and techniques you can apply to your virtual SmartStorms.

Preplanning

As you learned in Chapter 5, every successful SmartStorming session is planned in advance. The Pilot (and project owner, if appropriate) considers exactly what will take place in the room—what the specific goals, objectives, and challenges are; what technique will be used to align the group's attention; what ideation techniques will be utilized; who to invite; what criteria will be used to measure a good idea; and what steps will be taken to ensure follow-through. And so, just as you would with any live SmartStorming session, take time to preplan your virtual SmartStorm.

Go through each section in your SmartStorming Pre-Session Planner, just as you would for a live SmartStorm. But remember to keep in mind the requirements and limitations of the virtual environment. How can you best accomplish the very same objectives, but in a virtual setting?

A special note about selecting participants, since the scope of open innovation initiatives can vary wildly. If your goal is to open the floor to a vast universe of participants, then go for it. If, however, you are being somewhat more selective, then consider the same principles discussed in Chapter 5. Will you simply invite the usual suspects (or just send invitations to everyone)? Or will you thoughtfully invite those participants with the best understanding, skills, experience, expertise, and can-do attitude to successfully tackle the challenge? In many ways, a virtual SmartStorm is no different from a live one. You want people who will not only contribute but also inspire greater contribution from others. More is not necessarily better. Consider who will best collaborate for your initiative's ultimate success. And of course, always remember to bring in some unexpected thinking by inviting diversity!

Establishing Rules of the Game

While it is true that virtual SmartStorming minimizes the potential for the interpersonal conflicts that can take place in a live session, there still must be rules and guidelines for participation. How will ideas be submitted, how will comments and discussion take place, and what evaluation and selection criteria will be applied?

Send participants a set of inspirational rules along with the challenge (e.g., "Don't self-judge your own ideas—be spontaneous," "Go for quantity, not quality," "Go for wild, edgy ideas," "Challenge assumptions," "Think outside the box").

Of course, even in a virtual SmartStorm, there is the potential for negative judgment. And while judgment expressed remotely might sting a little less than it does when delivered live, it can still shut down a group. Make sure participants understand that they must suspend judgment during the idea-generation process (until later on during the evaluation and selection process). By doing so you will ensure that participants feel safe to share even the most audacious ideas—which is precisely what you want.

Stocking the pond

Again, just as with any SmartStorming session, you want your participants to have plenty of stimuli on which to build new connections and, ultimately, innovative, new ideas. Stocking the Pond (providing participants with fresh, new, and exciting sources of inspiration) in a virtual SmartStorm is essentially the same process as in a live session. Just make sure that even though you won't be in the room with your team, you don't overlook this important piloting skill.

One innovative approach to stocking the pond might be to enlist someone on your team to serve as "Inspiration Director." This person's job is to assemble an online "Inspiration Room" that contains a variety of interesting images, articles, videos, TED talks, anecdotes, background information, data, etc.—anything that can inspire new ideas. If you employ a commercial innovation-management tool, there may well be an area where such information can be stored. Otherwise, set up a simple website, or use a free online file-sharing tool such as Dropbox or Google Drive. Make sure everyone receives a link to the site, and consider allowing participants to share documents of their own. Also, send out weekly inspiration/motivation blasts to the participants, to help ensure continued enthusiasm.

Statement of challenge and goals

Defining clear goals and objectives, as well as a compelling challenge statement (as discussed in Chapter 7), is just as important in a virtual SmartStorm as it is in a live session. And once again, the approach is essentially identical.

One difference, however, might be related to the length of time often devoted to remote collaboration and idea-generation initiatives. Although some teams may complete such projects over the course of a few days, the process can sometimes extend for weeks or even months. In these protracted time frames, consider sending out weekly challenge prompts that highlight different facets, aspects, or perspectives on the challenge. In this way, you will have a better chance of keeping the challenge alive and compelling.

Use of compelling and effective idea-generation techniques

In many (probably most) cases, those conducting virtual brainstorms simply post a challenge and invite participants to contribute ideas. But as we know, utilizing proven idea-generation techniques can significantly improve the quantity and quality of ideas submitted—by inspiring new, different ways of thinking, and facilitating more spontaneous sharing and building on ideas.

Of course, the techniques you select must be appropriate for the technology you are using, but the very same principle applies. Just use your imagination and ingenuity. Think about various techniques you have learned and how they might be applied in a virtual SmartStorm.

Try to adapt live techniques so that they can be effectively applied virtually. For example, at first glance, Idea Sprinting may not seem like a viable technique for certain types of virtual SmartStorms. But consider setting up a timed exercise, where an email blast is sent to participants, challenging them to submit one hundred new ideas by midnight tonight. Create an atmosphere of friendly competition—offer a prize (even a virtual one) to the person who submits the most concepts. And then see what happens! A virtual Idea Sprint? Why not? Of course, if you are using video conferencing for a real-time virtual SmartStorming, Idea Sprinting could be an excellent technique to employ.

As you can see, this is just another reason why preplanning is so critical. Use your imagination. Consider all the techniques you have learned here—which would be appropriate and which can be adapted. And then research other, different techniques online, ones that might be effective in a virtual setting.

Here are some possible techniques to use in virtual SmartStorming:

- Idea Sprinting (as described above)
- Brainwriting (using a predefined email chain)
- Group Graffiti (utilizing an online whiteboard)
- SCAMPER (Take each letter, one a day, and have participants generate ideas based on that attribute of the challenge.)
- Channeling Genius (Do rounds of idea generation. First, solve this challenge as Steve Jobs would have. Next, solve this challenge as Walt Disney would. Then solve this challenge as Lady Gaga would, etc.)

- What If…? (If all limitations or restrictions were gone, what would become possible?)
- In Their Shoes (What are the emotional needs or wants, and how do we satisfy them?)

For more information and instructions on these ideation techniques, please see Chapter 20: Idea-Generation Techniques and Tools.

Selection criteria

As with any SmartStorming session, it is crucial that you define a clear, concise set of five to six selection criteria for the challenge. This should be done *before* the SmartStorm. These criteria are your definition of a great idea. Without them, how do you know if an idea is really good or viable?

Communicate the criteria to participants at the start of your virtual SmartStorm so they understand the yardstick by which the merits of ideas will be judged. Only when participants understand, up front, what defines a good idea can they work toward that objective in a decisive manner.

For more information, see Chapter 9. You will also find an Idea Selection Criteria Worksheet on page 264.

Additional piloting skills

In addition to the various SmartStorming elements detailed above, here are a few other important piloting skills to employ in your virtual SmartStorms.

- Effective questioning. Prompting participants with carefully crafted questions can significantly increase participation and, therefore, the quality and quantity of ideas contributed. Periodically pepper questions throughout the ideation period. Keep participants engaged and thinking about the challenge.

- Segregate divergent and convergent thinking. In many ways, this is easier to do in a virtual setting—since there is less chance of participants injecting criticism or judgment spontaneously. If you have the opportunity to monitor or review input, you can exercise complete control over this.

- Optimize participation and maintain enthusiasm. Unfortunately, people rarely consider how to make a virtual brainstorm more fun! Well-crafted challenge statements are even more critical here. Strive to use provocative, even audacious language. When possible, include visual stimuli. Send out daily or weekly "mind candy"—or inspirational verbal or visual prompts to spark ideas or new thinking.

- Encourage friendly competition. It is human nature that we love to compete. Stage techniques as contests—and publicly acknowledge the winners. For example, the highest number of ideas for a given exercise or time frame; the most audacious idea; the most creative, original, or innovative idea. And if possible, actually award prizes—lottery tickets, gift cards, etc. Or simply recognize winners in an "Ideation Genius of the Week" email blast.

- Allow participants to see what happens to their ideas. One of the most common mistakes made by those conducting remote brainstorms is not allowing participants to see what happens to their ideas as they move forward. In order to inspire and maintain enthusiastic participation, people must have a sense of ownership. Build in some process by which participants can follow the progress of their ideas. Foster a social networking/virtual community either through your innovation management tool, if you use one, or via online messaging platforms, chat rooms, Facebook, etc. Encouraging and facilitating collaboration and peer-to-peer interactions will significantly improve outcomes.

The lesson here is to always strive to conduct your virtual SmartStorming and open innovation initiatives as you would any session—with forethought, imagination, ingenuity, flexibility, and application of the proven SmartStorming methodology!

What to remember

- Virtual SmartStorming and remote collaboration offer significant benefits in situations where participants are scattered across a range of geographic locations.

- Crowdsourcing allows organizations to effectively leverage talent and contributions across an entire organization and even outside its corporate walls.

- Any number of technologies can be used for virtual SmartStorming: telephone, email, video conferencing, Web conferencing, wikis, and sophisticated open innovation management tools.

- Virtual SmartStorming and remote collaboration face many of the very same challenges as live, in-the-room brainstorms.

- Many SmartStorming principles, skills, and techniques can be applied to virtual brainstorms to increase their effectiveness: active piloting of participants, preplanning your initiative, establishing rules of participation, stocking the creative pond with inspirational stimuli, defining clear goals and objectives, crafting a provocative challenge statement, utilizing proven ideation techniques (adapted for a virtual environment), identifying evaluation and selection criteria, and many more!

Part Seven
A Bird's-Eye View

CHAPTER 24

SmartStorming: Putting It All Together

"Details create the big picture."

—Stanford I. Weill, businessman

The goal of this SmartStorming book is to help you forever rethink the way you approach creative problem solving and, specifically, brainstorming. You've now learned a powerful, proven system for planning, structuring, and leading highly productive group ideation sessions, time after time—a system that eliminates all of the fundamental weaknesses of traditional brainstorming by providing you the three essential components necessary for effective group ideation:

1. **Structure**—a proven, repeatable, six-step process designed to optimize the flow of activities, energy, and ideas to ensure more consistent results from the beginning of a session to the end.

2. **Leadership Skills**—the specific skills needed to effectively lead, inspire, and guide groups to greater productivity with less effort, such as how to get groups off to a fast start, engage the silent thinkers, ask powerful questions, and keep your group's idea generation momentum high throughout the session.

3. **Tools and Techniques**—a diverse portfolio of proven idea-generation tools and techniques that can be used for any challenge. These tools and techniques will help your groups explore a wider range of viewpoints and solve challenges in new and different ways. (Detailed descriptions and instructions for the SmartStorming tools and techniques can be found in Chapters 20 and 21, Pilot's Toolkit.)

In short, you now have everything you need to be a masterful SmartStorming Pilot—one who can plan and lead the most effective, most productive brainstorming sessions, whenever and wherever a challenge or opportunity presents itself.

The following is a comprehensive summary of all key principles and processes you will need to pilot highly effective SmartStorming sessions.

The SmartStorming six-step session structure

The SmartStorming six-step session structure is carefully designed to help you preplan your session, quickly achieve group alignment, clearly state goals and objectives, inspire enthusiasm, and create the momentum for spontaneous idea contribution and selection.

Like the carefully sequenced acts in a tightly choreographed play, each of the six steps builds on the one before, helping channel your group's creative problem-solving performance and productivity.

Familiarize yourself thoroughly with this proven structure and the meaning and value of each step. Each will be an important element of your session's ultimate success.

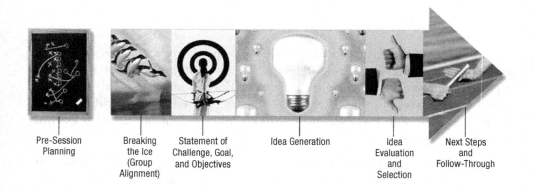

| Pre-Session Planning | Breaking the Ice (Group Alignment) | Statement of Challenge, Goal, and Objectives | Idea Generation | Idea Evaluation and Selection | Next Steps and Follow-Through |

Here is a brief overview of the six SmartStorming steps:

Step 1: Pre-Session Planning (purpose: to create the blueprint for a highly productive session)
You can dramatically improve the yield of new ideas generated by preplanning your session. Use the SmartStorming Pre-Session Planner (on page 260) to help you clarify your session goals and objectives, determine the best participants to invite, and identify the best icebreaker activity and idea-generation techniques to use. The checklist will help you organize and structure your session easily and quickly. It is the best way to guarantee that your group stays focused and on track.

Step 2: Breaking the Ice (purpose: to create group alignment and collaboration)
One of the keys to a successful SmartStorming session is to transform a room full of individuals into a collaborative team aligned toward a common goal. The fastest, most effective way to do this is by engaging the group in a playful activity that helps break down interpersonal barriers and free up participants' attention from outside concerns.

This activity is referred to as "breaking the ice." By taking just a few minutes to play before the work begins, participants are able to let go of formal roles, relate to one another as peers, and foster an atmosphere for spontaneous contribution, camaraderie, and teamwork.

Step 3: Defining the Challenge, Goals, and Objectives (purpose: to create a shared vision, understanding, and agreement)
As leader, you set the stage by clearly defining the challenge to be addressed and the specific goals and objectives for the session, establishing the rules of engagement, and also answering any questions participants may have before the SmartStorming process begins.

Step 4: Idea Generation (purpose: to inspire and guide your group's best creative problem-solving thinking)
Idea generation is the heart of the SmartStorming process. This is what your group came to do—generate ideas! The SmartStorming leader assumes the role of Pilot, actively engaging the group and guiding its exploration of ideas. The SmartStorming portfolio of proven ideation tools and techniques helps the group to think about the challenge in new and different ways and to generate more (and better) executable ideas than ever before.

Step 5: Evaluation and Selection (purpose: to harvest the creative genius of your group)
A SmartStorming session can generate dozens, if not hundreds of ideas—of which only a handful may have real potential. It is the Pilot's role to efficiently and accurately guide his or her group (or a separate selection committee, if more appropriate) through the process of separating the wheat from the chaff and identify those diamonds in the rough.

This step incorporates a systematic process for harvesting your group's best ideas as you go along, and then evaluating the most promising ideas against a predetermined set of objective selection criteria.

Step 6: Next Steps and Follow-Through (purpose: to initiate the action steps necessary to bring ideas to life)
Most typical brainstorms end when an acceptable idea is generated. But even the best ideas are worthless if they aren't implemented. The final step in the SmartStorming

process provides a systematic approach to establishing ongoing roles and responsibilities, ensuring accountability and compliance, and ultimately, taking the action steps necessary to bring promising ideas to life. .

As you can see, this SmartStorming six-step structure offers a comprehensive and systematic approach to brainstorming. It is built on the principle that a successful brainstorming session involves much more than just idea generation. It is a process that should be planned and skillfully led from start to finish. Once you understand this structure, you will be able to easily design and conduct highly productive group Smart-Storming sessions whenever necessary.

Preparing for your session: Use the SmartStorming Pre-Session Planner

The SmartStorming Pre-Session Planner is one of the most important tools in a Pilot's toolkit. The Planner helps you address the necessary elements for blueprinting a great session, each and every time.

The parts are simple. They are designed to prompt your best thinking and get you well organized. You will find the Planner an easy-to-use tool that will help your group stay focused and on track.

SmartStorming preplanning requires a small investment of time, but will pay you big dividends as your session flows more efficiently and enjoyably, and produces far superior results. Make it a habit to complete your SmartStorming Pre-Session Planner

SmartStorming Pre-Session Planner

Goal/Objective — 1. **Goal/Objective:** What specific outcome, end result, or deliverable do you wish to achieve from this session?

Challenge Statement — 2. **Challenge Statement:** What is the simplest, most concise and compelling way to present this challenge? (Formulate a thought-provoking question, e.g., "In what ways can we...?")

Participants — 3. **Participants:** Who are the best people (based on talent/knowledge/experience) to help you succeed? Create a problem-solving dream team. Be sure to invite diversity.

Background Info — 4. **Background Information:** What essential information, data, or context does your group need to know? What sources of inspiration would be helpful?

Icebreaker — 5. **Icebreaker:** What activity would quickly foster a spirit of collaboration and focus the group's attention? (See 25 Great Icebreaker Activities on page 255.)

Ideation Techniques — 6. **Ideation Techniques:** What idea-generation techniques would best inspire your group's problem-solving thinking in new, innovative ways? (Select two or three different techniques for your session. See Ideation Techniques in Chapter 20.)

Selection Criteria — 7. **Selection Criteria:** What specific objective criteria will you use as a yardstick for measuring the merits of a winning idea? (See Idea Selection Criteria Worksheet on page 264.)

Next Steps — 8. **Next Steps:** What specific action steps need to occur immediately after this session? Who are the best people to assign responsibilities to?

before each session, and you will soon discover why this simple part is so valuable.

Following is a brief overview of each part of the SmartStorming Pre-Session Planner.

1. Clarify Your Goals and Objectives (the specific end result you wish to achieve)
As the Pilot, the more clearly defined your goals and objectives are for the session, the more likely it is your group will achieve them. It's that simple!

Goals and objectives are not the same thing. Goals are broader and more conceptual in nature. Objectives are specific and measurable. And so in a SmartStorming session, your goal may be to develop strong, executable ideas (marketing strategies, product ideas, process innovations, etc.) that can be used to effectively solve a particular challenge (increase sales, leverage new technological capabilities, improve operational efficiencies, etc.). But your objective might be to generate fifty new ideas, six fresh strategies, or ten new tactics, or to more fully develop an existing idea during your ideation process.

2. Craft a Compelling Challenge Statement (a clear and provocative description of the issue, challenge, or opportunity being addressed)
It is extremely important that you define the specific challenge to be addressed in your session, in a simple, concise, and inspiring challenge statement. First, be certain you are clear on precisely what challenge you will be addressing in your session. Then, express that challenge in a powerful and motivating way. Use provocative language that will energize your group. Make your challenge statement a springboard for the imagination that jump-starts your group's creative thinking process. Take the time to craft a compelling challenge statement, and notice how much more innovative your group's ideas will be.

These first two sections, clarifying your goals and objectives and crafting a compelling challenge statement, help to focus the group's attention, set a high bar, and establish exactly what you expect your group to achieve.

3. Choose Participants (selecting the best people to invite to your session)
You can dramatically increase the quantity and quality of the ideas your group produces by strategically selecting the right kind of participants—those individuals with the most appropriate backgrounds, skills, knowledge, and experience for the challenge—instead of simply inviting the usual suspects. This is a critically important consideration to ensure success.

Think like a championship sports team manager: recruit an all-star dream team of individuals who possess the skills and understanding necessary to assure success. This third part of the planning process helps you do just that—evaluate exactly who the best SmartStormers would be for the challenge. Be sure to invite diversity! (See Participant Selection Planner on page 263.)

4. Provide Background Information (what your group needs to know)

In a typical brainstorming session, participants enter the room with only a vague notion of the task at hand. The most effective way to get your sessions off to a fast, productive start is by providing your SmartStormers with all the information they need to succeed—*before* the session begins.

This section helps you identify the right mix of information and inspiration to challenge a group and fuel its imagination. Naturally you will want to prepare a thorough brief or overview of the issue, situation, or challenge, plus the goals and objectives for the session (as identified in Steps 1 and 2).

But why not also direct your group to interesting websites that contain related information, provide some relevant articles, or pose a few provocative questions for them to consider before the session? Or instruct them to do some firsthand fieldwork in the real world, researching the subject of your session or observing or talking to representatives of your end user group or target audience. Be creative! Your upfront efforts will reap enormous rewards.

5. Choose Your Icebreaker (create group alignment)

When participants enter the room, chances are they arrive with scattered attention; they are preoccupied with outside concerns. The first job of a good Pilot is to help the group focus on the challenge ahead, free their attention from distractions, break down interpersonal barriers, and galvanize participants as a collaborative team aligned toward achieving a common goal.

The fastest way to accomplish this is through a brief, playful icebreaker activity. Icebreakers can be truly magical. Within a few short minutes, a group will be fully present, focused, and ready to tackle the challenge.

SmartStorming provides a wide range of fun and effective icebreaker exercises for you to choose from; or you can create your own. (See 25 Great Icebreaker Activities on page 255.)

6. Select Ideation Techniques (inspire fresh, new thinking)

While every part of a SmartStorming session is important, arguably the most important is the time devoted to idea generation.

This book provides a variety of different ideation tools and techniques for stimulating the flow of original thoughts, helping participants expand and enhance the ideas of others, and creating totally new areas of exploration.

This rich portfolio of proven idea-generation tools and techniques will help your group develop a wider range of fresh, new ideas, session after session. This part helps you decide which tools and techniques will be most appropriate for your challenge and group to ensure outstanding results. Be sure to select two to three different techniques per session to keep the process engaging and productive. (See Chapter 20: Idea-Generation Techniques and Tools.)

7. Establish Selection Criteria (the standards you will use to evaluate ideas)
A SmartStorming session can produce a surprisingly large number of ideas. The process of organizing, evaluating, and selecting the best of the bunch can often be a daunting challenge.

The SmartStorming method actually makes this potentially complicated and overwhelming process quite simple—and improves your chances of actually selecting the best ideas generated. Your objective selection criteria will be developed directly from your challenge, goals, and objectives established in parts 1 and 2. By predetermining the yardstick you will use to measure the effectiveness of potential ideas, you will have a clear, unambiguous evaluation tool, ready to implement. (See Idea Selection Criteria Worksheet on page 264.)

8. Planning Next Steps and Follow-Through (begin the process of bringing your ideas to life)
Most people believe a brainstorming session ends when ideas have been selected. In fact, the end of the idea-selection process launches an entirely new process—follow-through. Few people even consider that this is part of effective ideation. But even the most innovative and potentially valuable ideas are totally useless unless they are transformed from ethereal concepts into tangible realities.

To ensure that new ideas are brought to life, next steps and timetables need to be determined, responsibilities assigned, milestones established, and progress meetings scheduled. The eighth and final part of the SmartStorming Pre-session Planning process is to outline, ahead of time, preliminary next steps and follow-through plans. (See 5-As Action Planner on page 266.)

Key roles in the SmartStorming process

There are three key roles in the SmartStorming process: the Pilot (session leader), the Reporter (idea-catcher/scribe), and the SmartStormers (idea generators).

The Pilot's role is to confidently and skillfully direct his or her group through the SmartStorming process, as smoothly and efficiently as possible.

The Pilot navigates the group through the ups and downs and twists and turns of the ideation process. If the energy level of the group drops, the Pilot helps to elevate it. If the discussion veers off topic, the Pilot guides it back on course. A good Pilot makes the session a seamless, enjoyable experience.

Important reminder: The Pilot's job is to inspire and aid the group's exploration of ideas. He or she should not participate in contributing ideas.

The Reporter is a group member selected to write down every idea contributed by the group. This role is critical, as the Reporter frees up the Pilot to focus fully on leading the group. The Pilot should never act as his or her own Reporter. A good Reporter writes down all ideas accurately and clearly for all to see, and always numbers ideas to provide continuity and spatial memory.

The role of the SmartStormers is to understand the goals, objectives, and rules of the session, enthusiastically contribute insights and ideas, and participate (if appropriate) in selecting the strongest ideas to help the group achieve its goals. The best Smart-Stormers arrive at the session fully prepared and ready to focus on the task at hand.

Be sure to invite diversity—not just the usual suspects. The more varied the viewpoints and perspectives among your SmartStormers, the wider the range of ideas they will generate.

Preparing your SmartStorming session space

The ideal place to hold your SmartStorming session is a comfortable, well-ventilated room that is large enough to accommodate the number of SmartStormers participating. It is always preferable to find a space that is also visually or architecturally interesting (inspiring), and private enough to exclude outside noise and distractions.

In addition, the room should have plenty of open wall space, adequate desks and seating, plus all the equipment, materials, and supplies necessary for your planned session.

There are two important items to post on the walls before every session:

1. A poster-size list of the Rules of the Game

2. Several blank sheets of poster-sized paper to serve as your Idea Bank (the place where you will safeguard your group's most promising ideas). Allow one sheet for each ideation technique to be used in your session. If using a whiteboard, allocate a separate area for each technique.

Rehearse your instructions like a pro

They say the three most important things to remember when purchasing real estate are "location, location, location." When it comes to leading a group through the instructions of an icebreaker activity or a series of idea-generation techniques, the prevailing wisdom recommends, "Rehearse, rehearse, rehearse!"

Your Pre-Session Planner will help you select the best icebreaker activity and ideation techniques to use in your SmartStorming session. But it is up to you as the session Pilot to familiarize yourself with the instructions for each activity and rigorously practice explaining them. This behind-the-scenes activity of rehearsing will guarantee that your live instructions are clearly understood and flow smoothly.

Piloting Tip: It's helpful to make a photocopy of the instructions for each activity or technique you plan to use and bring it with you to the session. Also, be sure to bring a copy of your Pilot's Cheat Sheet of 25 Piloting Questions for Any Challenge (see page 259).

Managing your session for optimal productivity

Here are some important tips to help you more effectively and efficiently lead a group through a SmartStorming session.

Always break the ice. Begin every session with an engaging icebreaker activity; it will help free attention from outside concerns, break down interpersonal barriers, and foster a spirit of collaboration and teamwork.

Keep your session focus clear. Clearly define the group's goals and objectives for the session. In his book *The Art of Innovation*, IDEO's Tom Kelley states, "Start with a well-honed statement of the problem. Edgy is better than fuzzy. The session will get off to a better start—and you can bring people back into the main topic more easily—if you have a well-articulated description of the problem at just the right level of specificity."[19]

Make your challenge statement a launch pad for the imagination. Present the challenge statement in the most compelling and thought-provoking manner possible—make it a call to action, a statement that ignites the group's enthusiasm and catapults it into the realm of the imagination. The most powerful and effective challenge statements contain these characteristics:

Concise: It is simple, direct, clear, and easy to understand.

Intentional: It provides the group's *raison d'être* (purpose and goal).

Directive: It creates a sense of urgency by stating an immediate call to action.

Provocative: It sparks the imagination and inspires new associations and connections.

Open-ended: It encourages exploration and the discovery of a range of new possibilities.

Set the bar high: Set an ambitious, but achievable expectation for the specific quantity and types of ideas you want the group to generate in the session. Give the group a specific target number (or range) of ideas you would like them to achieve. For example:

"Let's shoot for fifty new ideas in the next twenty minutes."

"Let's come up with six new strategies by end of session."

"Let's identify ten new market opportunities in the next fifteen minutes."

Establish the Rules of the Game: People participate more freely when there is a safe, supportive environment in which to share insights and ideas. If negativity and judgment seep into a session, participants quickly feel self-conscious and defensive; they shut down and stop sharing. The role of the Pilot is to keep the SmartStorming session a judgment-free zone. Here are important rules to share with your team:

Suspend all judgment

There is no such thing as a bad idea

Maintain an ego-free zone

Go for quantity, not quality

Embrace wild, audacious ideas

Build on one another's ideas

One conversation at a time

Nothing is impossible

No texting or emailing during the session

The Boss speaks last

Get your group off to a fast start: The goal of every SmartStorming session is to achieve or surpass your goals in the time allotted. To that end, a Pilot needs to get his or her group off to a fast start. The faster a group becomes fully absorbed in its problem-solving activity, the more productive and enjoyable the session will feel to everyone—and the greater the odds the session goals will be achieved. Here are a few effective tips:

- Begin your session with a fast-paced, beat-the-clock type of icebreaker exercise to get the creative juices flowing.

- Establish a quick, rapid-fire tempo of questioning and answering for your session. Change directions by asking new questions every few minutes.

- Use a high-velocity, idea-generation technique like Idea Sprinting that sets a tight deadline for achieving an ambitious goal. "Let's shoot for twenty-five new ideas in five minutes!"

- Inject some friendly team competition: Divide the group into small competitive teams of three to five participants. Announce that the team that generates the most ideas within a given time frame wins bragging rights.

Engage the Silent Thinkers: Peer pressure and fear of judgment are two of the most common reasons shy or introverted participants may not be contributing ideas. To help them feel more comfortable, divide a large group into smaller teams with two to three members. These teams will provide a safer, more intimate collaborative environment (and minimize the problem of peer pressure). You can also use nonverbal, writing ideation techniques such as Brainwriting or Group Graffiti, or simply ask participants to submit ideas anonymously in writing.

Challenge assumptions: When a group experiences difficulty thinking outside its comfort zone, there's a good chance its perspective might be limited by assumptions and limiting beliefs—about what might or might not be possible, or the group's ability to successfully address a challenge. Use SmartStorming techniques such as Escaping the Box and What If...? to help a group identify and move beyond any perceived impediments, limitations, or barriers. (See Chapter 20 for full instructions.)

Manage your group's thinking direction: A group's thinking can flow in two possible directions: 1) it can diverge outward, in a broad, 360-degree anything goes exploration of ideas; or 2) it can converge inward, narrowing focus in an effort to discern, judge, and select ideas.

Divergent thinking allows a group to generate as many fresh, new ideas as possible. During this process all judgment is suspended; the group is encouraged to go for quantity of ideas (rather than quality) and push the boundaries of the imagination. Even wild, crazy, audacious ideas are welcome.

Convergent thinking, on the other hand, narrows down a large number of ideas through the process of analyzing, judging, eliminating, and selecting.

To keep your SmartStorming sessions super-productive, it is important to keep these different thinking processes from interfering with each other. A simple formula for success: Begin your session with divergent thinking to maximize the number of ideas. Then later, when your group is finished generating ideas, switch to convergent thinking to narrow down, evaluate, and select the very best ideas.

Ask provocative questions: SmartStorming piloting at its essence is the art of asking great questions. The more thought-provoking the questions you ask, the more insightful or imaginative the answers you receive will be. You can influence the directions in which a group's attention flows, what it focuses on, how deeply it probes, and ultimately, how many new ideas it generates, all by the type of questions you ask.

Asking questions is a very powerful tool for group discovery. Questions possess the power to transform the unknown into valuable information and understanding, simplify complex issues, stimulate leaps in imagination, shift a group out of the doldrums, refocus its efforts when it has veered off purpose, and catapult it to higher levels of discernment and insight.

Use questioning tools (such as the Pilot's Cheat Sheet of 25 Piloting Questions for Any Challenge, available on page 259) and techniques to dramatically increase your group's range of new ideas. (See Chapter 13 for more information about questioning.)

Use a variety of ideation techniques: A wide range of problem-solving techniques can be used to help a group generate ideas more effectively. Each approach is unique in the way it engages a group's thinking and imagination, providing a fresh perspective on the challenge and channeling the group's collaborative efforts. For example, an associative-thinking approach like Mind Mapping will engage a group's thinking in a very different way than an adrenaline-pumping, beat-the-clock type of ideation approach like Idea Sprinting. It is important to understand the differences between ideation techniques and select the best ones to use in your SmartStorming sessions.

Note: Plan to use two to three different techniques in your sessions to keep participants engaged and thinking in new and different ways. (See Chapter 20: Idea-Generation Techniques and Tools.)

Harvesting the genius of your group

The evaluation and selection phase of your SmartStorming session is the official crossover point from expansive, anything goes divergent thinking to the narrowing discernment of convergent thinking.

Earlier you learned about the importance of establishing a set of selection criteria to use as a yardstick for measuring the merits of an idea—how to harvest the most promising ideas after each ideation activity.

Here is a brief summary of the SmartStorming evaluation and selection process:

Step 1: Before your session—Predetermine a set of objective selection criteria for evaluating the merits of ideas.
Identify the specific characteristics, attributes, or benefits a winning idea must possess in order to address or solve the challenge at hand.

To determine your criteria, visualize the perfect solution, end result, or end product you wish to achieve. Then extrapolate the *must have* characteristics a winning idea would need to possess in order to create that desired reality.

Try to limit the number of selection criteria you develop to a manageable, easy-to-remember short list of five to six items (too many criteria can bog down your selection process and make it feel cumbersome).

Do your best to communicate each of your criteria in the simplest, most concise way possible. A good format to follow is to distill the essence of each criterion down to a single key word, usually an adjective or verb, followed by a concise one-sentence descriptive definition. For example:

Innovative—new, uniquely different, and better than other products

Distinctive—one of a kind, must stand out from the crowd

Provocative—challenges conventional thinking, creates buzz

Step 2: While generating ideas—Harvest the most valuable ideas as you go along, after each idea-generation activity. Transfer those ideas to your Idea Bank.

This is the simplest, most effective way to avoid the pitfall of "idea overwhelm" (the prospect of facing an overwhelming number of ideas to evaluate at the end of your freewheeling ideation activities). We recommend that Pilots plan to use at least two to three (or more) different ideation techniques during the course of a SmartStorming session; that means you and your group will harvest ideas two to three times during your idea-generation session (once after *each* technique).

To harvest ideas, set up an Idea Bank at the start of your session. At the conclusion of each ideation activity, have the group quickly select the most promising ideas generated during that activity (using their intuition and best reasoning abilities). Then have the Reporter transfer these ideas to the Idea Bank for safekeeping. Repeat this harvesting process after each ideation activity. By the end of your idea-generation process, you will have an easy-to-manage short list of the best ideas to evaluate during the final selection process.

Step 3: For final idea selection—Narrow down the total number of ideas in your Idea Bank using your objective selection criteria as a yardstick.

Before beginning the final selection process, take a few minutes to review your selection criteria, one at a time, with your group to make sure everyone understands the meaning of each. This step will create group alignment and, most importantly, establish a common framework for the activity of evaluating and selecting final ideas.

Next, provide each person with a limited number (five to seven) of peel-and-stick dots for voting. Instruct your group members to silently cast their votes by placing colored dots next to the ideas in the Idea Bank they feel are the very best. When the voting has been completed, those ideas with the greatest number of colored dots next to them represent the group's subjective short list of winners. (Note: You can also try other effective voting methods, including using a secret ballot, a show of hands [majority wins], Yes/No or Green/Red voting cards, or even an electronic handheld audience response polling device.)

Assess the short list of winning ideas to determine if any similar ideas can be combined or eliminated.

For a greater degree of confidence that the ideas selected measure up to the selection criteria, run the short list of ideas through the optional Step 4 (below).

(Optional) Step 4: Use the SmartStorming Idea Selection Diagnostic Matrix to identify the specific strengths and weaknesses of your best ideas.
This simple and effective tool helps groups clearly identify the most promising ideas with minimal personal subjectivity or bias.

The diagnostic checklist is a simple matrix grid on which each of your selection criteria is posted across the top and your most promising ideas are written down the left-hand side. The ideas are then judged against each of the criteria. Those ideas that meet all (or most) of the criteria are solid winners; those ideas that fail to meet three or more of the criteria should be discarded.

(See Chapter 9 for more information about the evaluation and selection process.)

Next steps and follow-through— The SmartStorming 5-As Idea Implementation Process

In order to ensure that your fresh, new, innovative ideas don't simply wither on the vine, it is important to initiate next steps and follow-through. While many things contribute to an idea making the final journey from concept to reality, we believe it is the responsibility of a SmartStorming Pilot to begin the process—ideally before the session has ended.

SmartStorming includes its own simple process—The 5-As Idea Implementation Process—to help you start your ideas on their journey to reality. Following is a brief overview:

Step 1: Act—Proactively foster an action-oriented attitude.
As a leader, model a *do it now* attitude for your team, and nurture this mindset in them. Acknowledge and reward those who take action—and coach those who do not to help them improve. Always be on the lookout for organizational or process-oriented obstacles to productivity, and address them. In short, make action taking a highly valued quality among your team, and observe the impact it has on productivity.

Step 2: Assess—Size up the big picture, then break it down into action steps.
As quickly as possible, assess how big, time-consuming, and complex the project of bringing your ideas to life will be. Break large projects down into smaller, more manageable steps—determine first what major subprojects will be part of your overall initiative; then break each of those subprojects down into major milestones and, finally, specific sequential tasks required to reach each of the mile-

stones. Maintain reasonable, but motivating pressure on the team. Carefully consider the time it will take to move the project to the next level—and strive to keep your timeline as tight as is reasonable. Remember, when someone has two weeks to accomplish a task, they will most often take two weeks. Ask for the same task to be completed in ten days, and they will get it done in ten days.

Step 3: Assign—Establish specific roles, responsibilities, and deliverables.
Identify the best person/people for each task. Consider the talents, skills, and expertise of each member of your team—who is self-igniting, goal-oriented, resourceful, dependable, has good organizational skills, etc.—and assign roles to the most appropriate person. Try to create an A-Team that can overcome any challenge and get things done!

Step 4: Agree—Create team alignment and personal accountability.
Make every effort to assign initial responsibilities and get agreement from participants on specific timelines and deliverables *before* leaving the room. Establishing specific roles, responsibilities, accountability, and consequences helps eliminate ambiguity and creates team alignment toward achieving a shared goal.

Step 5: Activate—Pull the trigger; make it happen!
Once you have quickly and efficiently gone through the first four steps, it's time to press the start button. Remember, the longer you wait to put the implementation process in motion, the greater the chance your project will never see the light of day.

The big picture

The flowchart on the next page illustrates the sequential steps in the SmartStorming process. As you'll see, each step flows seamlessly into the next like a tightly choreographed play; each step builds momentum on the one before, helping to maximize a group's creative problem-solving performance and productivity. By following this process, the group leader is free to focus attention on the group dynamics, allowing him or her to more effectively inspire and guide the group's exploration.

SmartStorming Six-Step Session Flowchart

1 **Pre-Session**
In step 1, you create your blueprint for leading the session; send out invitations, including all necessary background information the group may need.

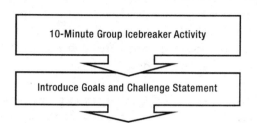

2 **Icebreaker**
In step 2, you help participants get to know one another and create group alignment with an enjoyable icebreaker activity.

3 **The Challenge**
In step 3, you introduce the session's goals and objectives, and announce the challenge statement—make it a provocative call to action!

4 **Idea Generation**
In step 4, you inspire and guide the group through a series of 2-3 different idea generation activities.

Be sure to harvest the group's best ideas after each ideation activity and have the session Reporter write them down on the Idea Bank.

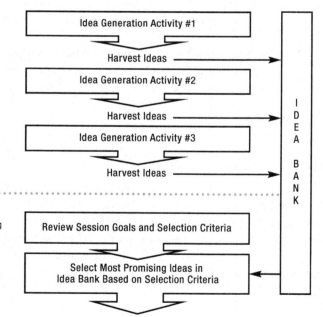

5 **Evaluation and Selection**
In step 5, you begin by reviewing the selection criteria with the group before evaluating ideas.

The selection criteria establish the benchmarks by which the group (or a selection committee) can more objectively evaluate the strengths and weaknesses of ideas.

6 **Next Steps**
In step 6, you announce the action steps necessary to move winning ideas forward to the next stage of their development. Be sure to specify deadlines and assign roles and responsibilities.

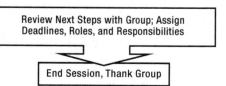

CHAPTER 25

Welcome to a New Paradigm in Idea Generation

"Do not follow where the path may lead.
Go instead where there is no path and leave a trail."

—Harold R. McAlindon, author

Congratulations! You now know everything you will need to become a brainstorming expert.

It's true! While that may seem like a big statement, after reading this book you really do know more about this critical part of the innovation process and how to implement it effectively than over 90 percent of those leading brainstorming sessions in any industry or field.

Becoming a highly effective brainstorming leader is an extremely valuable skill that you can carry with you on your professional journey and that delivers enormous benefits to any organization you are a part of. All it will take is a little time and practice applying the principles, tools, and techniques you've just learned.

In today's chaotic world, success in any endeavor is dependent on the ability to constantly reinvent oneself and one's offering. To constantly satisfy your customer, client, or audience in this era of ever-changing tastes and demands, you will need a continuous supply of fresh, new ideas. Ideas are the seeds of innovation, and ideas are very often born in brainstorming sessions. Brainstorming, in all its various forms, will continue on its current path toward becoming one of the most critical business processes practiced in organizations. And you now know how to brainstorm better than just about anyone else.

Whether you do it in a conference room, classroom, or on a video chat; use sophisticated online idea management tools, or flipcharts, whiteboards, or sticky notes;

in a group of one hundred or ten or all by yourself—SmartStorming is a better way to brainstorm.

Change can sometimes seem difficult, even uncomfortable. But like it or not, change is the only constant in our world today. The only business as usual is that there is no business as usual anymore. Today, you have only two choices—be an innovator or be irrelevant. Fortunately, you are now armed with everything you need to generate fresh, innovative ideas whenever you need them.

We encourage you to embrace this powerful new methodology. Make use of its proven structure; try out its varied techniques; practice and perfect your piloting skills. Then continue to expand upon your knowledge. Adapt the techniques to your specific needs, search for new ones you can learn and try, even try creating some! Make Smart-Storming your own.

Remember, every accomplishment, big or small, began with an idea. Smart-Storming really can help you break new ground, change the game, perhaps even change the world!

Be bold. Play this exciting game of change. And reap the rewards.

To learn more about SmartStorming training programs
and how they can help your organization achieve its innovation goals,
please visit our website at http://www.SmartStorming.com
or contact us via email at Partners@SmartStorming.com.

NOTES

1. Kambil, 2002.
2. Osborn, 1963.
3. SmartStorming, 2012.
4. Offner, Kramer, & Winter, 1996.
5. Oxley, Dzindolet, & Paulus, 1996.
6. Brazel, Carpenter, & Jenkins, July 2010.
7. Sawyer, 2007.
8. Sawyer, 2007.
9. Cameron, 1992.
10. Kelley, 2001.
11. Wolf, 1996.
12. Covey, 2004.
13. Kambil, 2002.
14. Belsky, 2010.
15. Belsky, 2010.
16. Kelley, 2001.
17. Osborn, 1957.
18. Osborn, 1963.
19. Kelley, 2001.

REFERENCES

Belsky, S. *Making Ideas Happen: Overcoming the Obstacles Between Vision and Reality.* New York: Portfolio, 2010.

Brazel, J. F., T. D. Carpenter, and J. G. Jenkins. "Auditors Use of Brainstorming in the Consideration of Fraud: Reports from the Field." *The Accounting Review* 85, no. 4 (July 2010): 1273–1301.

Cameron, J. *The Artist's Way: A Spiritual Path to Higher Creativity.* New York: Jeremy P. Tarcher/Putnam, 1992.

Covey, S. R. *The 7 Habits of Highly Effective People.* New York: Free Press, 2004.

Kambil, A. "Good Ideas Are Not Enough: Adding Execution Muscle to Innovation Engines." *Accenture Survey of* Chief Executive Magazine *Readers.* Accenture, 2002.

Kelley, T. *The Art of Innovation: Lessons in Creativity from IDEO, America's Leading Design Firm.* New York: Crown Publishing Group, 2001.

Kern, F. "What Chief Executives Really Want." *Bloomberg Businessweek* (May 18, 2010) http://www.businessweek.com/innovate/content/may2010/id20100517_190221.htm

Offner, A. K., T. J. Kramer, and J. P. Winter. "The Effects of Facilitation, Recording, and Pauses on Group Brainstorming." *Small Group Research* 27 (1996): 283-298.

Osborn, A. F. *Applied Imagination,* 10th Printing, Rev. Ed. New York: Charles Scribner's Sons, 1957.

———. *Applied Imagination,* 21st Printing, 3rd Rev. Ed. New York: Charles Scribner's Sons, 1963.

Oxley, N. L., M. T. Dzindolet, and Paulus, P. B. "The Effects of Facilitators on the Performance of Brainstorming Groups." *Journal of Social Behavior and Personality* 11 (1996): 633-646.

Sawyer, K. *Group Genius: The Creative Power of Collaboration.* New York: Basic Books, 2007.

SmartStorming Survey of over 500 SmartStorming workshop participants, blog, and website visitors. SmartStorming LLC, 2012.

Wolf, G. "Steve Jobs: The Next Insanely Great Thing." *Wired* (April 1996): 102-107, 158-163.

ABOUT THE AUTHORS

Mitchell Rigie

A top creative professional for over 25 years, Mitchell has expertise spanning the fields of art, design, communications, strategic marketing, and human development. He is a thought leader in the emerging field of peak creative performance; his "Creative Flow Principles" have helped hundreds of creative professionals in different industries achieve higher levels of productivity.

As a Vice President and award-winning creative supervisor for advertising agencies including Saatchi & Saatchi and Foote Cone Belding, and as a consultant for Grey Worldwide, he has managed creative teams in the development of campaigns for Fortune 500 clients including: Johnson & Johnson, American Express, GlaxoSmithKline, Merck, and General Electric.

Mitchell is a graduate of the Rhode Island School of Design and Coach University, the world's leading training organization for professional coaches. He also served as a member of the Board of Trustees for the Rhode Island School of Design.

Keith Harmeyer

Keith's professional background includes over 25 years in advertising and strategic marketing; sales and business coaching; and advanced communication and presentation skills training.

As a marketing and creative executive at agencies in the Omnicom and Publicis networks, as well as founder and principal of his own marketing communications firm, Keith created countless successful brand marketing programs and business presentations for many of the world's best known and most successful companies, such as American Express, JPMorgan Chase, Sony, Time Warner, ABC, Disney, Philips, Fujifilm, Conde Nast, Sports Illustrated, GlaxoSmithKline, Roche, McDonald's, Footlocker, and many others. He has also coached and trained numerous business leaders on their sales and presentation techniques, utilizing his proprietary system for persuasive communication.

Keith is a graduate of Loyola University and Tulane University, both in New Orleans, and of Coach University, the world's leading training organization for professional coaches. Formerly, he was the Executive Vice President, Marketing & Creative Services, at C2 Creative in New York City.

INDEX

Analogy/metaphor, 86, 224–227, 277
Associative thinking, 40, 80, 86, 91, 142, 215
Assumptions, 4, 70, 86, 89, 141, 151–155,
    196–199, 276, 309
  common assumptions, 153–154
  definition, 151–152, 196
  importance of challenging, 151–155, 196
  moving beyond, 154
Attention, nature of, 59

Belsky, Scott, 117, 118
Boss, managing, 36, 39–40, 106, 112, 253, 254
Brainstorming, viii–ix, 8, 11–16, 17–21
  elements required for success, 19, 299
  lack of training, 13–14
  specific failings of typical brainstorms, 14–15
Breaking the ice, 27, 57–65, 301

Cameron, Julia, 40
Capturing your group's ideas, 40–44
Challenge statement
  clarifying focus, 72–73
  crafting a powerful, 73–74
  mistakes to avoid, 72–73
Challenges, types of, 68–69, 95, 183
  solving wrong problem, 69
  symptom vs. source, 69–71
Challenging conventions, 86, 89, 93, 196, 246
Competition, friendly, 163, 173, 188, 293, 294
Convergent thinking, 84, 99–100, 133–137, 309
Counterintuitive/180-degree thinking, 86, 88,
    187, 276
Covey, Stephen, 101
Creative problem-solving, 12, 18, 85, 154, 232
  different approaches, 85–87, 87–93, 276–278
Csikszentmihalyi, Mihaly, 30

Distractions, managing, 38–39, 304
Divergent and convergent thinking, 84, 133–137
  benefits of convergent thinking, 134
  benefits of divergent thinking, 134

how to manage, 134–137
Diversity, inviting, 31–32, 260, 263, 303
Dream team, 31

Empathy-based insights, 86, 90, 212–214
Environment for session, 53–54
Escaping the box, 89, 151–155, 196–199, 276
Exploring viewpoints, 87, 89, 93, 234–240

Fast start, getting off to a, 90, 157, 161–164,
    209–211, 308
  before the session, 161–162
  during the session, 162–163
  dynamic tension, benefits of, 163
5-As Idea Implementation Process, 116,
    117–121, 266, 280–282, 312–313
Forced associations, 87, 90, 205–206

Goals and objectives, 27, 50, 67–68, 77, 262,
    292, 301, 303
  setting the bar high, 75–76, 307
Group dynamics, 13, 18, 127–131
Group genius, 18, 30, 32, 41, 60
Group size, 170–174
  challenges of managing large groups, 170
  configuring sessions for easier piloting, 171–173
  friendly competition, 173
  ideal, 170–171
  strategies for leading different size groups,
    172–173

Harvesting ideas, 101, 103–105, 110, 267, 310
  idea bank, 103–107, 311
  idea overwhelm, 41, 98, 103, 311
High-velocity thinking, 87, 90, 162, 209, 309

Icebreakers, 51, 57–65, 178, 255–258, 304
  activities, 255–258
  how to pilot, 60
  how to select, 60
  tips for successful, 62–64

Idea Bank, 101, 103–107, 111, 306, 311
Idea evaluation and selection, 28, 97–113, 310
Idea generation, 27–28, 79–96, 286–288, 301, 315
  stimulating new connections, 80–84
Idea-generation techniques, 87–95, 182, 304
  Bad2Good, 88, 187–189, 276
  Brainwriting, 88, 190–191
  Channeling Genius, 89, 192–195
  Escaping the Box, 89, 151–155, 196–199, 276
  Frankensteining, 89, 200–202, 276
  Group Graffiti, 89, 203–204
  guide for determining when to use, 94–95, 183
  how to choose, 94
  Idea Mashup, 90, 205–206
  Idea Speed Dating, 90, 207–208
  Idea Sprinting, 90, 209–211, 276
  In Their Shoes, 90, 212–214, 276
  Mind Mapping, 91, 215–218, 277
  1-4-All, 88, 185–186
  Pre-Storming, 91, 219–220, 245, 255
  Pump Up the Value, 92, 221–223, 277
  Reimagine It!, 92, 224–227, 277
  SCAMPER, 92, 228–233, 277
  SmartSWOT, 93, 234–240, 277
  Think Much, Much Bigger, 93, 241–243, 277–278
  Vision Boards, 93, 244–245
  What If...?, 93–94, 246–248, 255, 278
Idea selection, 28, 97–113
  and convergent thinking, 99–100
  common challenges, 98–99
  emotion vs. reason, 99
  evaluation and selection process, 28, 97–113
  harvesting, 103–105
  tips for managing, 111
  who should be selecting ideas, 100
Idea Selection Diagnostic Matrix, 107–109, 250
Ideas
  definition, 80
  evaluating, 28, 97–113
  generating, 79–96
  harvesting, 103–105
  selecting, 101–109
Innovation, 3–10, 30, 32, 40, 79, 116
  and ideas, 7–9

definition, 7–8
new Darwinism, 3–7
three types of, 7

Jobs, Steve, vii, 8, 80, 83, 89, 192, 195, 247, 248, 255, 293

Kelley, Tom, 72, 157–158, 307

Leadership skills, 19, 125–131, 172–173, 175–178, 299
  frequently asked questions, 175–178
  Pilot's presence, 125–127
  situational awareness, 127–130
Length/duration of session, 53–54, 175–176

Negativity, managing, 37, 176–177
Next steps and follow-through, 52–53, 115–121, 266, 280–281, 305, 312–313

Open innovation and virtual SmartStorming, 285–296
Osborn, Alex, 11–13, 18, 35, 171, 228

Personality types, disruptive, 33
Pilot, role of, 28–29, 305
Pilot's Toolkit, 179–268
Pre-Session Planner, 49–53, 260–261, 273, 291, 300, 302–305
  steps, 49–53, 302–305
Pre-session planning, 26, 47–55, 302–305
Productivity, maximizing, 157–160
  fueling momentum, 157–158
  making jumps, 159–160

Questions, art of asking powerful, 139–150
  tips for successful questioning, 146–148
  25 Piloting Questions for Any Challenge, 149, 259
  types of piloting questions, 140–146

Reinvention, continuous, 3–4, 7, 315
Reporter, role of, 29
Roles, 28–30
Rules of the Game, 34–36, 253, 274–275, 292, 308

enforcement, 37–40

Sawyer, Keith, 30, 32
Selection criteria, objective, 28, 99, 101–102,
    107–109, 113, 177, 178, 250, 264–265
Self-interest, managing, 38
Silent Thinkers, 165–168, 308
    definition, 165–166
    tips for inspiring, 166–167
Situational Awareness, 127–130
Six-step process
    Step 1—Creating Your Blueprint for Success,
        47–55
    Step 2—Aligning Your Group for Collabora-
        tion, 57–65
    Step 3—Creating a Springboard for the
        Imagination, 67–78
    Step 4—Generating Ideas! Unleashing Your
        Group's Creative Genius, 79–96
    Step 5—Harvesting Your Group's Most
        Innovative Ideas, 97–113
    Step 6—Transforming Ideas into New
        Realities, 115–121
SmartStormers, role of, 30
SmartStorming
    differences from traditional brainstorming,
        19–21
    5-As Idea Implementation Process, 116,
        117–121, 266, 280–282, 312–313
    guides, planners, and worksheets, 251–268
    idea generation techniques, 181–250
    leadership skills, 19, 125–131, 172–173,
        175–178, 299
    Pilot's toolkit, 179–268
    Pre-Session Planner (see separate entry)
    principles and best practices, 25–44
    putting it all together, 110, 299–314
    roles, 28–30
    rules, 34–36, 253, 274–275, 292, 308
    six-step process, 26–28, 47–121, 300–305
    three pillars for success, 19, 299
    Value Compass, 92, 221–222, 223, 249
Solo idea-generation techniques
    Bad2Good, 189, 276
    Escaping the Box, 199, 276
    Frankensteining, 202, 276

Idea Sprinting, 211, 276
In Their Shoes, 214, 276
Mind Mapping, 218, 276–277
Pump Up the Value, 223, 277
Reimagine It!, 227, 277
SCAMPER, 231, 277
SmartSWOT, 238, 277
Think Much, Much Bigger, 243, 277–278
What If...?, 248, 278
Solo SmartStorming, 271–282
    solo pre-session planner, 261, 273
Source of a problem, 69–71
    five ways to discern, 70–71
Statement of Challenge, Goal, and Objectives,
    27, 67–78, 262, 292
Stimuli, mental, 80–84
    different types, 82–84
Stocking the creative pond, 80–84
    ten ways to stock the pond, 82–84

Thinking outside the box, 89, 94, 151–155,
    196–199
Time of day for session, 53–54

Value Compass, 92, 221–222, 223, 249
Virtual SmartStorming, 285–296
    how to, 290–295
    idea-generation techniques, 293–294
    management tools, 288–290
    pros and cons, 286–287
    technologies, 287–290

CPSIA information can be obtained
at www.ICGtesting.com
Printed in the USA
FSOW04n1129210916
25225FS